THE
WHOLE ART
OF THE
STAGE

THE

WHOLE ART

OF THE

STAGE

François Hédelin, Abbé d'Aubignac, François H.

BENJAMIN BLOM New York/London 1968

88928

First published London 1684
Reissued 1968 by
Benjamin Blom, Inc., Bronx, New York 10452
and 56 Doughty Street, London W.C. 1

Library of Congress Card Catalog Number 68-21218

Printed in the United States of America

THE
Whole ART
OF THE
STAGE.

CONTAINING

Not only the Rules of the *Drammatick Art*, but many curious Obfervations about it.

Which may be of great ufe to the Authors, Actors, and Spectators of Plays.

Together with much Critical Learning about the Stage and Plays of the Antients.

Written in French by the command of Cardinal *Richelieu.*

By Monfieur *Hedelin*, Abbot of *Aubignac*, and now made Englifh.

LONDON,

Printed for the Author, and fold by *William Cadman* at the *Pope's-Head* in the *New Exchange* ; *Rich. Bentley*, in *Ruffel-ftreet*, *Covent-Garden*; *Sam. Smith* at the *Prince's Arms* in St.*Paul*'s Church-Yard; & *T.Fox* in *Weftminfter-Hall*. 1684.

The Translator's

PREFACE.

SOme may wonder that this being a
work of such use, and replenished
with such judicious Remarks, as
well as deep learning, in the whole
course of it, has hitherto scaped the
pen of our Translators out of a Language that has almost tyr'd our Presses
with continual productions. But the
reason of that may be that it was published in a time when we were Embroil-
ed in civil Wars here in England, and
that having laid aside all those Inno-

cent

cent Theatral Repreſentations the whole Kingdom was become the Stage of real Tragedies ; So that till his Majeſties happy Reſtauration, with whom the Muſes ſeemed to have been baniſhed this Iſland, it could not be expected that a book of this nature could meet with any kind reception in the world ; but by that time I ſuppoſe the Impreſſions were all ſold off, and it was to be met with no where but in the Libraries of the curious. It was by Communication from a Perſon of that ſort that the Tranſlator firſt had the thoughts of making it Engliſh, which he obtained leiſure to do, by an unhappy confinement to a retir'd life for his health ſake from more ſolid ſtudies and buſineſs which his profeſſion elſe involves him in. So Reader thou haſt here the whole Art of the Stage,

of

The Tranſlator's Preface.

of which there needs little to be ſaid,
the Book being its own Commendation ;
As for the Author he was a perſon of
a good Family in **Paris**, and of Exqui-
ſite Learning in Antiquity; much che-
riſhed by Cardinal **Richelieu** that
great **Mæcenas** of Ingenious men, and
by him for his deſerts made Abbot of
Aubignac & deſign'd Overſeer or Su-
per-Intendant General of the Theatres
in **France**, if the project of reſtoring
them to their Ancient glory (of which
you will ſee an abſtract at the end of
the book) had gone on, and not been
Interrupted by the Cardinals Death.

  The Tranſlator has made ſome
Alterations in the Authors method
& order of his Chapters, for the Author
having promiſcuouſly placed much of the
crabbed Antiquity Learning among the
other Obſervations upon the Dramma-
                                        tick

The Tranflator's Preface.

tick Art; and that being likely to difguft fome Readers The Tranflator has put it all in one Book at the latter end, where thofe who love that critical Learning may have it altogether, and the others who delight in a fmoother career of Reafons and Obfervations may go on in the firft three Parts without too ftrong an Application in matters of fome Intricacy.

There is nothing more, but that thou excufe the Errata, which by the negligence of the Printer are but too many.

THE

THE
CONTENTS.

Book I.

Book III.

The Contents.

Book III.

THE

THE

Whole Art

OF THE

STAGE.

The Firſt BOOK.

CHAP. I.

Being inſtead of a Preface to the whole Work , wherein is treated of the neceſſity of Publick Spectacles, of the Eſteem the Ancients had them in , and in what ſtate they are now amongſt us.

LL thoſe Incomparable and Famous Genius's which, from time to time, Heaven Deſigns for the Government of
Mankind , do not only indeavour to
make the Nations ſubject to their Conduct, Triumph with victorious Arms
over their Enemies, and thereby become Formidable

B   to

to the World ; but alfo having enriched them with all the wonders of Nature and Art, by the means of Commerce with Foreign Nations, they do ftrive to foften and fweeten their Difpofitions, by all the Noble Sciences that Mankind is capable of; and confidering that Nature its felf in its Nobleft Productions, after having adorned them with all Qualities neceffary to their Perfection, gives them a certain Contentment and Rejoycing in them, which is the greateft of its Favours ; thefe great Politicians, in imitation of her, do ufe to Crown all their Endeavours for the publick fafety, with publick Pleafures and Entertainments , making their own glorious Labours either the means or the pretexts of all general Diverfions. Their Victories are noted by days of Rejoycing and publick Games ; and all the Spoils and Riches of Foreign Nations, are brought from the extremity of the Earth, only to compofe the Pomp and Decoration of their Spectacles, as well as the moft curious Sciences are Cultivated to produce men capable of inventing new Entertainments.

And to fay Truth, what greater marks can there be of a flourifhing Greatnefs in any State, than to fee many of thefe Diverfions ? Thereby in Peace appears the Superfluity of its Riches, the Abundance of its People, who without being a Charge to the Publick, can fpare many days to their Pleafure, from thofe Employments which are neceffary to the fubfiftance of the great Body of the People ; and befides, the Number of rare Wits bufied in the publick Diverfion, with all forts of Inventions, and the greater number of excellent Artificers, employed to execute the ingenious thoughts of the firft, cannot but be a great Ornament to a Nation.

All the Common-wealths of *Greece*, had each their publick Games , where their Neighbours were as it

were

were obliged to affift, that they might all appear equal in Magnificency, as well as in Power and Authority: And if the Common-wealths of *Italy* were forced to come fhort of the Grandeur of *Rome* in that point, yet by their particular Cirk's and Theatres they have fhewed the World that they yielded only to the Miftrefs of it, and not to one another.

But whenever in the midft of War all thefe Diverfions are continued in a ftate, 'tis giving an evident demonftration, that the Riches of it are without meafure, and the People inexhauftible, when the dangers and labours of a Campaigne paffed in the toyls of War, and the profpect of one to come, does neither change the Humour nor the Courage of thofe that compofe the Armies, nor of thofe that ftay at home; that they undertake with Joy in Summer thofe glorious actions, of which they fee an Image upon the Stage in Winter with fo much Pleafure; and that the Advantages their Enemies reap from the War, are fo inconfiderable as not to difquiet, or interrupt the publick Joy.

Thus the *Athenians*, having received in the very Theatre the news of an entire defeat of their Army before *Syracufa*, would not fo much as interrupt the publick Games, but went on with thofe Spectacles as they had begun; and Foreign Embaffadours, who themfelves were by, and Spectators of this undaunted Generofity, admired it more than their real Power, as thinking it harder to fubdue. And to come nearer our times, if we confider what has paffed at *Vienna* and *Paris*, the Heads of two Rival Empires, under the Miniftry of the great Cardinal *Richelieu*; we muft confefs that thefe two Capitols feem'd by the Magnificencies of their Plays, Ballets, and other publick Entertainments, to try to perfwade the World, that the Event of the War, which fo warm-

ly

ly they carried on againſt each other, was indifferent to them, both as to their good or evil Fortune.

We are not neverthelefs to imagine that thefe pub-lick Spectacles afford nothing but a vain Splendour, without any real Utility ; for they are a fecret Inftru-ftruction to the People of many things, which it would be very hard to infinuate into them any other way. As for Example, Thofe publick Diverfions where there is any image of War, do infenfibly make them acquaint-ed with Arms, and make thofe Inftruments of Death familiar to them, infpiring them at the fame time with Courage and Intrepedity againſt all dangers ; befides, Vanity often prevails more with us than Reafon ; and that Jealous humour, of which our Nature can hardly ever well diveſt it felf, does continually foment within us a certain defire of Conpuering, which often carries us to overcome all our natural Weakneffes, and go be-yond our felves in great Attempts: Thus the Glory which one receives in publick for fome handfom action ; and the recital or reprefentation of the Heroick Virtues of thofe who are not even in being, at the time we hear them, does neverthelefs raife in us a prefumptuous be-lief that we are able to perform the like ; and this pre-fumption becoming a nobler fort of Envy, called Emula-tion, produces in us an infatiable defire of Honour, and elevates our Courage to undertake any thing that may effect that Glorious Defign.

As for thofe Spectacles which confiſt as much in Dif-courfe as Action, fuch as formerly were the Difputes upon the Stage between the *Epick* and *Drammatick* Po-ets: They are not only ufeful but abfolutely neceffary to inſtruct the People, and give them fome tincture of Moral Virtues.

The minds of thofe who are of the meaneſt Rank
and

and Condition in a State, are generally ſo little acquainted with any notions of Morality,that the moſt general Maximes of it are hardly known to them ; 'tis in vain therefore to make fine Diſcourſes,full of convincing Reaſons, and ſtrengthened with Examples to them, they can neither underſtand the firſt, nor have any deference for the latter. All the elevated Truths of Philoſophy are lights too ſtrong for their weak Eyes: Tell them of theſe Maximes, that Happineſs conſiſts leſs in the poſſeſſion of worldly things, than in the deſpiſing of them ; that Virtue ought to ſeek its recompence in its ſelf; that there is no Intereſt in the World conſiderable enough to oblige a man of **Honour** to do a baſe thing ; all theſe, I ſay, are Paradoxes to them, which makes them ſuſpect Philoſophy it ſelf, and turn it into Ridicule ; they muſt therefore be inſtructed by a more ſenſible way, which may fall more under their ſenſes ; and ſuch are the Repreſentations of the Stage, which may therefore properly be called the Peoples School.

One of the chiefeſt, and indeed the moſt indiſpenſible Rule of Drammatick Poems, is, that in them Virtues always ought to be rewarded, or at leaſt commended, in ſpight of all the Injuries of Fortune ; and that likewiſe Vices be always puniſhed,or at leaſt deteſted with Horrour, though they triumph upon the Stage for that time. The Stage being thus regulated, what can Philoſophy teach that won't become much more ſenſibly touching by Repreſentation ; 'tis there that the meaneſt Capacities may viſibly ſee,that favours of Fortune are not real Enjoyments,when they ſee the ruin of the Royal Family of *Priamus*; all that they hear from the Mouth of *Hecuba* ſeems very probable, having before their Eyes the ſad Example of her Calamities ; 'tis there that they are convinced that Heaven puniſhes the horrid Crimes of

the

the Guilty with the remorse of them; when they see *Orestes* tormented by his own Conscience, and driven about by Furies within his own Breast; 'tis there that Ambition seems to them a very dangerous Passion, when they see a man engaged in Crimes, to attain his Ends, and after having violated the Laws of Heaven and Earth, fall into Misfortunes as great as those he had overwhelmed others in, and more tormented by himself than by his Enemies: 'Tis there again that Covetousness appears a Disease of the Soul, when they see a Covetous man persecuted with continual Restlesness, and fears of want in the midst of all his Riches. And lastly, 'tis there that a Man, by Representation, makes them penetrate into the most hidden secrets of Humane Nature, while they seem to touch and feel in this living Picture, those Truths which else they would scarce be capable of: But that which is most remarkable, is, That they never go from the Theatre without carrying along with them the idea of the Persons represented; the knowledge of those Virtues and Vices, of which they have seen the Examples; their memory repeating continually to them those Lessons which have been derived to them, from sensible and present Objects.

Besides, in all Governments there is a number of idle People, either because they hate taking pains, or because they need not do it to live; this idleness carries them generally to many Debaucheries, where they consume in a very little time, what might suffice for the keeping of their Families many Months, and are then forced upon ill actions for a supply to their present wants. Now, I think nothing worthier the care of a Great Prince, than to prevent, if possible, his Subjects from taking these extravagant Courses; and as it would be too severe to enjoyn them perpetual labour,

so

Comœdiis & Tragœdiis o-tiosis damus: nemo enim in Theatrum venit qui non libens velit id tempo-ris amittere. Scalig. l. 3. c. 24. poet.

so I think that publick Spectacles and Entertainments would most innocently amuse those who have no other employment; their own pleasure would carry them thither without constraint, their hours would slide away without regret, and their very idleness being busie, they would there lose all the thoughts of doing ill.

Thus whether out of the consideration of procuring that Joy and Content to Mankind, which makes their greatest Felicity, and without which they can relish no other Happiness; or whether to shew the greatness of a *State*, either in Peace or War; to inspire the People with Courage, or to instruct them in the knowledge and practice of Virtue; or lastly, to prevent Idleness, (one of the greatest mischiefs of a State) Princes can never do any thing more advantageous for their own Glory, nor for their Peoples Happiness, than to found, settle, and maintain at their own Charges, publick Spectacles, Games, and other Diversions, in the greatest Order; and the noblest Magnificence that their Crown will afford.

And without doubt they have always been thought very important to the very Political part of the Government, since the Philosophy of the *Greeks*, and the Majesty and Wisdom of the *Romans*, did equally concern their Magistrates, in making them Venerable, Noble, and Magnificent. They made them Venerable, by Consecrating them always to some of their Gods, and by putting them under the direction of their Chief Magistrates; and they were beyond measure Magnificent, because the Expence was allowed out of the publick Treasure; and the liberal Contributions of their greatest Men in employment, who endeavoured to surpass each other in Magnificence, that they might make the time of their Administration more memorable. Very
often

often the Chief of the Nobility were at the whole Expence, only to gain the Peoples Favour; and they obliged all the Eminent Artificers in all kinds, to ſhew their Excellency in them: they did uſe to ſend to the remoteſt Nations for Men, Beaſts, or any Rarity that could increaſe the Pleaſure of their Spectacles; and laſt of all, they had Crowns for the Conquerors in all Exerciſes, and Statues for thoſe, who with any extraordinary Magnificence had been at the charge of them.

It had been neverthelefs little for theſe two Noble Nations to enjoy theſe Pleaſures alone, if they had not propagated them to all the others of their Knowledge. The *Greeks* filled *Afia* with them, and the *Romans* carried them all over *Africa* and *Europe,* and after they had Conquered the beſt part of the known World, to ſhew that their Domination was Gentle, and not Tyrannical; they received the Gods, and the Religions of all Nations into *Rome,* and ſent them the Games, Spectacles, and Diverſions of that famous Capitol, to let them ſee that they had not made War upon them to oppreſs them, but to increaſe their Happineſs, by ſharing their Felicity with them. The Theatre of *Sardis* in *Afia,* that of *Carthage* in *Africa,* and thoſe of *Douay, Niſmes,* and *Autun* in *France,* are convincing Teſtimonies of this, though ruinous ones; and when *Conſtantine* carried the Siege of the Empire to the City of his Name, he made there ſuch publick Buildings for Spectacles, as ſhewed he would make it the Seat of his Pleaſures, as well as of his Power.

But the Ancients did not only aim at obliging the preſent Age with their Noble Structures, but endeavoured to endear Poſterity to them, by making of them, as much as in them lay, immortal: Thus their Cirques, their
                                                        Theatres,

Theatres, and Amphitheatres, were built with the moſt poliſh'd and laſting Marble, and with ſo much Art, that if any thing they might reſiſt the ſuppreſſion of Time ; but alas! as if man imprinted the Character of his own Mortality upon all his Works, theſe Glorious Monuments of their greatneſs have yielded to the ſame deſtiny ; the Torrent of Time which overwhelms and deſtroys all things, has ſcarce left us the Image of them in ſome old ruines, half demoliſh'd.   And Reaſon and Cuſtom ſeem to have join'd with Time in aboliſhing many of the Ancient Spectacles.   Thoſe Bloody Combats of Gladiators againſt each other, and of Men againſt Beaſts, till certain Death followed, have not been deriv'd to us, becauſe they are contrary to that Humanity which the Law of the Goſpel recommends, as the Foundation of Chriſtian Charity. Something of that conſideration made their Naumachia's or Naval Battels, in which ſometimes there were fifteen or ſixteen thouſand men engag'd, be left of ; but indeed the Expence of that was ſuch, as nothing but the *Roman* Empire could ever furniſh.   The Courſes of their Chariots, and the Races of their Horſes, with the other Games of the Cirque, have been neglected as uſeleſs. And the running at the Ring in Turnaments, and fighting on Foot at the Barriere, which ſucceeded them in our Anceſtors Days, have been likewiſe laid aſide ; Lances being as little in uſe with us in War, as Chariots : For as to the Courſes of Bulls and Horſes, which yet remain in *Italy*, they are rather to be numbred among the ridiculous Sights of our Age, than compared to the Spectacles of the Ancients.

The Javelin is of little uſe neither ; and therefore.

C   we

we have neglected the Art of throwing it with flight in War.

The Difcus or Coite is onely a diverfion of the

meaner fort of People.   Boxing or fighting with Cudgels or Clubs, becomes the roughnefs of none but Savages,   and it would in my Opinion be a   very fcurvy Diverfion in the Gallantry of the *French* Court.

Tennis, or Playing at Balls, which the Ancients called *Sphæromachia*, has nothing of its firft   manner and glory,   but is fo chang'd as hardly to be known,   and there being no Crowns nor Rewards for the Actors, it is only become a voluntary Diver-

fion.

As for Wraftlers, they are in fome of our Provinces, but very few :   Firft,   becaufe it is againft the Rules of Modefty to fee not only Men, but   Women naked,   try their Strength and Skill againft one another,   (for fo both Sexes did   formerly) but   now the Women are banifh'd from that Immodeft Exercife: And befides there was a neceffity of being Dieted, and living up to the ftrictnefs of certain Rules of Health, which has made it be forfaken ; and having nothing Noble left in it,   is onely become the Diverfion of the meaner fort.

The fame thing has befallen the Amphitheatres, where from   all Parts of the Earth were   brought wild Beafts to fight againft one another :   For to fee, as we do fometimes, a Fellow lead a Lyon about to be Worried by a Dog of his Acquaintance, is a ridiculous fight ; and fo are thofe other Combats of Beafts, which are yet in *Italy*,   unworthy the greatnefs or care of a State.

Bonfires and Fireworks have had   a better defti-

ny;

ny ; for if ours do not obferve that Order and Art which the Ancients did in theirs,they are not at all Inferiour to them in Magnificence. I may fay the fame of our Balls and Balets, of which we have happily maintained the Splendour, though our way of Dancing has nothing in it like that of the *Greeks* and *Romans* : But ftill thofe which we have feen at *Paris*, and which have deferved the Admiration and Applaufe of the two greateft Kings in *Europe*, and of their Courts ; thefe Balets, I fay, in which twice the whole Machine of this World, the Heavens, the Sea, the Earth, and Hell the bottom of it, were reprefented, furpafs in my Opinion any thing that we can by reading obferve of that kind among the Ancients.

As for the Theatre, or Stage, it has not been much happier than the Cirque. For not to fpeak of thofe other Diverfions which were given the People *in it*, the Art of compofing Drammatick Poems, and reprefenting of them, feems to have had the fame Deftiny with thofe Famous Structures where they were Acted. It has lain long buried with the Ruines of *Athens* and *Rome* : And when at laft it was reftor'd in fome fmall meafure amongft us, it ftill appear'd like a Carcafs taken out of the Grave, without any Shape or Vigour. All the firft Pieces of the Stage were without either Art or Learning, or any other Ornament than that of Novelty ; the Compofition was without Skill, and the Verfes without any Politenefs ; the Actours no waies underftood their bufinefs,and the whole Reprefentation was defective all over ; infomuch that they had not a painted Cloth to hide thofe who were to go off the Stage ; but they were reputed abfent who did not prefent themfelves to fpeak.

'Tis

Nunc in Gallia
ita agunt fabu-
las, ut omnia in
conspectu sint, u-
niversus appara-
tus dispositus sub-
limibus sedibus
personæ ipsa nun-
quam discedunt,
qui silent; pro
absentib. habent.
Stalig. lib. 1. c.
21. Poet.

'Tis true, that in our Age our Poets having recovered the Way to *Parnaſſus,* upon the Footſteps of
Euripides and *Terence,* and there happening to
be Actours amongſt us, who might in *Rome* it ſelf
have match'd with *Æſopus* the famous Tragedian,
and *Roſcius* the no leſs Renown'd Comedian,
the Stage has got a new Face, and the Wrinckles
that were upon that Old one have begun to grow
ſmooth, and altogether to look with leſs deformity.
Happy in this, that the greateſt Genius of our Time,
the great Cardinal *Richelieu,* ſmil'd upon her. It was by
his Liberality that ſhe firſt receiv'd new Strength, and
began to challenge her Old Rights, her Beauty, Nobility and Splendour; and it was by his care that moſt
of what was either Ingenious, Learned, or Magnificent
among the Ancients, was ſeen by degrees upon our
Theatre: And yet after all, we muſt own that the
Stage was fallen from ſo high a degree of Glory, into
ſo much contempt and abjectneſs, that it was impoſſible to heal entirely thoſe Wounds which it had
received in its fall, nor to reſtore it, but after much
Labour and Time. But ſince the ſame hand, which
begun the Cure, has not been able to finiſh it, 'tis to
be feared that the Drammatick Art will never arrive to its perfection, and I doubt will hardly maintain it ſelf in the ſtate it is, any long time. And if
ſo, its relapſe will be ſo much the more dangerous,
becauſe it is not every Age that produces Genius's
both underſtanding and Liberal, and accompliſh'd
with all the Qualities neceſſary to ſo great a Deſign.
The Life of this great man has form'd an Age of
great and new things: but all thoſe which did not
arrive to perfection, according to their Nature, in
his time, will hardly meet with an Opportunity to
do

do it after his Death. And indeed it belong'd to no body more to adorn the Kingdom with all delightful Spectacles, than to him ; who every day encreas'd our Victories, and Crown'd us with new Lawrels. 'Twas but reasonable that he, who was in War so like *Cæsar* and *Pompey,* should imitate them likewise in the restoring of Theatres, and other Princely Diversions ; and in a Word, the magnificence of Publick Spectacles could not be better deriv'd than from him, who was himself the most glorious and noble Spectacle in the World.

It was to please him that I Compil'd this Practice of the Stage, which he most passionately had wish'd for ; in hopes it would ease our Poets of the great labour, they must else have undergone, if with great Expence of Time they would have collected these Observations, which I have made ready for them, out of the different Authors, and from nice and accurate Remarks on the Stage it self. It was likewise by his Order, that I made a Project of restoring the *French* Theatre to the Splendour of that of the Ancients, and what Remedies were to be used against all our Impediments. He had conceiv'd such hopes of succeeding in this design, that he made me treat to the whole extent of the matter, upon that which I had first but summarily touch'd, and was resolv'd to employ all his Power and Liberality in compassing this Noble Enterprise. The Death of that great man made those two Works miscarry, but here is the first, which as it is I give to the publick, upon the follicitation of my Friends. As for the second, I shall only Communicate to the World the Project of it, it not being proper to Expose any more of it,

since

since there were not above five or seven Chapters of it Writ, which are imperfect too, and out of Order.

CHAP. II.

The Design of the whole Work.

THE Glory to which the *French* Theatre is arriv'd, may perhaps make some think that this Discourse is useless, since our Poets, having given to the World so many compleat Poems, with a general Approbation, may be thought to be above those Instructions, which seem to be the Remedy for Faults to which they are no longer subject ; I will not therefore be guilty of so great a Vanity, as to say that the Scope of this Work is to inform them of things which we see they Practice every day with success, but it is to let the World know the Excellency of their Art, and to give People subject to admire them so much the more, in shewing what Learning, Invention, Abilities, and Care there are requir'd to finish those Poems which make one of the greatest of our Pleasures, while they only give the Players the Trouble of reciting them. And in this I shall not onely raise the Fame of our Poets, but contribute considerably to encrease the Pleasure we take in seeing and reading their Works: For it is natural to every body to relish any agreeable object so

much

Much the more, by how much they are capable of difcovering the Reafons that render it agreeable ; and as we have more Value for Precious Stones, when befides their noble natural Qualities, we confider to what dangers they expofe themfelves, who bring them from the remoteft Parts of the Earth ; fo I think we fhall feel fo much the more admiration and joy in the Reprefentation of Theatral Diverfions, if by the knowledge of the Rules of the Art we are able to penetrate all the Beauties of them, and to confider what Meditations, Pains, and Study they have coft to be brought to that Perfection. So noble and fo vaft a defign requir'd, I confefs, a Genius much fuperior to mine, and a Body more capable of fupporting the Fatigue of ftudy and application. But I think that this being rather a Summary, than a compleat Treatife, and as it were rather a Collection of my own Obfervations, than a profound Differtation, full of knotty Difputes and Contestations with our modern Authors, whofe Opinions are it may be more reafonable than mine, I may be the eafilier Excufed. All that will be feen here is but the Compendium of thofe Matters which I had once refolv'd to treat at large, if many Confiderations had not taken from me both the defire and power of performing it : If by chance it be obferv'd, that fome Places are touch'd with more Strength, and better Finifh'd than others, it is becaufe I deliver'd thefe Memoires to my Friends as they were, unequal and unpolifh'd, according to thofe Heats and Colds which accompany all Writers, who following the firft ardour of their Projects, do not review with Care the whole Product of their Endeavours,

If

If any thing appear reafonable and pleafing, that will be enough to hinder me from repenting the reprieve I have given my Book from thofe Flames to which I had once refolutely Condemn'd it; and at leaft, though my matter and Order be not approv'd, yet fome one more laborious, finding the way open, and having the Affiftance of fome Illuftrious Protectour, will purfue to the utmoft Perfection that which I have but hinted, and as it were flightly imagin'd.

CHAP.

the Theatral Action, the Connexion of the Scenes, the intervals of the Acts, and a thousand other particulars, of which there is nothing left in Antiquity, of which all the Moderns have said so little, that it is next to nothing ; all this, I say, is that which I call the Art or Practice of the Stage.   As for the Ancients, if they have writ nothing about it, as to the practical part, it is because that perhaps in their time it was so common, that they could not believe any body capable of not knowing it ; and indeed if one look into their works, and make but the least reflection upon the Art they use, one may perceive it almost every where.

But for the Moderns; they for the most part have been entirely ignorant of it, because they have neglected the reading the Poems of those great Masters; or if they have read them, it was without taking notice of the nicest beauties with which they are adorn'd ; therefore it must be set down for a Maxime out of contest, that 'tis impossible to understand Drammatick Poetry without the help of the Ancients, and a thorough meditation upon their Works.

CHAP. IV.

Of the Rules of the Ancients.

I was, I muſt confeſs, extremely ſurpriz'd ſome years ago, to ſee ſome Plays in great eſteem both in *Paris*, and at Court, in which there was ſcarce a Scene, that did not in ſome meaſure offend the Rules of Decency and Probability ; but I was much more aſtoniſh'd, when going about to ſay ſomething of thoſe Rules, and to Explain the ways how to obſerve them, I was taken for an Hypochondriack, who had ſtrange ſingular fancies of his own, of things that never were, nor could be. All the Rules of the Ancients, by which I pretended Poets were to be guided in the conduct of their Plays, were look'd upon as dangerous innovations, like thoſe in Government, or in Religion. There was no asking, what time the action repreſented took up, and in what place the things expos'd to our view were ſuppos'd to be perform'd, nor how many Acts a Play had ? I was anſwer'd preſently, that the Play had laſted three hours, that the Action had been all upon the Stage, and that the Fiddles had mark'd the Intervals of the Acts ; in a word, 'twas enough to pleaſe, to have the name of Commedy given to a

great

great many Verfes put together, and recited upon
the Stage. But at laft having grown acquainted
with fome of the learned men of our Age, I found
amongft them many very well acquainted with the
Art of the Stage, particularly in the Theory and the
Maxims of *Ariftotle*, and fome too, who did apply
themfelves to the confideration of the Practical part.
All thefe were of my opinion, and condemning the
voluntary blindnefs of our times, did extremly
help me to confound the ftubbornnefs of thofe, who
refus'd to yield to Reafon.

Thus by little and little the face of the Theatre
has been entirely changed, and is at laft come to that
perfection, that one of our moft celebrated Authors
has publickly confefs'd, and that often, that in looking over fome of his own Plays, which had been acted
with great approbation of the Town, about ten
or twelve years ago, that he was much afham'd of
himfelf, and did extremly, pity thofe who had applauded him. I have neverthelefs had the misfortune to incur the difgrace of fome little Authors, who
having neither Genius, nor Learning enough, to
come up to thefe Rules in the excellency which they
propounded, fided with part of the Players, to run
me down. As for thefe latter, their defign being only
to gain by their Profeffion, and not to excel in it,
they thought that the ftrictnefs and feverity of thefe
Rules would frighten all the young Authors, and
deter them from writing ; by which means they
thought themfelves in danger of being forc'd to leave
the Stage, to feek for fome other Employment, for
want of new Plays : but the Event has confounded
this piece of Ignorance, for there were never feen
more Drammatick Poems, nor more agreeable ones,
than

than fince ; although we have not for Actours fuch as *Valeran, Veautray,* and *Mondory* were.

But yet fince fome perfons of Judgment, for want of being well vers'd in Antiquity, have endeavour'd with fome appearance of Reafon to maintain the errours of our Age, I think my felf oblig'd to anfwer their fcruples, and to fatisfie a great number, who yet feem unwilling to be undeceiv'd. Therefore here are five Objections which have been ordinarily made to me, againft the Rules of the Ancients.

Firft, That we are not to make Laws to our felves from Cuftom and Example, but from Reafon ; which ought to prevail over any Authority.

Secondly, That the Ancients themfelves have often violated their own Rules.

Thirdly, That divers Poems of the Ancients had been tranflated, and acted upon our Stage with very ill fuccefs.

Fourthly, That divers of our modern **Plays,** though quite contrary to thefe Rules, had been acted with great applaufe.

And laft of all, That if thefe rigorous Maxims fhould be followed, we fhould very often lofe the greateft beauty of all true Stories.   Their Incidents having moft commonly happened at different times, and in different places

As to the firft Objection; I anfwer, That the Rules of the Stage are not founded upon Authority, but upon Reafon ; they are not fo much fettled by Example, as by the natural judgment of Mankind ; and if we call them the Rules and the Art of the Ancients, 'tis only becaufe They have practis'd them with great regularity, and much to their Glory ; having

firft

firſt made many Obſervations upon the Nature of Moral Actions, and upon the probability of Humane Accidents in this life, and thereby drawing the Pictures after the truth of the Original, and obſerving all due circumſtances, they reduc'd to an Art this kind of Poem, whoſe Progreſs was very ſlow, though it were much in uſe among them, and much admir'd all the world over. But however I am very ſparing of citing their Poems, and when I do it, it is only to ſhew with what agreeable Artifice they kept to theſe Rules, and not to buoy up my opinion by their Authority.

As for the ſecond Objection, it ſeems not conſiderable; for Reaſon, being alike all the world over, does equally require every bodies ſubmiſſion to it; and if our modern Authors, cannot without offence be diſpens'd from the Rules of the Stage, no more could the Ancients; and where they have fail'd, I do not pretend to excuſe them. My Obſervations upon *Plautus*, ſhew very well that I do propoſe the Ancients for Models, only in ſuch things as they ſhall appear to have followed Reaſon in; and their Example will alwaies be an ill pretext for faults, for there is no excuſe againſt Reaſon. In things which are founded only in Cuſtom, as in Grammar, or in the Art of making a Verſe with long or ſhort ſyllables, the Learned may often uſe a licenſe againſt the receiv'd practice, and be imitated in it by others, becauſe Cuſtom may often have countenanc'd a thing not well of it ſelf. But in all that depends upon common ſence and reaſon, ſuch as are the Rules of the Stage, there to take a licenſe, is a crime; becauſe it offends not Cuſtom, but Natural light, which ought never to ſuffer an Eclipſe.

Non omnia ad Homerum referenda tanquam ad normam cenſeo, ſed & ipſum ad normam. Scalig. l. 1. c. 5.

I

I muſt not omit, for the Glory of the Ancients, that if they have ſometimes violated the Art of Drammatick Poems, they have done it for ſome more powerful and inducing Reaſon, than all the Intereſt of the Play could amount to. As for Example, *Euripides*, in the *Suppliants*, has preferr'd the glory of his Country to that of his Art, of which I have ſpoken elſewhere.

The third Objection has no force, but in the Ignorance of thoſe that alledge it. For if ſome Poems of the Ancients, and even thoſe which were moſt in Eſteem with them, have not ſucceeded upon our Stage, the Subject, and not the want of Art, has been the cauſe of it; And ſometimes likewiſe the Changes made by the Tranſlators, which deſtroyed all the Graces of the Original: They have added improbable Scenes between Princes, and have ſhew'd out of time that which the Ancients had carefully conceal'd with Art; and very often changed a fine Relation, into an impertinent ridiculous Spectacle. But That which is more worthy our conſideration, is, that there were certain Stories, fitted for the Stage of *Athens* with great Ornaments, which would be in abomination upon Ours: For Example, the Story of *Thyeſtes*; ſo that we may ſay, that either the Moderns have corrupted the Ancients, by changing their whole Oeconomy, or the Imperfection of the Matter ſtifled the excellency of the Art.

To deſtroy the 4th Objection, we need only to remember, that thoſe Plays of ours, which took with the people, and with the Court, were not lik'd in all their parts; but only in thoſe things which were reaſonable, and in which they were
con-

conformable to the Rules: When there were any paffionate Scenes, they were prais'd; and when there was any great Appearance or noble Spectacle, it was efteem'd; and if fome notable Event was well manag'd, there was great fatisfaction fhewn; but if in the reft of the Play, or even in thefe beauties of it, any irregularities were difcover'd, or any fault againft Probability and Decency, either in the perfons, time, or place, or as to the ftate of the things reprefented, they were condemned as Faults. And all the favour that was fhewed the Poet, was, that out of the defire of preferving what was fine, the Spectatours were fomewhat more indulgent to what was amifs.

Therefore that fuccefs fo much bragg'd on, is fo far from contradicting the Rules of the Stage, that quite contrary it eftablifhes their Authority. For thefe Rules being nothing but an Art to caufe the fineft Incidents to pleafe with decency and probability, it fufficiently appears how neceflary they are, fince by common confent, all that comes up to them is approved of, and all that varies from them is in fome meafure condemn'd. Examples would extremely illuftrate this truth, if I were not afraid to anger fome of our Poets, by inftructing the others at their coft.

The 5th Objection is abfolutely ridiculous. For the Rules of the Stage do not at all reject the moft notable Incidents of any Story, but they furnifh us with Inventions, how fo to adjuft the Circumftances of the Action, Time, and Place, as not to go againft

E all

all probable appearance, and yet not to reprefent them always as they are in Story, but fuch as they ought to be, to have nothing but what's agreeable in them. 'Tis That then that we are to feek, and of which in the following Difcourfe I fhall communicate my Thoughts.

CHAP.

C H A P. V.

How they ought to Inſtruct themſelves, who intend to write a Drammatick Poem.

IN the Univerſities, the Drammatick Poets, as well as others, are given to young Scholars to read and ſtudy, and they affording great variety by moral Sentences, of which they are full, and by the Dialogues of different perſons conteſting with paſſion, as alſo by the imagination of thoſe Machines, which one muſt neceſſarily ſuppoſe to have been employed in the repreſentation of them; to which may be added the ſudden Turns and Events of the Stage, they cannot but procure an Extrem delight to theſe young Students, and make a ſtrong impreſſion in their minds; and though the whole, it may be, is both ill explain'd by thoſe that Inſtruct them, and as ill underſtood by Them; yet they have infinite ſatisfaction in the thing.

It may be after this, they ſee ſome Play compos'd by their Maſter, and acted in the ſame Schools ; and though that be done by very ill Actors, and carry with it in all its circumſtances the true Character of

pedantry,

pedantry, neverthelefs this is perform'd with fo much noife, buftle, and preparation, that they conceive a mighty Idea of it, having feen nothing better, and being incapable of finding out the faults of the piece.

If then there happens to be amongft thefe Youths a fiery Lad with Fancy, and fome Inclination to Poetry, finding himfelf at leifure to employ his parts his own way, he fixes upon Drammatick Poetry; and out comes a piece of his. To make which he generally follows this method; he pitches upon fome ftory that pleafes him, without confidering, whether it be fit for the Scene or no, or ever reflecting what is to be avoided in it, or what Ornaments may be added; he is refolv'd to hide under the Curtain any thing that fhall incommode him, to put *France* at one corner of the Stage, *Turkey* at the other, and *Spain* in the middle, his Actours fhall be fometimes in the *Louvre*, then in a Wood, or High-way, and then in a Garden full of Flowers, and no body knows how they came there; and if any body is to pafs by Sea from *Denmark* to *France*, 'tis done with the drawing of a Scene. Having thus fill'd every thing with ridiculous Imaginations, and things oppofite to all probability, he makes his firft Scene; which he has no fooner done, but finding himfelf at a ftand, he repairs to fome of the Theatres, to fee if he can fteal any Invention from them, that fhall pleafe him. Then he gets into the company of fome celebrated Poet or Critick, and from them he is fupplyed with fome new thought, or paffionate incident, or fome flight of the Art, which he immediatly employes quite contrary,

and

and out of all time; and having thus with the help of some Songs and Elegies, made formerly for *Cloris*, muster'd up three or four hundred Verses, he resolves to call it an Act. Thus going on in the same method, he gets to the death or marriage of some Prince, and then 'tis privately whisper'd among his Friends, that he has made a very pretty Play: The Ladies desire to see it, and 'tis by the Author red to them in secret, they are charmed with some Florid Expressions, or smart Repartees, and call in the Gentlemen of their acquaintance to hear it. Every body applauds and flatters the Author, reserving to themselves the privilege of laughing at him, as soon as his back's turn'd ; and in short, he acquires thus the honourable title of a Poet.

Without doubt, not only one must have prodigious good fortune, but more than that, an infus'd science, like *Adam's*, to make at first and by such methods a piece (not comparable, I say, to those whom twenty Ages have reverenced) but to make a thing like that of the Poet *Rhodophilus*, of whom *Scaliger* says, that his *Comedie* rather excited pity than mirth. To say truth, the Complaisance or Ignorance of the Spectatours is extreme, when they condemn others, as too severe, who cannot applaud such stuff, as this is. There is no Mechanick trade in the World that does not oblige to a long Apprentiship under a Master, and when the Artists set up for themselves, they are examin'd by the Company, to whom they must produce some Master-piece of their own making. And shall we then think, that to succeed in the greatest Art that is, in which the mind has all the share,

and

Extat illius Comædia, qua nihil aversum magis a comitate ; adeo enim insulsa est, ut misericordiam potius quàm risum excitet. Scal. l. 6. c. 3.

Diu non nisi optimus quisque, & qui creden-

tem sibi minime fallat, legendus est; sed diligenter aut pene ad scribendi solicitudinem, nec per partes modo scrutanda omnia; sed perlectus liber utique ex integro resumendus. Quintil. l. 10. cap. 1.

and which is not only the hardest, but the least understood Art that we have, there needs nothing, but to have the Impudence to undertake it; no certainly, there goes a great deal more to it, and therefore I will now counsel, as well as I can, any body that undertakes to be a Poet, and tell him, what he is to do.

In the first place, let our Poet suppress all those impetuous desires of glory and applause, and leave thinking, that to make a good Play, 'tis enough to have a vein for Poetry. He must begin with applying himself to the reading of *Aristotle's* Poeticks, and those of *Horace*, and he must read them attentively, and meditate upon them; then he must turn over those that have made Commentaries upon them, as *Castelvetro* in *Italian*, who in his Jargon says very fine things, *Hieronymus Vida, Heinsius, Vossius, la Menardiere*, and a great many more; and let him remember, that *Scaliger* alone says more than all the rest; but he must not lose a word in him, for all his words are of weight and importance. As for the book of *Boulenger*, he must value him only for his Collection of Passages out of other Authors, and not mind the Consequences he draws from them; for I believe for my part that the things he has writ, came into his head just as he was writing them, and without any precedent Meditation.

Horat. de art. poet. verf. 268. Vos exemplaria Græca Nocturnâ verfate manu, verfate diurnâ.

I add to these Authors *Plutarch, Athenæus, and Lilius Giraldus*, who all in many places have touch'd the chief Maxims of the Stage; in a word, he must not let slip any thing of the Ancients, without examining every period of them; for very often a word thrown out by the by, and out of the fubject of the Stage, contains in their books fome important fecret, and the refolution of fome great difficulty.

Having thus ftudied the Theory, he muft read all the Greek and Latin Drammatick Poems, which by good fortune have been preferv'd to our times, as likewife their old Scholiafts or Commentators, but ftill take the liberty to examin them impartially, for they are fubject to a great many Errours, and delight in falfe and vain fubtleties of no ufe at all; and all along one muft be fure to make conftant reflexions, and examine why a Poet has rather done one thing than another, and he may obferve that often a word ingenioufly caft out by an Actour, to prepare fome Incident, or to explain the Circumftances of place or time, is not a thing flightly to be pafs'd over; and if after all, I durft be fo vain, as to make one amongft his Mafters, I could wifh he would join the Precepts of this practical part of the Art, to what he may difcover in the Ancient or Modern Poets; for though I cannot brag of giving him confiderable and important fuccours in his Defign, yet I am fure I fhall not be ufelefs or incommodious to him, and though it fhould appear that I am miftaken, yet I am fure he will thank me for the very means I afford him of inftructing himfelf better.

Our Poet having thus acquir'd a perfect Notion of the Art of the Stage, may much more certainly, and with greater fuccefs undertake fome noble defign.

As

As for me, without repeating here what may be learnt in *Ariſtotle*, and his Interpreters, both Ancient and Modern, I will only endeavour to treat of new matters, or at leaſt to give new Inſtructions upon thoſe things, which have been treated of by others.

CHAP.

C H A P. VI.

Of the Spectators, and how they are to be considered by the Poet.

MY Intention is not here to teach the Spectators of a Play, the attention that they ought to have, nor the silence that they ought to keep, no more than the caution they ought to observe in judging of the Play ; nor what they should do to avoid those Errours which Complaisance, or a Prejudice against the Author, often runs them into; though all this might be usefully enough, and to good purpose, treated of here.

But I onely mention the Spectators in reference to the Poet, that is, how he ought to consider them when he is making a Play.

I borrow here the Comparison of a Picture, of which I shall often make use in this Treatise ; and I say that my Picture may be considered two ways.

First, as a Picture ; that is, as the work of the Artist ; where there are Colours, and not real things ; shadows, and not substances ; artificial lights, false elevations, prospective distances, or lontananzas, deceiving shortnings, and in a word, appearances of things that really are not in the Picture.

F

Secondly,

Secondly, It may be confider'd as containing a Story painted, whether a true one, or fuppos'd to be fo; whereof the Place is certain, the Qualities natural, the Actions undoubtedly true, and all the Circumftances of them obferv'd accordingto order and reafon.

This may be all applyed to Drammatick Poems: One may at firft confider the Shew and Reprefentation of things, where Art gives you Images of them which really are not. There are Princes in appearance; Palaces upon painted cloth, dead men in fhew; and 'tis for this that the Actors carry all the Marks of thofe whom they reprefent. The Decoration of the Stage, is the Image of thofe places where the thing is fuppos'd to be tranfacted. There are Spectators, and the perfons that appear upon the Stage talk in the Mother Tongue of the Audience, all things being to be made fenfible and plain to them. 'Tis to arrive to this Reprefentation of the thing, that the Poet caufes fometimes one, fometimes another Actor to appear, and difcourfe upon the Stage: making recitals of things that ought to be known, and yet ought not to appear; and Employing Machines, and other Contrivances, for the appearance of thofe things which are to be fhew'd to the Audience.

Thus *Efchylus* makes the Palace of *Clytemneftra* open, that the body of *Agamemnon* may be feen upon the Step of the inward door, where a dead man lies along upon the Threfhold. In *Ajax, Tecmeffa* opens his Tent to fhew his madnefs, by the number of the dead fheep which lye round about him. In *Euripides, Hecuba* fwouns away upon the Stage, to exprefs the greatnefs of her Mifery: And in *Plautus*, the

the Captives exprefs their condition of flavery, by being bound, and having an appearance of Guards about them; and after this the difcourfes made by the Actors, upon thefe different Appearances, perfect the Reprefentation.

Or elfe we may confider in thefe Dramatick Poems, the true Hiftory, or that which is fuppo-fed true, and of which all the Adventures have re-ally come to pafs, in that order, time, and place, and according to thofe Intrigues which appear to us. The perfons are there confider'd according to their different Characters, of their Condition, Age and Sex; and the things they fay, as having been really pronounced by them, as well as perform'd in their actions; and in a word, all things as we fee them upon the Stage.

I know very well that the Poet is the Mafter, and that he difpofes the order of his Poem as he thinks fit; taking the time, which he lengthens or fhortens as he pleafes; chufing likewife what place he will in the whole world; and for the Plot he Invents it according to the ftrength and finenefs of his own fancy; and in a word, he gives what form he pleafes to the matter he has in hand; but ftill 'tis certain, that all thefe things muft be fo adjufted, as to feem to have naturally both the rife, progrefs, and end which he gives them; fo that though he be the Author, yet he muft write the whole with fuch Art, that it may not fo much as appear that it was by him Invented. So in *Efchylus's* Trage-die of *Agamemnon*, all things appear as if really *Agamemnon* had been murder'd; and in *Sophocles*, as if *Ajax* were really furious; and fo of all the other Pieces of the Ancients. And likewife when

we

we judge of any Play on our Stage, we suppose the
thing either true, or that ought to be so, and
might be so; and upon that suppofition we approve of all the Words or Actions that are done or
faid by thofe who fpeak or act; and of all thofe E-
vents which might probably follow the firft Appearances; becaufe that in this cafe we believe
that things might really happen as they feem, nay
that they have happened, and ought to happen
fo. And on the contrary, we condemn all that
ought not to be done, or faid, according to the
qualities of the perfons, the place, the time, and
the firft appearances of the Play.

Now to underftand how the Poet is to govern
himfelf, with regard to the Spectators, and when
they are to be confiderable to him, or not fo, we
need but reflect upon what we have faid of a Picture; for looking upon it only as the Work of the
Artift, the Painter does what he can to make it
Excellent, becaufe it will be feen, and that he expects to be known and admir'd by it; but if he
confider it as a Story painted, he keeps as clofe as
he can to the Nature of the thing he reprefents,
and does nothing but what will feem probable in
all its Circumftances, becaufe it is all to be confider'd as true, and fuppos'd fo. For example, if he
will draw *Mary Magdelen* in her penitent retire-
ment, he will not omit any of the moft important
parts of her Story, becaufe if he fhou'd do otherwife, they that fhould fee it would hardly know
it. He muft place her in a decent pofture, elfe fhe
will be a difagreeable Object. He will not draw her
proftrate and groveling with her face upon the
ground, becaufe that would hide the fineft part of
                                                her,

her, but rather he muſt ſet her upon her knees.
He ought not to cover her all over with a Cilice, or
haircloth, but leave her half naked, that the Charm
of her beauty may appear the more. He muſt not
place her in the bottom of a deep Cavern, for then
ſhe cannot be ſuppos'd to be ſeen, but at the entrance of it, with ſo much light as is juſt neceſſary;
and this he muſt do, becauſe he conſiders his work
as a Picture which ought to fall under the Senſes,
and pleaſe at the ſame time.

But when he conſiders this Picture the other way,
that is, keeping to the truth of the Story, he muſt
give her a Complexion pale and wan, becauſe it is
not credible it could be otherwiſe in the midſt of
ſo much auſterity; ſhe ſhall not have a Crown before her, but a Croſs; ſhe muſt not be plac'd upon
a rich embroider'd Bed, but upon the ground;
there ſhall not be a Palace near her, but a horrid
Wilderneſs; he muſt not environ her with Pages,
and Women Attendants, but rather with wild Beaſts,
but they muſt be in a quiet poſture, that ſhe may
be ſuppos'd to live among them; the Cave ſhall be
cover'd with Moſs, not gilded and finely ſet out.
The very trees are not to be made full of Flowers and Fruits, but rather half-dryed, and wither'd;
and all the Country about them barren and wild.
And in a word, he ſhall adorn his work with all
thoſe things which probably might become the
ſtate of penitence, according to the perſon, place,
and other dependencies of the Story, becauſe here
he conſiders the truth of what he is to repreſent.

In the ſame manner, the Poet conſidering in
his Play the Repreſentation or Spectacle of it, does
all that he can to make it agreeable to the Spectators;

tors; for his bufinefs is to pleafe them. And
therefore he fhall preferve all the nobleft Incidents
of his Story, he fhall make all his Actors appear with the beft Characters he can, he fhall employ the fineft Figures of Rhetorick, and the
Moving'ft Paffions, obferving to hide nothing that
ought to be known and pleafe, and to fhew nothing that ought to be hid, and may offend ; and
in fine, he fhall try all means to gain the efteem
and admiration of the Audience.

But when he confiders in his Play the true
Story of it, or that which is fuppos'd to be fo, he
muft particularly have a care to obferve the Rules
of probability in every thing, and to make all the
Intrigues, Actions, Words, as if they had in reality
come to pafs ; he muft give fit thoughts and defigns, according to the perfons that are employed,
he muft unite the Times with Places, and the Beginning with the Confequences ; and in a word, he
follows the Nature of things fo, as not to contradict neither the State, nor the Order, nor the
Effects, nor the Property of them ; and indeed
has no other Guide but Probability and Decency,
and rejects all that has not that Character upon
it. He muft contrive every thing as if there were
no Spectators ; that is, all the Perfons in the Play are
to act and fpeak as if they were truly (for example)
a King, and not *Mondoroy* or *Bellerofe*; as if they
really were in the Palace of *Horatius* in *Rome*,
and not at *Paris* in the *Hoftel de Bourgogne* ; and
as if no body faw them, or heard them, but thofe
who are acting with them upon the Stage. And
by this Rule it is that they often fay that they are
alone, that no body fees them, nor hears them,

Two famous Players.

that

that they need not fear being interrupted, or difturb'd in their Solitude, no more than hindred in
their defigns ; though all this is fpoken in the prefence of it may be two thoufand perfons; becaufe in
this the Nature of the Action is followed according
to truth, for then the Spectators were not by ;
and this onght to be ftrictly obferv'd, for all that is
affected in favour of the Spectators is falfe and
faulty.

I know very well that the Poet does not work upon the Action as true, but only fo far as it is fit
for Reprefentation, and therefore it may feem that
there may be fome mixture of thefe two Confiderations, therefore I fhall propound the way how he
fhall diftinguifh them. He examines firft all that he
defigns to make known to the Audience, either by
their Eyes or their Ears, and accordingly refolves
either to let them fee it, or to inftruct them by fome
recital of the thing which they ought to know.
But he does not make thefe Recitals or Spectacles
onely becaufe the Spectators ought to know or fee.
How then ? Why he muft find in the Action,
which is confider'd as true, fome motive, colour, or
apparent Reafon, for which it may appear that thefe
Shews or Recitals did probably happen, and ought
to come to pafs ; and I may fay that the greateft Art
of the Stage confifts in finding out thefe Motives
or Colours. An Actor muft come upon the Stage,
becaufe the Spectator muft know his Defigns and
Paffions. There muft be a Narration made of things
paft, becaufe elfe the Spectator being ignorant of
them, would not underftand what's prefent, and under reprefentation. There muft be a Shew or Spectacle, to move the Audience with pity or admi-
rations ;

ration; and that is working upon the action as reprefented; and it is his duty as well as his chief defign;
but he muft hide this under fome colour drawn from
the truth of the Action it felf; infomuch, that the
perfon who is to inftruct the Audience, muft come
upon the Stage upon the pretext of looking for
fome body there; or to meet one who had given him an Affignation. So the perfon who is to
make a Narration of things paft, muft do it fo as it
may feem neceffary, and done to advife about fomething in agitation at prefent, for which there is fome
help wanting. If there be a Spectacle, it muft be
to fome end, as to excite fome body to be reveng'd,
or fo; and this is call'd working upon the truth of
the Action, without minding the Spectators; becaufe 'tis probable, that, taking things only in themfelves. all this might fall out fo.

Let us come to the Examples alledg'd before. *Æfchylus* caufes *Agamemnon* to be murder'd in his Palace; but the Audience muft know this, and how
does he inform them of it? He makes that Unfortunate Prince cry out like a man that expires under
the violence of thofe who murder him. *Sophocles*
obferves the fame thing in the murder of *Clitem-
neftra* by the hand of *Oreftes*. And I cannot but admire at fome who tax both thofe Poets of having
defil'd the Stage with blood, when 'tis apparent
that they are kill'd in the Houfes reprefented upon
the Stage, and out of the fight of the Spectators,
who only hear their cries and lamentations, and fee
the body afterwards when 'tis dead.

In the fame *Sophocles*, *Ajax* is outragiously furious,
and yet there is a neceffity of his appearing upon
the Stage with *Ulyffes*, without hurting him, and

¶   to

to that end *Minerva* brings him out of his Tent, and
suspends for a while his fit of madness.

In *Euripides* the Spectators must know that *Polydorus* is dead, that *Hecuba* may receive a new height-
ning to her afflictions ; and to do it with appearance of reason, one of her Women goes to fetch wa-
ter at the Sea side, to wash and purifie the dead body
of her Daughter *Polyxena*, whose Funeral she was to
perform, where she finds, as it were by chance, the
body of the unhappy young Prince, which she brings
to his more unhappy Mother, and so discovers very
handsomely the series of all that sad Adventure.
(And by the by it appears, how much they are mistaken, who think that the Poet sends *Hecuba* her
self to the Sea side, and that there she had found the
Body of her Son).   But we should be bound to too
tedious an enumeration, if we would by Examples
shew the conduct of the Ancients in this point.

For upon their Stage there is not a Recital, a
Passion, nor an Intrigue, that has not its colour ; if
you take the Story as true, though it be a Fable invented by the Poet only for Representation.   In a
word, the Spectators are not considerable to the Poet, in the Truth of the Action, but only in the Representation ; and upon this Maxim, if we examine
the best part of our Modern Poets, we may easily
perceive, that they go against all probability, even in
those things which have been esteem'd the most; Because the Authors, when they expos'd them to the
people, did it without any colour that might make
us suppose them reasonable.   Thus in the truth of
the Action it happens that a man makes a necessary
Narration, that's well, for the Spectators ought not

to be ignorant of it ; but this man could not know the very thing he tells, then 'tis againſt probability for him to make this recital. A Lover appears upon the Stage in a violent paſſion to pleaſe the Spectatours ; but he could not naturally make theſe complaints in the place repreſented by the Stage; there muſt then ſome colour be found out for his being there extraordinarily, or elſe you go againſt probability : As much may be ſaid of a thouſand other Adventures which appear upon our Stages, where every day we have Images of things that never were, never can be, and by conſequent ought not to be.

CHAP.

C H A P. VII.

Of the Mixture of Reprefentation with the Truth of the Theatral Action.

I Believe the Title of this Chapter will be at firft fight feverely cenfur'd, becaufe it may be it will not be underftood ; but when I fhall have explain'd my meaning, I hope all the judicious will be reconcil'd to the Terms, as well as to my Sentiments about the thing.

I call Truth of the Theatral Action, the whole Story of the Play, fo far as it is confider'd as a true one, and that all the Adventures in it are look'd upon as being come to pafs. But I call Reprefentation, the Collection of all thofe things which may ferve to reprefent a Drammatick Poem, confider'd in themfelves and in their own Nature, as the Players, the Scenes, the Mufick, the Spectators, and a great many other things. As for Example, in the Play of *Cinna,* made by Monfieur *Corneille* ; that that *Cinna,* who appears upon the Stage, fpeaks like a *Roman,* that he loves *Æmilia,* counfels *Auguftus Cæfar* to keep the Empire, confpires againft him, and is pardon'd by him ; all this I fay, is the truth of the Theatral Action. That the fame *Æmilia* hates

G 2 *Auguftus,*

Auguftns, and loves *Cinna*, that fhe defires to be reveng'd, and yet apprehends the Event of fo great an Undertaking; all this too is of the truth of the Action. That *Auguftus* propofes his thoughts of leaving the Empire to two perfidious Friends, and that one advifes him to keep it, and the other to leave it, is likewife of the truth of the Action. In a word, all that in the Play either is confider'd as a part, or has a neceffary dependence upon the Story, ought to be of the truth of the Action; and 'tis by this Rule that one ought to Examine the probability of all that's done in the Play; as the fitnefs and decency of the Expreffions, the connexion of the Intrigue, the patnefs of the Events, &c. And one naturally approves of all that ought to have been don according to the truth, though it be a fuppos'd Story, and one condemns all that one thinks contrary to truth, or not becoming the actions of life.

But that *Floridor* or *Beauchafteau* act the part of *Cinna*, that they are good or ill Actors, well or ill drefs'd, that they are feparated from the people by a Stage, which is adorn'd with painted cloth, reprefenting Palaces and Gardens, that the Intervals of the Acts are mark'd by ill Fidlers, or excellent Mufick; that an Actor goes behind the Stage, when he fays he goes into the Kings Clofet, and fpeaks to his Wife, inftead of fpeaking to a Queen, that there are Spectatours, and thofe either from the Court, or the City; that they are filent or make a noife, that there are quarrels in the Pit, or none, all thefe things are, and do depend on the Reprefentation.

Therefore *Floridor* and *Beauchafteau* are to be look'd

look'd upon as reprefenting, and that *Cinna* or *Horatius*, whom they reprefent, are to be confider'd as real aud true perfons, acting and fpeaking as *Cinna*, and *Horatius*, and not as thofe who reprefent them, and *Floridor* and *Beauchafteau* muft be look'd upon as transform'd into thofe men, whofe names and concerns they take upon them, fo that part of the *Hoftel de Bourgogne* which is rais'd and adorn'd for a Stage, is the place reprefenting, and the Image of another place which is reprefented at that time, whether the Palace of *Auguftus* or *Horatius*; and it muft in the Play be look'd upon as the true place where all things pafs, fo the time which is employed in the Reprefentation, being a part of our natural currant year, is but a reprefenting time, but the day reprefented, and in which one fuppofes the action of the Stage to come to pafs, ought to be taken for a real true time in regard to the Action.

I fay then that one ought never to mingle together what concerns the Reprefentation of a Play, with the true Action of the Story reprefented.

It would not be well lik'd off, that *Floridor*, while he is reprefenting *Cinna*, fhould talk of his own domeftick affairs, or of the lofs and gains of the Play-houfe; or that while he is repeating the Speech made by *Cinna* to the Confpirators at *Rome*, he fhould addrefs himfelf to the People of *Paris*, and make fome Reflections upon them; or that while he is examining the hatred and haughtinefs of *Æmilia*, he fhould go about to talk of the fweetnefs and good breeding of our Ladies; In a word, he would not be endur'd to confound *Rome* and *Paris*, nor actions pafs'd fo many years ago, with prefent Adventures,

ventures ; becaufe that is not only offending againſt all the Rules of decency, but thoſe of common ſenſe.

I know very well that our Modern Poets have not hitherto been very guilty of this fault, but becaufe the Ancients, whom I generally propoſe for Examples, have been ſo indulgent to the Peoples pleaſure, as not to take care to avoid this Errour, I thought it would not be amiſs to ſay ſomething of it, leſt our Poets ſhould follow their Example, after the rate of that ſcurvy Orator, whom *Cicero* ſpeaks of in *Brutus*, for never imitating the great men in any thing, but ſuch things where they were faulty. *Ariſtotle* ſays that ill Poets fall into Errors, becauſe they are ignorant of the means of doing better, and that good ones do the ſame thing out of Complaiſance to the Players, and for the Diverſion of the Audience ; but I think that a true Poet ought not to ſeek any other way of being profitable to the firſt, nor of pleaſing the laſt, but by the excellence of his Play.

Comedy in its riſe, and when it firſt begun to be acted, as Tragedy was, by ſet Actors, was nothing but a Satyrical Poem, which by little and litle, under pretext of inſtructing the People, by inveighing at their Vices, came at laſt to be ſo bitter and ſcandalous, as not onely to expoſe the moſt Eminent Citizens, but not to ſpare the Magiſtrates themſelves, nor the moſt Illuſtrious Perſons of the State, whoſe Names, Faces, and actions were brought upon the Stage ; and this was that the Authors call Old Comedy.

Not but that at firſt even this was much more innocent than afterwards ; for under *Epicharmus*, and
the

firſt Comicks who ſucceeded him, Comedy was merry and laughing, but not injurious and affronting; it had Salt and Railleries, but not Gall and Vinegar; but at laſt that liberty degenerated into ſo much libertiniſme, that *Ariſtophanes*'s Plays did not a little contribute to the death of the famous *Socrates* by exciting the People againſt him. The Repreſentation in thoſe days was ſo confounded with the Truth of Action, that they were almoſt the ſame thing; and that which was ſaid againſt the *Socrates* upon the Stage, was often applicable to the *Socrates* who was in the Pit. 'Tis but reading *Ariſtophanes*'s firſt Plays, and you ſhall ſee that all along he confounds the intereſt of the Actors with thoſe of the Spectators, and even the Hiſtory repreſented with the Publick Affairs of the State, upon which he founds his Jeſts and Railleries; In a word, his Plays are down-right Libels, containing the Names, Qualities, Actions, and viſible Portraicts of thoſe whom the Poet undertook to expoſe; and that without any other conduct or rule, but that of his Satyrical wit and paſſion; ſo far were they from being ingenious rational Poems, regulated by Art; and the Magiſtrates foreſeeing the dangerous Effects of ſuch licenſe, forbid them any more naming particular perſons in their Plays.

But as one is always Ingenious in miſchief, the Poets found means, though they left out the Name, to repreſent the Perſon ſo livelily, that every body knew preſently, who they meant; and this was ſince call'd Middle Comedy; and ſuch were the laſt Plays of *Ariſtophanes*.

But this way of Satyr, though ſomewhat milder than the other, was ſtill thought to be of as

ill

ill Confequence, and by the Magiftrates accordingly prohibited. This put the Poets to fome ftand,
and forc'd them at laft to invent not only the
Names, but likewife the Adventures of their Stage,
and then Comedy, being an ingenious Product
of wit and Art, was regulated upon the model of
Tragedy, and became (to define it rightly) the true
Picture and Imitation of the Common Actions of
life. Then the Reprefentation was no longer confounded with the Truth of the Action, and all
that was done upon the Stage was confider'd as a
true Story, in which neither the State, nor the
Spectators, were fuppos'd to have any part. The
Adventures were generally taken from fome remote Country, with which the place where they
were reprefented had little communication, and the
Actors feem'd to act only by the confideration
of thofe things, which were reprefented. Thus that
which came to be call'd New Comedy was made,
of which *Terence* was one of the firft that gave
us a Model, and that fo good a one, that it is never feen that he ever confounds the Reprefentation with the Truth of the Theatral Action. *Plautus* who went before him, and was nearer the
time of Middle Comedy, is not fo regular, but
does fo often fall into that inconvenience, that
the reading him becomes tedious, and not feldom
his Plays are confus'd and obfcure by it.

*Parùm ferið
res agi videtur,
fi Actores ipfi
populum com-
pellent.
Voſs. lib. 2. c.
26. fect. 15.
Poet.*

*Act. 3. Sc. 1.
Nunc hùc hono-
ris veſtri ve-
nio gratiâ, ne
hanc inchoa-
tam tranfigam
Comædiam, fi-
mul Alcumenæ
quam vir &c.*

In his *Amphytrion, Jupiter* is fuppos'd to be at
Thebes in the time that *Hercules* is born, and when
he appears under the form of *Amphytrion*, he tells
the Spectators, *I am Jupiter, and I am chang'd to*
Amphytrion *when I pleafe, which I do,* (fays he to
the Spectators) *to oblige you by Continuing this Play,*
and

*and for the love of Alcmena that she may appear Inno-
cent.* Where we see he mingles the concerns of the
Actors with the Interest of the Spectators, and makes
an Interfering of *Romans* who were present, with
those who were suppos'd to act in *Greece*, which certainly cannot be but very ridiculous, and must confound the understanding of the Spectators, by for-
cing them to imagine a man double, and to distinguish in him both words and sentiments very different, without any necessity or reason for it. Certainly when a man appears before us with the
Clothes, Countenance, Words, and Gesture of a
person, whom he represents, he is not to be consider'd otherwise than according to that Image, which
from our Eyes we imprint in our mind; and therefore all that unmasks him, to shew him, as he really
is, such a Player, whose Name is so or so, confounds
the Attention of the Audience, who expect nothing
from that Actor, but things proper to the person
whose Appearance he takes.

In his *Aulularia*, *Euclio* is at *Athens*, where he has
been rob'd, and while he is seeking the man that ran
away with his Treasure, he says such things to ex-
press his despair, that the Audience falls a laughing;
upon which *Euclio* turning to them, says, *why do
you laugh, I know you all well enough, and know that
amongst you there are Thieves enough.* Now *Euclio*
is suppos'd to be at *Athens,* where no *Romans* could
be for Spectators, much less could they be suspected
to conceal among them the man that had stoln
his Money. He is so full of these faults, that
there is scarce a Play of his without them; but in
two places the raillery is so ingenious, and so plac'd

at the end of the Play, without being interwoven in the Story, that it may very well be excufed.

The firſt is at the end of *Pſeudolus,* where his witty Slave having invited *Ballio* to drink with him, he anſwers, *Why don't you likewiſe invite theſe Gentlemen?* pointing to the Spectators; to which *Pſeudolus* replies, *I don't uſe to invite them, nor they me; but Gentlemen, if you will ſay that our Houſe and Play pleaſes you, I invite you again to morrow.*

Bal. Te ſequor, quin vocas Spectatores ſimul? Pſ. Hercle me iſti haud ſolent vocare, neque ergo ego iſtos; verùm ſi voltis applaudere atque approbare hunc gregem & fabulam, in craſtinum vos vocabo. Pſeudol. Act.5.Sc. 2.

The other is at the end of his *Rudens,* where *Dæmones* having invited *Labrax* to Supper, tells the Spectators. *I would invite you too, Gentlemen, but I have little to give him; and beſides I hope you are all engaged; but if you pleaſe to give your approbation to this Play, I will Invite you all to ſup with me this day ſixteen year.*

Spectatores vos quoque ad coenam vocem, ni daturus nihil ſim, neque ſit quicquam pollucti domi, neue adeò vocatos credam vos eſſe ad cænam foras. Verùm ſi Voletis plauſum fabulæ huic clarum dare, Comiſſatum omnes venitote ad me ad annos ſexdecim.

In theſe caſes, the Action of the Stage being over, the Railleries that are made can no longer confound the *Ideas* of the Spectators.

As for Tragedies, as their ſubject is more noble and ſerious, they are ſeldom infected with this corrupt way; except in *Euripides's* Prologues, where often the chief Actor, or a God in ſome Machine, makes a Narration of things happened before the the opening of the Stage. Which I muſt confeſs I cannot approve of, becauſe often theſe things are clear enough in the thread of the Story; and when Poets do not explain their Subject, by the

Mouth

Mouth and Actions of their Actors, 'tis a fault without excuse, and Prologues are but ill shifts to repair such a neglect. *Sophocles* never does it, and I cannot but advise all Poets to follow him in this.

H 2 CHAP,

C H A P. VIII.

How the Poet muſt make his Deco-
rations, and other Neceſſary Acti-
ons in the Play, known to the Au-
dience.

THE moſt remarkable and indeed an eſſential
difference between Epick and Dramatick
Poems, is, that in the firſt, the Poet ſpeaks alone,
the perſons that he produces all uttering themſelves
by his mouth ; 'tis he that ſays, that ſuch and ſuch
people made ſuch and ſuch diſcourſes, and not
they that come and make them themſelves. But
in the Dramatick Poem, the Poet is ſilent, and
none but the perſons introduc'd by him, do ſpeak ;
and during all the Theatral Action, he appears no
more than if the perſons were really thoſe whom
they repreſent.

Therefore in the Epick Poem, the Poet makes all
the deſcriptions that may grace his work, when
and where he pleaſes. If he has a mind to ſhew a
Temple or a Palace, he frames the Architecture of
it according to his own fancy. If there be a ſhip-
wrack, he expreſſes as he pleaſes the horror of the
Tempeſt

Tempeſt, the fear of the Seamen, the cryes of thoſe who are caſt away, and the conſtancy of his Hero, and for all this he chuſes that place in his Poem, which he thinks fitteſt for theſe or other Deſcriptions. But in a Dramatick Poem, the Poet muſt ſpeak by the mouth of his Actors, he cannot employ any other means, and what they omit, can no ways be ſupplyed by any induſtry of his ; if there be a Shipwrack, the Actors muſt explain it, and ſpeak of the misfortune of thoſe who have been caſt away; and ſo for any Ornament or Action extraordinary : They muſt all be explain'd by thoſe whom he brings upon his Stage. The Ancient Poets have been very exact and judicious in this pàrticular, but our Modern Authors have committed ſuch faults in it, as have much disfigur'd their Plays.

A Play may be regarded two ways; it is made to be acted by perſons, who are to do every thing, as if they were the true perſons repreſented; and likewiſe Plays are made to be read by people, who without ſeeing them acted, can by their imagination, and the ſtrength of the impreſſions the Poet gives, make thoſe perſons as it were preſent to their Idea. Now whether a Play be acted or read, it muſt be underſtood by the Spectators, and by the Reader ; it cannot be known to the Spectators, but juſt as the Actors ſhall make it ſo ; and the Reader can underſtand no more of it, than the Verſes or Expreſſions do inform him, ſo that either way all the Decorations, Clothes, or neceſſary Motions, for the underſtanding the Play, muſt be had in the Verſes, or other expreſſions in Proſe, which are by the Actors recited.

To

To this may be said, that our Poets ufe to be by at the Rehearfals, and fo tell the Players every particular that they are to do; but befides the negligence of the Players in the execution of this, how fhall any body do, that would act the Play without the Poet? how fhall they know where the Scene lies? what Decorations belong to it, and what Clothes the Actors have, and fo in any other Circumftances neceffary to the underftanding and Ornament of the Play? *Efchylus* his Tragedies have been often acted at *Athens*, after he was dead.

The fame thing was done by *Plautus*'s Comedies at *Rome*; and is done every day at *Paris* by our old Plays; all which could not well have been perform'd, if the Poet had not been careful to explain all things by the Actors. I know indeed that to help the dulnefs of fome Readers, many of our Poets have made Marginal Notes in their printed works, which exprefs that which is not faid in the Play; As *here appears a Temple open, here a Palace adorn'd with divers Columns of noble Architecture, here the King whifpers his Favourite,* and the like. But in all thefe Notes 'tis the Poet that fpeaks, which he is not allowed to do in this fort of Poems, and it cannot be done without interrupting the Reader in the midft of paffions, and dividing his application, and fo diffipating fome of thofe Ideas which he had receiv'd already for the underftanding and relifhing the Play.

But I fay more than all this, a Play ought to be made with fo much Art, and the Actors are to fpeak fo, that it fhall not be neceffary to marke the diftinction of the Acts, nor Scenes, nor fo much as to put the Names of thofe that fpeak, and to

prove

prove what I fay, we need only to confider, that
when an Actor comes upon the Stage, the Poet
does not come to tell his name, it muft be known
by himfelf, or fome other of the Actors ; and the
failing in this has made, that in fome Plays, that
I have feen, three Acts were over, before the
Audience knew the Name of the chief Actor,   and
that without any apparent neceffity of hiding
either That or his Qualitie ; for fometimes it is
neceffary he fhould be *Incognito*, but then 'tis as
neceffary that it fhould be known he is fo.

In this particular the Ancients have been fo
accurate, that I dare boldly fay, that let one have
a Tragedy, either of *Sophocles*, or *Euripides*, or a
Comedy of *Terence*, or *Plautus* without Title, Diftinction, Names of the Actors, or any Character
particular, to make either Them, or the feparation of the Acts and Scenes known, I would prefently difcover both the Name, Quality, Equipage,
Clothes, Gefture, and Interefts of all thofe who
fpeak ; the place of the Scene, its decorations, and
in a word, all that can make any part of the Theatral Action ; and all Plays, which cannot in the
fame manner make all things known to the Reader, are certainly defective. But to do this well,
there are many Ingenious Artifices to put fuch words
in the mouth of an Actor, as may be a reafonable
pretext for him to explain what is neceffary for
the underftanding of the Subject ; and thefe following Contrivances may ferve for an Example.

Sometimes the furprize of an Actor is a very
agreeable way of doing it; fo in *Plautus's Curculio*,
Palinurus, is furprized to fee *Phædromus* come
out of his Houfe before day with *Flambeaux* and
Servants

Servants loaden with Bottles of Wine.

Sometimes one employs the compaſſion which he ought to have of the miſerable ſtate of ſome other Actor, as *Electra* in *Euripides* does, to make it known that her Brother was before the Gates of his Palace, laid all along wrap'd up in his Cloke, and tormenting himſelf with his own diſquiets.

It may be done likewiſe by way of raillery; as in the *Trinummus* of *Plautus*, where *Charmides*, to deſcribe the great broad brimm'd Hat of a Cheat, diſguiz'd like a Souldier, ſays, *I believe this fellow is of the race of the Toadſtools, for he is all head.*

Or elſe it may be contriv'd, that two Actors ſhall ſhew one another ſome thing extraordinary; as in the firſt Act of the *Rudens* of *Plautus*, where by that Artifice one is inform'd, that there has been a Shipwrack, that there are ſome perſons yet alive ſwimming to the ſhore, that two women are alone in a ſmall Bark, and are by the Waves carried upon the Sands, where they fall into the Sea, and then getting up again with much ado gain the ſhore.

Sometimes by the Actions themſelves the Actors are ſufficiently known, as in *Euripides*, *Polyphemus* and the Satyrs drinking and growing drunk.

Very often an Actor by a cholerick word or action makes known what another Actor is doing; as in the *Caſina*, *Cleoſtrata* ſeeming angry, makes it appear that her Husband is chucking of her with his hand, to bring her into good humor again. Theſe may ſerve for Examples, many ſuch being obvious to an ingenious Fancy.

Not that a Poet need be very particular neither

ther, he is not bound to make an Exact defcrip-
tion of all the Columns, Portico's, or other Ornaments of Architecture in a Temple or Palace;
'tis enough that he mention in general terms, the
Decoration of his Theatre: And yet when any
Circumftance is to have an Effect in the Play,
then not only he may, but he muft ftay upon it
a little; as in the *Io* of *Euripides*, where it not
being permitted to the Women to go into the
Temple of *Apollo*, they ftay without and talk of
the painting, which made the Ornament of it on
the outfide; and in the *Moftellaria* of *Plautus*,
where *Tranio* defirous to perfwade his Mafter
Theuropides, that he had purchas'd the Houfe of
one of his Neighbours, onely to get fome Money
upon that pretext out of the old Man, he fhews
him the Avenue of it, and makes him obferve
it's Veftibule, Pillars, and other Singularities, which
muft be fuppos'd neceffary in the decoration of
the Stage, when the Play was acted.

There is no neceffity neither that many particulars fhould be explain'd, which are fufficiently underftood by natural Confequence; as when
a Poet fhall make *Horatius* a *Roman* fpeak, he
need not tell us what drefs he is in, nor endeavour to make us admire the Generofity of his
Sentiments; for 'tis of Neceffity, that he fhould
be drefs'd and fpeak like a *Roman*.

Two things, which muft never be forgot for the
underftanding of the Play, are the Time, which
the Poet gives to the Theatral Action, and the
Place where the Scene is laid. The Ancients have
Practis'd this with fo much Art, that often they
that read their Plays hardly take Notice of it at
firft;

I

firſt; *Plautus* opens the Stage in his *Amphytrio*, at the end of that long night which *Jupiter* had made on purpoſe to come and viſit *Alcmena* in, before ſhe was brought to bed ; which appears clearly by the diſcourſe of *Soſias*, who complains in the very firſt Scene of the length of the night, and ſays, *that he believes Aurora has a Cup too much, and cannot wake ſoon enough;* and the Play ends before Dinner, as it appears again by the Order which *Jupiter,* under the ſhape of *Amphytrio,* gives to *Soſias,* to go and invite *Blepharo* to Dinner, as ſoon as he ſhall have finiſh'd his Sacrifice ; for after this Order given, all the Events are ſo quick, that 'tis plain that all the Intrigues which perplex'd *Amphytrio* are firſt ſolv'd and made open.

The ſame Author has been as carefull to expreſs the place of his Scene, as has been already ſhew'd in his *Rudens* and *Curculio*; and the ſame is obſerv'd in the *Frogs* of *Ariſtophanes,* and the *Ajax* of *Sophocles.*

Very often it happens, that things are not ex-plain'd juſt as they are done, but a good while after ; as the Poet thinks moſt convenient, and where he can do it with the leaſt Affectation. I ſhall give no other example, but that of *Corneille* in his *Androme-da,* where when the winds carry her away, *Phine-as* is thrown to the ground by a Thunder-clap, of which at that time no further notice is taken, but 'tis made known in the ſecond Act, where *Phineas* complaining of the violence of the Gods againſt the endeavours he made to ſave *Andromeda,* ſays, That they were forc'd to ſtrike him to the ground, to take that occaſion to cary her away.

And ſince I am faln upon this Play, which is a-dorn'd

dorn'd with fo many Machines, I cannot but obferve, that all the Decorations and extraordinary Actions which are in the third and fifth Act, are very dexteroufly explain'd, and with an Art worthy of a *Grecian* Theatre; but for that great Palace, which makes the Decoration of the firft Act, and that Magnificent Temple, which does the fame in the 4th, I think there is not one word faid by which it may appear that they are there; and I was forc'd, when I read the Play, to have recourfe in thofe places, to the explanation which is before each Act, or elfe I had never known what the Decoration had been; and to fay truth, one may put the Temple in the firft Act, and the Palace in the 4th, and it will do altogether as well, without being oblig'd to any change in the Verfes, or order of the Subject; by which it appears, how requifite it is to explain the Decorations in the Play it felf, to joyn judicioufly the Subject with the Place, and Actions with Things, and fo make a Total full of fymmetry and ornament in all its parts.

The End of the Firft Book.

THE
Whole Art
OF THE
STAGE.

The Second BOOK.

CHAP. I.

Of the Subject of Dramatick Poems.

Uppoſing here what the Poet ought to know of that part of a *Drama*, which the Ancients call'd the *Fable*; we, the Story or Romance ; and I in this place, the Subject: I will onely ſay that for Subjects meerly inven- ted, and of which one may as well make a Trage- dy as a Comedy ; if they do not take, 'tis perfectly
the

the Poets fault, and a fault without excuse or pretext, which he can never clear himself of; for being Master as well of the Matter as of the Form, the miscarriage of the Play can be attributed to nothing, but to his want of Conduct in the thing, and to the Errors of his own Imagination. But as for Subjects drawn from Story, or from the Fables of the Ancients, he is more excusable if he misses of success in the Representation of them, for he may be many ways constrain'd; as if a great man command him to preserve certain Circumstances, not so fit for the Stage, or that he does it himself out of some consideration more important to him than the Glory of being a good Poet would be. But if he be free in his choice, he may be sure that he shall be blam'd if his Play does not take, it being certain, that Art out of an ill Story may make an excellent *Drama*; as for Example, if there be no Plot, the Poet must make one; if it be too intricate, he must make it looser and easier; if too open and weak, he must strengthen it by Invention, and so for the rest. On the other side, there is no Story so rich in it self, but an ill Poet may so spoil the beauty of it, that it will hardly be known to be the same Story.

Besides, one is not to think, that all fine Stories are fit to appear with success upon the Stage; for very often the beautifullest part of them depends upon some Circumstance, which the Theatre cannot suffer; and it was for this, that I advis'd one who had a mind to undertake the Loves of *Antiochus* and *Stratonica*, to let it alone; for the most considerable incident in it, being the cunning of the Physician in discovering the Prince's Passion, by

causing

cauſing all the Ladies in the Court to paſs one by one before the Princes Bed, that ſo by the emotion of his Pulſe, he might judge which of them it was, that cauſed his Diſeaſe; I thought it would be very odd, to make a Play where the Hero of it ſhould always be a bed, and that it would be hard to change the Circumſtance ſo, as to preſerve the Beauty of it; and that beſides, the Time and Place of the Scene would be difficult to bring together; for if *Antiochus* be ſuppos'd ſick a bed in the morning, 'twould be improbable to lay much action upon him all the reſt of that day; and to place the Scene in a ſick mans Chamber, or at his door, would be as unlikely.

'Twas for the ſame Reaſon, that the *Theodora* of *Corneille* had not all the approbation it deſerv'd: 'Tis in it ſelf a moſt ingenious Play; the Plot being well carried, and full of variety; where all the hints of the true Story are made uſe of to advantage, the Changes and Turns very judicious, and the Paſſions and Verſe worthy the Name of ſo great a man. But becauſe the whole buſineſs turns upon the Proſtitution of *Theodora* to the Publick Stews, it could never pleaſe; not but that the Poet, in that too, has taken care to expoſe things with great modeſty and nicety; but ſtill one is forc'd to have the Idea of that ugly Adventure ſo often in ones Imagination, particularly in the Narrations of the 4th Act, that the Spectators cannot but have ſome diſguſt at it.

There are a hundred Stories like theſe, and harder yet to manage for the Stage; and likewiſe on the contrary there are lucky ones, which ſeem to
have

have happened on purpofe; as that of *Sophonisba*, who is a Widow, and married again, lofes her kingdom, and recovers it all in a day.

The way therefore of chufing a Subject, is to confider whether it be founded upon one of thefe three things; either upon Noble Paffions, as *Mariamne* and the *Cid*; or upon an intricate and pleafing Plot, as *Cleomedon*, or the *Difguis'd Prince*; or upon fome extraordinary Spectacle and Show, as *Cyminda*, or the *Two Victims*; and if the Story will bear more Circumftances of this nature, or that the Poets imagination can fitly fupply the Play with them, it will be ftill the better; provided, he obferve a juft moderation, for though a Poem ought not to be without a Plot, nor without Paffions, or noble Spectacles, yet to load a Subject with any of them, is a thing to be avoided. Violent Paffions, too often repeated, do as it were numm the Soul, and its Sympathy; the multitude of Incidents and Intrigues diftract the Mind, and confound the Memory; and much Show takes up more time than can be allowed it, and is hard to bring on well. 'Tis for this reafon, that fome of our Poets who had contriv'd in every Act a memorable Incident, and a moving Paffion, did not find that the fuccefs anfwer'd their Expectation.

If I am ask'd, what is the meafure of employing thofe things? I fhall anfwer, 'tis every ones natural judment; and it may happen that a *Drama* may be fo luckily contriv'd, that the preparation of the Incidents, and the variety of the Paffions, fhall correct the defect of the abundance of them; and that the Art of the Machines fhall be fo well underftood, that they may eafily be made ufe of in

every

every Act, as I formerly propounded to Cardinal *Richelieu*, but hitherto they are little in use in our ordinary Theatres.

'Tis besides most commonly ask'd here, how far the Poet may venture in the alterations of a true Story, in order to the fitting of it for the Stage. Upon which we find different Opinions among both the Ancient and Modern Criticks; but my Opinion is, that he may do it not only in the Circumstances, but in the Principal Action it self; provided he make a very good Play of it: For as the Dramatick Poet does not much mind the time, because he is no Chronologist; no more does he, nor the Epick Poet, much mind the true Story, because they are no Historians; they take out of Story so much as serves their turn, and change the rest; not expecting that any body should be so ridiculous as to come to the Theatres to be instructed in the truth of History.

Arist. c. 15. Quis nescit omnibus Epicis Poëtis historiam esse pro argumento ? quam illi aut adumbratam, aut illustratam, certè aliâ facie quum ostendunt, ex historia conficiunt Poëma. Nam quid aliud Homerus ? quid' tragicis ipsis faciemus ? Scal. l. 1. c. 2.

The Stage therefore does not present things as they have been, but as they ought to be ; for the Poet must in the Subject he takes reform every thing that is not accommodated to the Rules of his Art ; as a Painter does when he works up on an imperfect Model.

'Twas for this Reason that the death of *Camilla* by the hands of her Brother *Horatius* was never lik'd of upon the Stage, though it be a true Adventure, and I for my part gave my Opinion, that to save in some measure the truth of the Story, and yet not to offend against the decency of the Stage, it would have been better that that Unfortunate Maid, seeing her Brother come towards her with his Sword drawn, had run upon it of her self ; for by that

K   means

means she would still have dyed by the hand of *Horatius*, and yet he might have deserved some compassion, as unfortunate but innocent, and so the Story and the Stage would have been agreed.

In a word, The Historian ought to recite matter of Fact, and if he judges of it, he does more than he ought to do; the Epick Poet is to magnifie all Events by great Fictions, where truth is as it were sunk and lost; and the Dramatick Poet ought to shew all things in a state of decency, probability, and pleasingness. 'Tis true, that if Story is capable of all the Ornaments of Dramatick Poetry, the Poet ought to preserve all the true Events; but if not, he is well grounded to make any part of it yield to the Rules of his Art, and to the Design he has to please.

Hinc Horatius cum dixisset, Famam sequere, quod pertinent ad τὸ ὅμοιον. Voss. lib 1. c. 5. Many against this do alledge the Authority of *Horace*, who sayes, *that he ought in Story to follow the common receiv'd Opinion, or at least to invent things that may be as conformable to it as possible.* But I answer, that *Horace* in that place does not treat of the Subject of the Play, but of the Customs and Morals that ought to be given the Actors; who ought not to be represented different from what they were believed; as it would be to make *Cæsar* a Coward, or *Messalina* chaste; and this *Vossius* has well observ'd in his *Poetick Art*, and I wonder that people should be abus'd by Citations applyed quite contrary to the Sense of the Author; and yet I am not of opinion that a known Story, yet fresh in the minds of the People, can suffer to be considerably chang'd, without great caution: but in such a case I should advise the Poet rather to abandon such a subject, than to make an ill Play of it, it, out of a humour of following truth; or at leaft to manage it fo, as not to check directly the receiv'd Opinion among the Vulgar. If we examine well the Senfe of *Ariftotle*, I believe he will be found to be of this Opinion; and as for the Ancient Poets they have always taken that Liberty, the fame Story having hardly ever been treated the fame way by different Poets. As for example, The Adventures of *Polydorus* are very different in *Euripides* and *Virgil. Sophocles* kills *Emon* and *Antigone*, but *Euripides*, who has made the fame Story in two Plays, marrys them together in one; contrary to what he himfelf had done before in the other call'd, The *Phænician* Ladies. The fame *Sophocles* in *Oedipus* makes *Jocafta* ftrangle her felf, and *Euripides* makes her live 'till the combat of her Sons *Eteocles* and *Polynices*, and then kill her felf upon their dead bodies. *Oreftes* and *Electra* are very different in many Circumftances, though both Works of the fame Poet. In a word, the four Tragick Poets of the *Greeks*, whofe Works we have, are all different in the difpofition of the fame Stories, and I believe that they were the caufe of that grand diforder and confufion there is in Story and Chronology in thofe old times, becaufe that they having chang'd both the Times and Events for their own ends, they have influenc'd fome Hiftorians, who thought to pick out of them the truth of Story, and fo made all things uncertain; any body that will read the *Electra* of *Euripides*, that of *Sophocles*, and the *Cæphores* of *Æfchilus*, will eafily fee that they made no difficulty of contradicting one another, and themfelves.

As for the different kinds of Subjects, letting
alone

alone thofe ordinary divifions of *Ariftotle,* and his Commentators, I here propofe three forts of Subjects

The firft confifts of Incidents, Intrigues, and new Events, when almoft from Act to Act there is fome fudden change upon the Stage, which alters all the Face of Affairs; when almoft all the Actors have different Defigns; and the means they take to make them fucceed come to crofs one another, and produce new and unforefeen Accidents, all which gives a marvellous fatisfaction to the Spectators, it being a continual diverfion, accompanied with an agreeable Expectation of what the Event will be.

The fecond fort of Subjects are of thofe rais'd out of Paffions; when out of a fmall Fund the Poet does ingenioufly draw great Sentiments and noble Paffions, to entertain the Auditory: and when out of Incidents that feem natural to his Subject, he takes occafion to tranfport his Actors into extraordinary and violent Sentiments, by which the Spectators are ravifh'd, and their Soul continually mov'd with fome new Impreffion.

The laft fort of Subjects are the mixt or compound of Incidents and Paffions, when by unexpected Events, but Noble ones, the Actors break out into different Paffions; and that infinitely delights the Auditory, to fee at the fame time furprizing Accidents, and noble and moving Sentiments, to which they cannot but yield with pleafure.

Now tis certain, that in all thefe three forts of Subjects the Poet may fucceed, provided the difpofition of his Play be ingenious; but yet I have
obferv'd

obferv'd fome difference, according to which they take more or lefs.

Subjects full of Plot and Intrigue are extreme agreeable at firft, but being once known, they do not the fecond time pleafe us fo well, becaufe they want the graces of Novelty, which made them charm us at firft, all our delight confifting in being furpriz'd, which we cannot be twice.

The Subjects full of Paffions laft longer, and affect us more, becaufe the Soul which receives the impreffion of them, does not keep them fo long, nor fo ftrongly, as our Memory does the Events of things; nay, often it happens, that they pleafe us more at fecond feeing, becaufe that the firft time we are employed about the Event and Difpofition of the Play, and by confequent do lefs enter into the Sentiments of the Actors; but having once no need of applying our thoughts to the Story, we bufie them about the things that are faid, and fo receive more Impreffions of grief or fear.

But it is out of doubt, that the mix'd or compound are the moft excellent fort, for in them the Incidents grow more pleafing by the Paffions which do as it were uphold them, and the Paffions feem to be renew'd, and fpring afrefh, by the variety of the unthought of Incidents; fo that they are both lafting, and require a great time to make them lofe their Graces.

We are not to forget here (and I think it one of the beft Obfervations that I have made upon this Subject) that if the Subject is not conformable to the Cuftoms and Manners, as well as Opinions of the Spectators, it will never take, what pains foever the Poet himfelf take, and whatfoever Ornaments

ments he employs to fet his Play off. For all Dramatick Poems muft be different, according to the People before whom they are reprefented; and from thence often proceeds that the fuccefs is different, though the Play be ftill the fame. Thus the *Athenians* delighted to fee upon their Theatre the Cruelties of Kings, and the Misfortunes befalling them, the Calamities of Illuftrious and Noble Families, and the Rebellion of the whole Nation for an ill Action of the Prince, becaufe the State in which they liv'd being Popular, they lov'd to be perfwaded that Monarchy was always Tyrannical, hoping thereby to difcourage the Noble Men of their own Commonwealth from the attempt of feizing the Soveraignty, out of fear of being expos'd to the the fury of a Commonalty, who would think it juft to murther them. Whereas quite contrary among us, the refpect and love which we have for our Princes, cannot endure that we fhould entertain the Publick with fuch Spectacles of horrour; we are not willing to believe that Kings are wicked, nor that their Subjects, though with fome appearance of ill ufage, ought to Rebel againft their Power; or touch their Perfons, no not in *Effigie*; and I do not believe that upon our Stage a Poet could caufe a Tyrant to be murder'd with any applaufe, except he had very cautioufly laid the thing: As for Example, that the Tyrant were an Ufurper, and the right Heir fhould appear, and be own'd by the People, who fhould take that occafion to revenge the injuries they had fuffer'd from the Tyrant; but Ufurpation alone, againft the will of the People, would not juftifie without horrour the death of the Soveraign by the hands of his rebellious Subjects: We have

feen

seen the tryal of it in a Play call'd *Timoleon,* whom no confideration of State or common Good, no love nor generofity towards his Country, could hinder from being confidered as the Murderer of his Brother and his Prince; and for my part I efteem that Author who avoided to have *Tarquin* kill'd upon the Stage, after the violence he had offer'd to *Lucretia.* The cruelty of *Alboin* infpir'd horrour into the whole *French* Court, though o-therwife it were a Tagedy full of noble Incidents and lofty Language.

We have had upon our Stage the *Efther* of Mr. *Du Ryer,* adorn'd with great Events, forti-fied with ftrong Paffions, and compos'd in the whole with great Art; but the fuccefs was much unluckier at *Paris,* than at *Roüen*; and when the Players at their teturn to *Paris* told us the good fortune they had had at *Roüen,* every body won-dred at it, without being able to guefs the caufe of it; but for my part I think that *Roüen,* being a Town of great Trade, is full of a great Num-ber of *Jews,* fome known, and fome conceal'd, and that by that reafon they making up a good part of the Audience, took more delight in a piece which feem'd entirely *Jewifh,* by the Conformity it had to their Manners and Cuftoms.

We may fay the fame thing of Comedies; for the *Greeks* and *Romans,* with whom the Debauches of young People with *Curtizans* was but a laughing matter, took pleafure to fee their Intrigues repre-fented, and to hear the difcourfes of thofe pub-lick Women, with the tricks of thofe Minifters of their Pleafures countenanc'd by the Laws. They were alfo delighted to fee old covetous men

over

over-reach'd, and cheated of their money, by the circumvention of their Slaves, in favour of their young Masters; they were sensible to all these things, because they were subject to them one time or another; but amongst us all this would be ill received; for as Christian Modesty does not permit persons of Quality to approve of those Examples of Vice, so neither do the Rules by which we govern our Families allow of those flights of our Servants, nor do we need to defend our selves against them. 'Tis for the same Reason that wee see in the *French* Court, Tragedies take a great deal better than Comedies; and that on the contrary, the People are more affected with the latter, and particularly with the Farces and Buffooneries of the Stage; for in this Kingdom the persons of good Quality, and Education, have generous thoughts and designs, to which they are carrried either by the Motives of Vertue or Ambition, so that their life has a great Conformity with the Characters of Tragedy; but the people, meanly born and durtily bred, have low Sentiments, and are thereby dispos'd to approve of the meaness and filthiness represented in Farces, as being the Image of those things which they both use to say and do; and this ought to be taken notice of, not only in the principal part of the Poem, but in all its parts, and particularly in the Passions, as we shall say more amply in a Chapter about them; for if there be any Act or Scene that has not that conformity of manners to the Spectators, you will suddenly see the applause cease, and in it's place a discontent succeed, though they themselves do not know the cause of it. For
the

the Stage and Eloquence are alike in this, that their Perfections and Faults are equally per-ceiv'd by the Ignorant and by the Learned, though the caufe is not equally known to them.

L   CHAP.

CHAP. II.

Of Probability and Decency.

The French word is vray-*semblance, for which we have not an English word Expressive of all its Sense.*

HEre is the bottom and ground work of all Dramatick Poems; many talk of it, but few underſtand it; but this is the general touchſtone, by which all that comes to paſs in a Play is to be tryed and examin'd, and it is the very Eſſence of the Poem, without which nothing rational can be done or ſaid upon the Stage.

Syneſ in Caluit. encom. p. 72. e-dit. Pariſ. an. 1612.

'Tis a general Maxim, that Truth alone is not the Subject of our Theatres, becauſe there are many Truths which ought not to be ſeen, and many that cannot be repreſented publickly; therefore *Syneſius* has ſaid very well, that Poetry and other Arts, founded in Imitation, follow not Truth but the common Opinion of men. It is very true, that *Nero* caus'd his Mother to be murder'd, and then had her cut up to ſee the place, where he had lain nine Months before he was born; but this Barbarity, though pleaſant to him that executed it, would yet be not only horrible to thoſe, to whom it ſhould be ſhew'd, but incredible becauſe ſuch a thing ought not to have come to paſs: I believe that amongſt the great number of Stories, from which the Poet may take

Subjects,

Subjects, there is hardly any one which in all its true Circumstances is fitted for the Stage, so as to be represented without altering something of the E-vent, the Time, the Persons, and many other par-ticulars.

That which is simply possible is left a Subject for Plays, for many things may come to pass by the rencounter of Natural Causes (or the adventures of humane Life) which yet would be ridiculous, and almost incredible, to be represented. 'Tis possible that a Man may dye suddenly, and that happens often; but That Poet would be strangely laugh'd at, who to rid the Stage of a troublesome Rival, should make him dye of an Apoplexy, as of a common Disease; and it would need exceeding ingenious and artful preparations.

There is nothing therefore but *Probability*, that can truly found a Dramatick Poem, as well as adorn and finish it; not that True and Possible things are banish'd off the Stage, but they are received upon it, only so far as they are Probable; and therefore all the Circumstances, that want this Character, are to be alter'd so as to attain it, if they hop'd to appear in publick. *Res esse oportet in ipsis etiam Comœdijs admodum verisimiles, ut tametsi ficta repræsentari magis quam fingi videantur Scal. lib.6. cap 3.*

I shall not here expatiate upon ordinary and ex-traordinary Probability, the Masters of the Art have made ample Treatises about it; and no body is igno-rant, that things naturally impossible become possi-ble, and even probable, by the Power of God Al-mighty, or That of the Devil; and that the Proba-bility of the Stage does not oblige to represent only those things which happen according to the com-mon course of Humane Life, but likewise gives leave to launch into the wonderful Accidents of it,

L 2   which

which makes the Events fo much the more furpri-
fing, if they are ftill probable ; but that which I have
obferv'd in this matter, is , That few have underftood, how far this Probability ought to reach ; every body indeed believing that it ought to be obferv'd in the principal Action of the *Poem*, and likewife in the moft fenfible Incidents of it , but they
went no further.   Now is it moft certain, that the
leaft Actions, brought upon the Stage , ought to be
probable, or elfe they are entirely faulty, and fhould
not appear there.   There is no Action of Humane
Life fo perfectly fingle, as not to be accompanied by
many little Circumftances, which do make it up ;
as are the Time, the Place, the Perfon, the Dignity, the Defigns, the Means, and the Reafons of the
Action ; and fince the Stage ought to be a perfect
Image of Action , it ought to reprefent it entire,
and that Probabilty and Decency be obferv'd in all
its parts.   When a King fpeaks upon the Stage , he
muft fpeak like a King, and that is the Circumftance
of his Dignity, againft which nothing ought to be
done with Decency ; except there be fome other reafon to difpenfe with this laft, as that he were in difguife.   Befides, without doubt a King fpeaking according to his Dignity muft be fuppos'd to be
fomewhere , and therefore the Stage muft carry the
Image of the place where he then was, for there are
things which in Probability ought not to be done or
faid, but in certain places.   It ought alfo to appear,
in what time he fpoke, for one ought to fpeak differently in different times, as a Prince before he
gives Battel, will fpeak otherwife than after he has
won it, or loft it.

Therefore

Therefore to preferve this Probability in the Circumftances of the Treatral Action, the Poet muft be Mafter of the Rules of the Stage, and Practife them, for they teach nothing elfe, to make all the parts of an Action appear with Probability and Decency, and to reprefent a whole and entire Image of them.

To this fome have faid, That Reafon and Common Senfe are fufficient of themfelves to Judge of all thefe things. I grant it, but it muft be Reafon and common Senfe, inftructed in the affairs of the Stage, and in what is defign'd to be reprefented : For fuppofe, that a Man of good Senfe fhould have never feen nor heard of a Play, and be brought to fee one, without being told what it is he is carried to ; 'tis certain that he will hardly know, whether the Players be true Kings and Princes , or only the Images of them ; and when he does know, that all that is but a Fiction, yet will he fcarce be able to judge of the Faults or Perfections of the Play, without making many Reflections to confider, whether what is reprefented be profitable or no ? For to judg perfectly of a Dramatick Poem, our Natural Reafon muft be inftructed and inured to that kind of Images, which are made ufe of by men to reprefent any Action, and know precifely, how Probability is to be preferved in all the ftrokes of this animated Picture ; and that cannot be attained to , but by a great number of Obfervations made by length of time and different Perfons.   The Art of the Stage was by thefe Obfervations framed by the Ancients, and had fo flow a Progrefs, that from *Thefpis,* who firft added an Actor to the Chorus , who before that acted Tragedies alone, to the time of *Ariftotle,* who reduced thefe Rules into an Art, there pafled two

hundred

hundred years : He therefore that, on a fudden without ftudy or reflection, will pronounce his Judgment of a Play, will often find himfelf miftaken ;
becaufe'tis very hard he fhould have before his Eyes
on a fudden all thofe Confiderations, which are requifite to examine the Probability of what has been
reprefented ; and it has often happened, that People of very good underftanding have at firft commended fome Actions of the Stage for well invented
things, which upon being better informed, they
have found contrary to all Probability and Ridiculous.

But it is a much ftranger thing, and yet very
true, that I have feen People, who had for many
years compos'd Plays themfelves, read a Play of anothers, and that over and over again, and yet never find out the length of time, nor the place of
the Scene, nor many of the Circumftances of the
moft important Actions, fo as to judge whether they
were probable or not. *Heinfius* himfelf, though

Plautus no-
vem menfes uno
Dramate com-
plexus eft, ut
vix maior am-
pliorque Home-
ricæ Iliados
quam Amphi-
tryonis fit peri-
odus : Alcume-
na autem conci-
pit & parit ;
quod fi fieret,
iam nullo epifo-
dio opus effet, i-
deoque nec ars
effet comœdiam
fcribere.
Heins. in Ho-
rat.
Voff. lib. 2. c. 3.

very Learned, and who has publifhed the Art of
compofing Tragedies, is fo far miftaken in the *Am-*
phitryon of *Plautus*, as to think it contains nine
Months, though it do not really contain above eight
hours, and at leaft is comprehended between Mid-
night and Noon the day following. *Voffius*, one of
the moft Learned of our time, and very underftanding in the Art of Poetry, writes as He does, that
Plautus in his *Amphytrion* makes *Hercules* be conceived and born in one Night, though 'tis certain he
fuppofes him Conceived feven Months before ; and
Mercury fays it twice exprefly in the Play ; therefore I think my felf bound to give my Readers warn-
ing, that of all that that excellent man has made,
                                    there

there is nothing to be fo carefully avoided, as his Third Chapter of his Firft Book, where he treats of the Errors of Poets, and pretends to Correct the Ancients. for he himfelf falls into much greater. *Scaliger* has faid in two places, that in *Æfchylus*, *Prometheus* is kill'd by a Thunder-Bolt, and yet 'tis certain that he is only carried away in the ftorm, and that appears by the words of *Prometheus*, and thofe of *Mercury*, who both fay it clearly enough. There are thofe who have read *Æfchylus* over and over, and yet have been fo negligent in obferving of him, that they believe (and amongft them, the Author of the Argument of his *Agamemnon* is one) that he makes *Agamemnon* be murdered upon the Stage, though it be faid by the Chorus, that they hear the Cries and Lamentations he makes in his Palace, and are ready to break in, to fee whats the matter; from which Refolution they are diverted by the Arrival of *Clytemneftra*, who comes and tells, how fhe had with her own hand committed that Cruel action. Many Learned Men have faid, That the Third Comedy of *Terence* contained two days; *Scaliger*, *Muretus*, *Voffius*, F. *Membrun*, and others have been of that Opinion; but it does not contain above ten hours, as I have made it appear, in my Differtation of *Terence Juftified*. And Monfieur *Menage*, who writ upon this Subject, only to contradict Truth out of Malignity, has not dar'd to allow it above 14 or 15 hours, and to compafs that, he has been fain, to pervert the Order of the *Athenian* Months, that he might fhorten the day, and lengthen the night, and fo overthrow the Oeconomy of Nature, to find fome Fault with the Difpofition of the Play.

Ridicule fe dat Plautus, cum in Amphitryone fingat eadem die Alcumenam & concipere & parere.

Hodie illa pariet filios geminos duos, alter decumo poft menfe nafcetur puer quam feminatus eft; alter menfe feptumo. Amphitry. Act. 1. fc. 2.

Lib. 7. c. 4. Poet. & lib. 3. c. 97.

ἰδίως δὲ Αἰχύλ⊙ τὸν Ἀγαμέμνονα ἐπὶ σκήνης ἀναιρεῖσθαι ποιεῖ.

Arg. Agam. Æfchyl.

I

I have feen fome others, whom I had much difficulty to perfwade, that in the *Phœnicians* of *Euripides*, the *Electra* of *Sophocles* , and the *Clouds* of
Ariftophanes, the Unity of place was obferved ; fo
much do old Errors fometimes blind us : And fo
true it is, that in this Art, as well as in all others,
our natural Reafon needs the knowledge of the Rules
of the Art, to judge well of the Perfection or Faults
of the product of the Art, and I dare boldly fay, that
whoever fhall read this Treatife, fhall condemn many things which they formerly thought very Rational.

C H A P.

C H A P. III.

Of the Unity *of* Action.

'TIS one of *Ariſtotle*'s Rules, and without doub.
a very Rational one, that a Dramatick Po
em ought to comprehend but one Action ; and he
does very pertinently condemn thoſe, who make a
Play of the whole Story, or Life of a Hero.   For
though we ſpeak but of one principal Part, on
which all the other Events, bad and good, do depend ; yet there are divers ſubordinate Actions. But
to explain this more particularly, I will here give
the Reaſon of this Rule, as I apprehend it ; and how
likewiſe one may comprehend upon the Stage divers Incidents in one Action.

'Tis certain, that the Stage is but a Picture or I-
mage of Humane Life ; and as a Picture cannot
ſhew us at the ſame time two Originals, and be an
accompliſhed Picture : It is likewiſe impoſſible that
two Actions, I mean principal ones, ſhould be repreſented reaſonably by one Play.   Let us conſider
what the Painter does, who is to make a Picture of
ſome Story ; he has no other deſign, but to give the
Image of ſome Action, and that Action is ſo limit-
ted, that it cannot repreſent two parts of a Story together, and leſs all the Story upon which he has
fix'd ; becauſe it would be neceſſary that the ſame
Perſon ſhould be Painted, and appear in different
M   places,

places, which would make a ftrange Confufion
in the whole Picture, and it would be hard to diftinguifh any Order amongft fo many different Actions; and by confequent, the Story would be very obfcure and confufed: Therefore inftead of that, the
Painter would chufe, amongft All the Actions which
made up the Story, the moft important One, and
the fitteft for the Excellency of his Art, and which
in fome meafure fhould contain all the others; fo
that with one look one might have a fufficient knowledge of all that he defigned to exprefs; and if he
defired to exprefs two parts of the fame Story, he
would make in fome corner of the Picture a Lonta-
nanza, where he would paint that other Action,
which he had a mind to reprefent, that he might
make it be underftood, that he defign'd the painting
of two different Actions, and that it was two Pictures, and not one.

As for Example, Suppofe he defigned to draw
the Story of *Iphigenia*, it would be hard for him to
comprehend in one Picture, all the Adventures of
that Princefs; therefore he would chufe that of the
Sacrifice, which the *Greeks* were going to make of
her to *Diana*, to appeafe her Anger, and the ftorms
of the Sea; for in this Action her whole Story
would in fome meafure be comprehended. The
ftorms of the Sea, which kept the Fleet in the Port
of *Aulide*, would be confidered as the Caufe; the
Grief of her Father, and the Compaffion of the o-
ther *Grecian* Princes, would be the Circumftances;
and her being carried away by that Goddefs her felf,
as an extraordinary Favour, by which fhe was to be
fav'd; and the if he had a mind to exprefs that
Diana carried her to *Tauris*, where fhe was upon
the

the point of Sacrificing her Brother *Oreſtes*, he would put her in one of the Corners of his Picture, in the particular dreſs of *Diana*'s Prieſteſs, with ſome other marks of this ſecond Adventure, and ſo make two Pictures of two different Actions of the ſame Story.

The Dramatick Poet muſt imitate the Painter, and when he undertakes the Compoſition of a Play, he muſt reckon that he undertakes to make a living ſpeaking Picture, and that therefore he cannot comprehend in it a whole Hiſtory, or the Life of an *Hero*, becauſe he would be neceſſitated to repreſent an infinite number of Events, and employ a vaſt number of Actors, and mingle ſo many things, that he would make up a work of perfect Confuſion, and would be forc'd in moſt places to offend againſt Probability and Decency, and to go beyond the time and extent, ordinarily allowed to Dramatick Poems ; or if he would keep within the limits of the *Rules* of his Art, he would be forced to haſten all the Incidents, and as it were heap them one upon another, without either Graces or Diſtinction, and ſo be obliged to ſtifle and ſuppreſs all the Paſſionate ſtrokes ; and in a word, ſhew ſuch a Monſtrous Extravagant Image, as They have done, who have repreſented in the Firſt Act of a Tragedy, the Marriage of a Princeſs ; in the Second, the Birth of her Son ; in the Third, the Amours of that young Prince ; in the Fourth, his Victories ; and in the Fifth, his Death ; in all which there was matter enough for above twenty Plays. Our Poet therefore, amidſt this vaſt extent, ſhall pitch upon ſome one remarkable Action ; and as one may ſay, a point of Story, notable by the Happineſs or Misfortune of

M 2 ſome

some Illuſtrious Perſon, in which point he may comprehend, as Circumſtances, all the reſt of the Story, and by repreſenting one chief part make the whole known by ſome ſleight to the Spectators, without multiplying the principal Action , and without retrenching any of the neceſſary Beauties to the perfection of his Work ; and if by chance he ſhould meet in the ſame Story with two or more Actions , ſo conſiderable, that they each of them deſerved a Play , and ſo independent or oppoſite to each other, as not to be reconciled ; he ought to make Two or More plays of them, or chuſe the moſt Important, and particularly, the moſt Pathetick for his Subject.

Thus the *Suppliants* of *Euripides* do not contain the whole War of *Thebes*, but only the Burial of the two Princes of *Argos*. *Hecuba* contains not the taking of *Troy*, but the laſt misfortunes of that Queen in her Captivity. The *Ajax* of *Sophocles*, ſhews not all the Exploits of War of that Hero , nor his Diſputes with *Ulyſſes* for the Arms of *Achilles* . but only repreſents his madneſs, which was the cauſe of his Death ; and ſo we may ſay of moſt of the ancient Plays. But in all theſe the Poets have ſhewed ſo much Art, as to inſtruct the Spectators , either by Narrations, Diſcourſes , Complaints , or other ſleights of the Art, in all the Circumſtances of thoſe Stories which they treated.

As likewiſe, when the Subjects, that fell into their Hands, were of too great an Extent to be comprehended in one Play, and having in them many Actions of equal importance, they have made different Pictures of that, which could not be comprehended under one Image.

Euripides

Euripides has not confounded the Sacrifice of *Iphigenia* in *Aulis*, with the Adventures of the fame Princefs in *Scythia*. *Æfchylus* in one Play caufes *Agamemnon* to be murdered by *Clytemneftra*; and in another brings her to punifhment for it ; and from thence it comes amongft the Ancients, many Plays have the fame Name, and often many Events of the fame Story are reprefented in different Plays, which indeed was fome ways neceffary in *Athens* ; for as their Poets were to work for the Solemnity of the four great Feafts or Holy-days, and to have four Plays for each of them ; of which there were three to be Serious, and the fourth Satyrical or Comical, which made up the *Tetralogy*. I am of Opinion, they took all their Subjects from the fame Story, as I have fhewed more at length in my *Terence Jufti-fied*.

Now, as to the manner of bringing many different Incidents into one Action, and to make a Poem of them, which fhall naturally contain many Acts, and different Scenes ; to explain this well, I return to the comparifon of Painting, which I have fo often us'd already.

We have faid that a Picture can reprefent but one Action, but it ought to be underftood one principal Action, for the Painter may very well place in the fame Picture many Actions, which depend upon that chief Action, which he pretends principally to reprefent. And indeed there is no one action of Life fo fingle, but it was preceeded, accompanied, and followed by many others, all which do compofe it, and give it its Being : Therefore the Painter muft, whether he will or no, draw thefe fubordinate Actions, or elfe his principal one is imperfect. If he

paints

paints the Sacrifice of *Iphigenia*, he cannot place her all alone at the foot of *Diana*'s Altar, or without any body, but *Chalchas* who is to facrifice her ; but rather, following the Example of the Painter *Timantes*, he will place there all the Grecian Princes with fad Countenances ; *Menelaus* her Uncle fhall be extreamly afflicted ; *Clytemneftra*, her Mother, fhall be expreffed all in Tears and defpair ; and *Agamemnon*, her Father, with a Vail upon his Face, to hide the weaknefs of his Nature to the chief of the *Greeks*, and yet allow fomething by this flight to the excefs of his Grief; he will not forget to make *Diana* appear in the Sky, ready to ftop the Arm and Sword of *Chalchas*, becaufe all thefe Actions do as it were wait upon, and make up this doleful Religious Action, which elfe would be weak and naked of all its Ornaments, without all thefe ingenious Circumftances.

'Tis in the fame manner, that a Dramatick Poem ought not to contain above one Action, but it muft be brought upon the Stage entire, with all its Dependencies, and nothing muft be forgot of thofe Circumftances, which naturally are appropriated to it: And of this I think I need not propofe any Example; but it will not be amifs to give our Poet one Advertifement, which is, That if the principal Action be in the Story loaded with too many Incidents, he muft reject the leaft important, and leaft pathetick ones; and on the contrary, if the Story want thofe Incidents, he muft fupply that want by his own Fancy, which he may do two ways.

Firft, either by inventing fome Intrigues, which naturally might make a part of the princi-

pal

pal Action : Thus the Author of the Tragedy of the *Horatius*'s has very well invented the Marriage of *Sabina*, Sister to the *Curiatius's*, with the Eldest of their Enemies, that so he might introduce the Passions of a Wife, to mingle with those of *Camilla*, who was a Maid, and in love with one of the *Curiatius's*.

Secondly, He may seek out in Story, things that have happened before or after the Action, which makes the Subject of his Play, and with Art joyn them to his Plot, saving still the differences of times and places, according as we shall shew in the following Chapters. This has been observed by the Author of *Cleopatra*, who makes *Octavia*, *Antony*'s Wife, come privately to *Alexandria*, and so has the pleasure of shewing so great a Lady with all her generous Sentiments.

But we are to observe here, that the Poet, as near as he can, ought to take his Action as single as possible ; because he will still be so much the more Master of the Passions, and other Ornaments of his Play, which by that means he can shew to the best advantage ; whereas, if he meets with them in Story, they will still be clogg'd with some Circumstances, which will constrain the whole Design, and give him a great deal of trouble; and in short, little and single Subjects in the hands of an ingenious Poet, who knows how to work them, cannot miscarry. 'Tis *scaliger*'s advice, and we have seen the proof of it in *Alcionea,* a Play of Mr. *Du Ryers*, which though it had no fund in Story, nevertheless ravished the Audience, by the force of the Passions, and richness of the Style. And on the contrary, all those, who in the same

Argumentum brevissimun sumendum, idque maxime varium multiplexque faciendum. l. 3. c. 97. Scal.

Poem

Poem, have brought in divers illuſtrious important Actions, have ſtifled the Beauty of them all, in not giving room enough to the Paſſions, as we have experienced in ſome Plays, where all the Actions, though in ſome meaſure depending on a principal one, yet were ſo ſtrong in themſelves, that they hindred each other, and were every one of them capable of being the ſubject of a Play.

CHAP

CHAP. IV.

Of the Continuity of the Action.

AFter the Poet has chofen the Subject or Story, which he thinks capable of the Ornaments of Dramatick Poetry, and that he has fix'd upon the point, in which he will make the Unity of his Theatral Action confift; he muft remember, that his Action ought to be not only one, but continued, that is, That from the opening of the Stage, to the very clofing of the Cataftrophe, from the firft Actor, that appears upon the Scene, to the laft that goes off; the principal Perfons of the Play muft be always in Action; and the Theatre muft carry continually, and without any interruption the face of fome Defignes, Expectations, Paffions, Troubles, Difquiets, and other fuch like Agitations, which may keep the Spectators in a belief, that the Action of the Theatre is not ceafed, but ftill going on. This is one of the Precepts of *Ariftotle*, as well as of Reafon; and his Interpreters have always obferved the Ceffation of Action for one of the greateft Faults of the Drama; 'tis of this fault, that fome People, but impertinently, do accufe *Terence* in his Third Comedy, call'd *Heautontimoreumenos*;

συνεχῶς ἠ μιᾶς. Arift. Poet. cap. 11. Gouean in Terent. Heaut. Scalig. lib. 6. cap. 3. Poet.

N   but

but I have fufficiently juftified him elfe-where. The Ancient Tragedians could hardly fail in the obfervation of this Rule, becaufe they had Chorufes, and the bufinefs of thofe Chorufes being to reprefent thofe who were prefent upon the Scene at the time of the Action, 'tis probable they would have gone off as foon as they fhould have feen the Action ceafe, as having no pretext to ftay there any longer.   'Tis befides certain, that if upon our Stages the Action fhould ceafe in the middle of the Play, or about the Second or Third Act, all the Intrigues being finifhed, nor no preparation for any new Incident or Paffion to come, the Spectators would be in the right to rife and be gone, fince they would have reafon to believe the Play done, and if they ftayed any longer, knowing there were two or three Acts to come, it would be only by the knowledge they had of what the Poet ought to do, and not by any hint of his, to prepare them for it; as if a man hapned to be there, who had never feen a Play, 'tis certain he would belive it at an end as foon as he had nothing new to expect ; and in this cafe, I have feen fometimes Ladies ask, if the Play were done, though they had often been at Plays, and knew they were generally of greater length ; fo much does the Ceffation of the Action upon the Stage furprize the Spectators, and perfwades them that there is nothing more to come.   If we feek the reafon of it, it is becaufe the Action would not be one, if it were not continued ; for Moral Actions, fuch as are thofe of the Theatre, come to be divided and multiplied , whenever they break off ; and are interrupted for then, if they begin again, they are two Theatral Actions , both of them Imperfect.   'Tis for this that the beft Drama-

tick

tick Poets always use to make their Actors say, where they are going, and what is their Design, when they go off of the Stage, that one may know, that they are not idle while they are absent, but are acting something of their part, though one sees them not.

But when we say, that the chief Persons in the Play are always to be in Action, we do not mean by that, the Hero or Heroine of the Play, for they often Act the least, and yet suffer the most in the whole Business; for in regard to the Continuity of the Action, the Principal Actors are those who carry on the Intrigue or business of the Play, it may be a Slave, a waiting Woman, a Cheat, or some such Person; and for the Continuity, 'tis enough if the least Actor is but doing, provided it be necessarily, and that the Spectator from his working may naturally expect some important change or adventure in the Subject.

'Tis worth observing too, that often in appearance the Action of the Stage ceases, though it be not really so; which happens when the Poet prepares an Incident, which is to appear afterwards, and of which one of the Actors speaks slightly, and *en passant*, which is an Artifice of the Poets.

The Example is very ingenious in the *Ajax* of *Sophocles*, where the Action seems entirely to cease in the beginning of the Third Act, but is continued by a Messenger, who comes and tells of *Teucers* Arrival in the Camp, and of all that had been done there since his coming, concerning his Brothers Fury, and the Cure of it, by which means the Action is not only well renewed, but continued; because in the precedent Acts, *Ajax* often speaks, and complains of the length of his Brothers absence, which makes all the Spectators wish his return, as a means to save *Ajax* himself, so that when the news of his Arrival is brought, it appears that the Action had not ceased at all, for *Teucer* was acting in the Camp for his Brother according to the expectation of the Audience; of all which nevertheless there comes nothing to pass of what they hop'd, and 'tis in that that consists the Poets chief Art, to promise that which never comes to pass, and to bring that to pass which he does not promise.

'Tis necessary to observe here besides, that the Theatral Action does not always cease, though all the Actors be in Repose, and as it were without Action; because that sometimes 'tis a necessary Action of the Play, that they all should be so; and the Spectator expects some Event from the Actors doing of nothing. This we shall make clear by Examples, and particularly by the *Plutus* of *Aristophanes*, where we see that after the Second Act, the Actors carry *Plutus* to the Temple of *Æsculapius*, to cure him of his Blindness, where they go to Bed to sleep, and remain without Action; for this Sleep and Repose was the Natural state, in which they were to be, to receive from that God, the favour of being cured, and is by consequent a necessary Action to the Stage. By

Resp. au discours sur l'Heautont. p. 7. ed. 2. p. 102.
which it appears, how much Monsieur *Menage* has been mistaken, to believe that the Action of the Stage ceased as to those who were asleep, and was only continued in the Person of *Carion* who was awake; for 'tis quite contrary, he that is awake is a Slave, who eats and steals the remainder of the Sacrifice without any regard to the Subject of the Play; and they who sleep do that which Custom prescribed to those, who were to expect a Cure from *Æsculapius*, and as *Plutus* and

his

his Companions did : One might fay, perhaps, that the Action of *Æfculapius*, who cures *Plutus* and what *Carion* faw, as he tells it afterwards, are enough to continue the Action; but ftill there would be a breach and fome time loft in it, from that in which the Actors lye down to the time of *Æfculapius*'s coming, if it were not true, that their very lying down and going to fleep, continues the Action of the Comedy.

This Chapter may receive fome more light by the Treatife I have made upon the third Comedy of *Terence*, where I have touch'd this matter, and by what I have done upon that Author, it will be eafie to find, how to examine the Ancients, if one would difcover the Artifices, which they ufe to obferve in this Continuity of the Action of the Theatre.

CHAP.

CHAP. V.

Of the Subjects with two Walks, whereof one is by Modern Authors called Epifode.

OUR Modern Authors do now by an Epifode mean a Second Story, which comes as it were crofs the principal Subject of the Play, and fome for this Reafon call it a Play with two Walks ; but the Ancient Poets have not known, or at leaft have not practis'd this Multiplicity of Subjects : *Arifto-tle* makes no mention of it, and I know no Example of it, except fome will fay that the *O-reftes* of *Euripides* is of this kind, becaufe there are two Marriages concluded in the Ca-taftrophe ; but there is not in the Body Body of the Play any mixture of Intrigues, to carry on thofe two Amours, and bring them to this Conclufion.

Comedy has been otherwife managed, for ha-ving received many more Changes than Tragedy, from what they Both were at firft; it has ad-mitted of this mixture of two Stories in the fame Play : And we have yet fome in *Plautus*, and a

great

great many in *Terence*, who may afford an In-
struction how to compose with Art and Grace
that sort of Plays better than *Plautus*.

But however, not standing here upon the word
Episode, which amongst the Ancients signified
quite another thing. I am content the signification of the Word should be according to our
Modern Authors; and do allow that Tragedy
may have some Episodes, as well as the Epick
Poems, and not unlike them; but in Tragedy
there are two things to be observed. First, That
these Episodes, or Second Stories be so incorporated into the chief Subject, that they cannot be
separated from it, without spoiling the whole
Play; for else the Episode would be looked upon
as a superfluous and troublesome part, which
would but hinder the Union of the chief Adventures, and slacken the motion of the Incidents, which tend to a Conclusion; as indeed
in the Play, of our time the most applauded, the
Episode of the Princesses love has been condem- *The Cid.*
ned by all, because it was absolutely useless.
Therefore to avoid that Inconvenience, 'tis necessary that the Person ingaged in the Episode,
be not only concern'd in the Success of the Affairs of the Stage; but besides, the Adventures of
the Hero or Heroine ought to be of that concern to the Persons of the Episode, as that the
Audience may rationally apprehend some mischief,
or hope some good out of those Persons for the
whole concern of the Stage; and for the interest
of those who seem strangers, and are not then unuse-
fully so.

The other Observation to be made about these E-
pisodes,

pifodes, is, That the fecond Story muſt not be equal in its Subject, nor in its Neceſſity, to that which is the foundation of the Play, but it muſt be ſubordinate to it, and ſo depend upon it, that the Events of the principal Subject cauſe the Paſſions of the Epiſode ; and that the Cataſtrophe of the firſt produce naturally and of its ſelf the Cataſtrophe of the ſecond, or elſe the principal Action would be no longer ſo. Theſe are the two Reflections, which I have made upon the Epiſodes of our Modern Poets, which may give hints to better underſtandings than mine, to make ſome more conſiderable ones.

C H A P.

C H A P. VI.

Of the Unity *of* Place.

AFter the Poet has order'd his Subject according to the Rules we have given, or it may be Better, which his own Industry and Study may furnish him with; he must reflect, that the best part of it must be represented by Actors, which must be upon a Stage fix'd and determinated; for to make his Actors appear in different places, would render his Play ridiculous, by the want of Probability, which is to be the foundation of it.

This Rule of Unity of Place begins now to be look'd upon as certain; but yet the ignorant, and some others of weak judgment, do still imagine that it cannot but be repugnant to the Beauty of the Incidents of a Play; because that they, happening often in great distance of place, cannot but lose by this constraint; and therefore whatsoever Reason you oppose against their imaginations, they fancy a false impossibility in the Execution, and reject stubbornly all that's said to convince them; on the other side, those that are but half read in Antiquity, do well perceive the strength of what it alledg'd for this Rule, but yet they make Objections so unbecom-

O   ing

ing a literate thinking man, that they have often mov'd pity in me, though I had more mind to
laugh at them. 'Tis the property of little Genius's
not to be able to comprehend many things at the
fame time, fo as to reduce them to a point ; their
judgment not being able to affemble fo many images as they muft have prefent all at once ; and therefore they make fo many difficulties, that 'tis eafie to
fee, they would be glad that there were Reafons wanting to convince them.

As for the truely Learned, they are thoroughly
convinc'd of the neceffity of this Rule, becaufe
they fee clearly that Probability can no ways be
preferv'd without it ; but I may boldly fay, that hitherto no one of them has explain'd this Rule, and
made it intelligible, either becaufe we do not take
the Pains of making all the neceffary reflexions upon the Works of the Ancients, to difcover the Art
which is moft commonly hid in them, and which
always ought to be fo, without an apparent neceffity
of the Subject or the Intereft of the Actors ; or
elfe becaufe no body ftrives to go beyond the firft
great Mafters, and what They have neglected is given over moft commonly by their Followers.

Ariftotle has faid nothing of it, and I believe he
omitted it, becaufe that this Rule was in his time
too well known ; the Chorus's, which ordinarily
remain'd upon the Stage from one end of the Play
to the other, marking the unity of the *Scene* too
vifibly to need a Rule for it ; and indeed, would it
not have been ridiculous, that in the Play call'd the
Seven before Thebes, the young Women who make
the Chorus, fhould have found themfelves fometimes before the Palace of the King, and fometimes

times in the Camp of the Enemies, without ever
ftirring from the fame place; and the Three famous
Tragedians of the *Greeks*, whofe Works we have,
are fo punctual in the Obfervation of this Rule,
and do fo often make their Actors fay, where they
are, and whence they come; that *Ariftotle* muft
have fuppos'd too much Ignorance in his Age, and
in thofe who fhould read thefe Poets, if he had
gone about to Explain fo fettled a Rule. But fince
the Ignorance and Barbarity of fome paft Ages have
brought fuch diforder upon the Stage, to make
people in the Play appear in different parts of the
World on the fame Stage, it will not be amifs to give
here at length the Reafon of this Rule, fo well
practis'd by the Ancients, and that in honour of
fome of our Modern Poets, who have very handfom-
ly imitated them.

To underftand it then, we muft have recourfe
to our ordinary Principle, which is, that the Stage
is but a Reprefentation of things; and yet we are
not to imagine, that there is any thing of what we
really fee, but we muft think the things themfelves
are there of which the Images are before us. So
Floridor is much lefs *Floridor*, than the *Horatius* of
whom he acts the Part, for his drefs is *Roman*, he
fpeaks, acts, and thinks as that *Roman* did at that
time; but as that *Roman* could not but be in fome
place acting and fpeaking, the place where *Floridor*
appears does reprefent that where *Horatius* was, or
elfe the Reprefentation would be imperfect in that
Circumftance.

*Loci ficti vera
Loca imitan-
tur. Scal. l. 1.
cap. 13.*

This Truth, well underftood, makes us to know
that the place cannot change in the reft of the Play,
fince it cannot change in the Reprefentation, for one

O 2 and

and the fame Image remaining in the fame ftate, cannot reprefent two different things ; now it is highly improbable, that the fame fpace, and the fame floor, which receive no change at all, fhould reprefent two different places; as for Example, *France* and *Denmark* ; or within *Paris* it felf, the *Tueilleries* and the *Exchange* ; at leaft to do it with fome fort of colour, one fhould have of that fort of Theatres which turn quite round and entire, that fo the Place might change as well as the Perfons acting ; and to do this, the Subject of the Play ought to furnifh fome Reafon for this change, and as that cannot well happen, but by the Power of God Almighty, who changes as he pleafes the Face of Nature, I doubt it would be hard to make a reafonable Play without a dozen Miracles at leaft.

Let it then be allowed for a certain truth, that the Place, where the firft Actor, who opens the Play, is fuppos'd to be, ought to be the fame place to the end of the Play ; and that, it not being in the ordinary courfe of Nature, that the place can receive any change, there can be none likewife in the Reprefentation ; and by confequent, that all your other Actors cannot rationally appear in any other place.

But we muft remember, that this Place, which cannot be fuppos'd to change, is the *Area* or floor of the Stage, upon which the Actors walk, and which the Ancients call'd by the name of *Profcenium* ; for as that reprefents that fpot of ground, upon which the perfons reprefented did actually walk and difcourfe, which could not turn about or change on a fudden, or without a Miracle, fo when you have once chofen the place

where

where you intend your Action to be begun, you muſt ſuppoſe it immovable in all the reſt of the Play, as it was in effect and really.

'Tis not the ſame with the ſides and end of the Theatre, for as they do but repreſent thoſe things which did actually environ the Perſons acting, and which might receive ſome change, they may like-wiſe receive ſome in the Repreſentation, and 'tis in that that conſiſts the changing of Scenes, and other Ornaments of Decoration, which always raviſh the People, and pleaſe the beſt Judges, when they are well done; ſo we have ſeen upon our Stage a Tem-ple adorn'd with a Noble Front of Architecture, which coming to be ſet open ſhew'd the inſide of it, where in Perſpective were deſcryed Pillars and an Altar, and all the other Ornaments of a Church extremly well done; ſo that the place did not change, and yet had a fine Decoration.

We are not nevertheleſs to imagine, that the Po-ets *Capricio* is to rule theſe Decorations; for he muſt find ſome colour and appearance for it in his Subject.

So for Example, he might feign a Palace upon the Sea ſide, forſaken, and left to be inhabited by poor Fiſhermen; a Prince landing, or being caſt a-way there, might adorn it with all the rich Furni-ture fit for it; after this by ſome Accident it might be ſet on fire; and then behind it the Sea might appear, upon which one might repreſent a Sea Fight; ſo that in all the five changes of the Stage, the unity of Place would ſtill be ingeniouſly pre-ſerv'd; not but that the very floor or *Proſcenium* may change too, provided it be ſuperficially, as if ſome River ſhould overflow it, as the *Tyber* did in

the

the time of *Auguftus*; or if Flames came out of the
Earth and cover'd the face of it, in all thefe cafes
the unity of place would not be broke. But as I
have faid already, the Subject of the Play muft furnifh probable Reafons for thefe changes, which I repeat the oftner, becaufe I am ftill afraid, that it will
not make Impreffion enough in the Reader.

'Tis not enough neither to fay, that the Floor or
Stage fhould reprefent a place immoveable; it muft
befides be a place fuppos'd open in the reality, as it
appears in the Reprefentation; for fince the Actors
are fuppos'd to go and come from one end of it to
the other, there cannot be any folid body between,
to hinder either their fight or motion; therefore the
Ancients did ufe to chufe for the place of their
Scene in Tragedies fome publick place, as that before
the gate of a Palace; and in their Comedies fome
part of a Town, where different Streets met, and
where the Houfes of the principal Actors were fuppos'd to be; becaufe thefe places were moft fitly
reprefented by the empty Stage, adorn'd with the
Figures of thofe Houfes. Not that they always followed this, for in the *Suppliants*, and in the *Ion* of
Euripides, the Scene is before a Temple; and in the
Ajax of *Sophocles*, the Scene is before his Tent,
pitch'd in the Corner of a Forreft; in the *Rudens* of
Plautus, it is before the Temple, and fome fcatter'd
Houfes, from whence one fees the Sea. And indeed
all this depends upon the Poets Invention, who according to his Subject chufes the place, the moft convenient for all that he has a mind to reprefent, and
adorns it with fome agreeable Appearance.

One may judge from all this, how ridiculous was
the Wall in the *Thisbe* of Poet *Theophile*, it being
plac'd

plac'd upon the Stage; and *Pyramus* and *She* whifpe-
ring through it, and when they went out, the Wall
funk, that the other Actors might fee one another:
For befides that the two places on each fide of
the Wall reprefented the two Chambers of *Pyramus*
and *Thisbe*; and that it was contrary to all appearance of Reafon, that in the fame place the King
fhould come and talk with his Confidents, and
much lefs that a Lion fhould come and fright
Thisbe there; I would fain know, by what fuppos'd means in the action it felf, this Wall could
become vifible and invifible? and by what enchantment it was fometimes in being, and then ceas'd quite
to be again? The fault is not lefs in thofe, who fuppofe things done upon the Stage, which have not
been feen by the Spectators, it not being probable
they could have been done without being feen, or
elfe things muft be fuppos'd to have been invifible
in the reality of the action; upon which I think
one of our Modern Poets fell into a great Errour of
this kind, having plac'd a Baftion upon the Stage,
and having afterwards caus'd the Town to be taken
by that Baftion, which was never feen to be either
attack'd or defended.

As for the Extent which the Poet may allow to
the Scene he chufes, when it is not in a Houfe
but open, I believe it may be as far as a man can fee
another Walk, and yet not know perfectly that 'tis
he; for to take a larger fpace would be ridiculous,
it being improbable that two people being each of
them at one end of the Stage, without any Object
between, fhould look at one another, and yet not fee
one another; whereas this diftance, which we allow often, contributes to the working of the Play
by

by the miftakes and doubts which a man may make by feeing another at a diftance ; to which the Thea-tres of the Ancients do very well agree ; for being, as they were, threefcore yards in front among the *Romans*, and little lefs among the *Græcians*, it was pretty near the proportion we allow them.

I defire the Reader befides to confider, that if the Poet did reprefent by his Stage all the Places and Rooms of a Palace, or all the Streets of a Town, he fhould make the Spectators fee not onely all that happened in his Story, but all that was done be-fides in that Palace, or in the Town ; for there is no Reafon to hinder the Spectators from feeing all that, nor why they fhould fee one thing fooner than another, particularly confidering, that fince they can fee at the fame time into the Garden of the Palace, and into the Kings Cabinet, according to the Subject of the Play, they muft likewife hear and fee all that is done there, befides the Theatral Action ; except there were an Enchantment to fhew onely that which the Poet had a mind to, and to hide all that was not of his Subject ; befides the Stage would never be empty of any of the Actors, ex-cept they went out of the Palace or Town, for fince the place reprefents the Palace with its Garden, Court, and other Appartments, one cannot forbear feeing any one who fhould go from any of thofe Appartments into the Court or Garden ; and by confequent, as long as any of the Actors were in the Extent reprefented by the Stage, they cannot avoid being feen: To which it cannot be anfwer'd, that to mark the different Appartments, there may be Curtains to fhut and draw ; for thefe Curtains

are

are fit for nothing, but to tofs their Inventors in them, like Dogs in a Blanket.

I have fpoken fo clearly of this in my *Terence Juftified*, that I have nothing more to fay againft this grofs Piece of Ignorance.

If it be faid befides, that the Poet has the liberty of fhewing and hiding what he pleafes ; I grant it, provided there be a probability that one thing be feen, and another not; but there would need a fin- gular Invention to contrive, that ever and anon the fame Perfons, acting and fpeaking in a Palace, fhould be feen, and not be feen ; for that would be making of the Walls to fink and rife, go backwards and forwards every moment. This may be enough to fhew the error of thofe, who upon the fame Scene reprefent *Spain* and *France*, making their Stage, not onely almoft as big as the Earth, but likewife cau- fing the fame Floor to reprefent at the fame time things fo far diftant from one another, and that without any apparent caufe of fo prodigious a change.

We may likewife obferve, how they are miftaken, that fuppofe in one fide of the Stage one part of the Town, as for example, the *Louvre*, and on the other fide another part, as the *Place Royal;* thinking by this fine Invention to preferve the unity of Place. Indeed if two Parts or Quarters of a Town, thus fuppos'd, were not far from one another, and the fpace between were really empty of Houfes, fuch a thing were not improper ; but if between the two places, there are many Houfes and folid bodies, I would then ask, how it comes to pafs that thofe Houfes do not fill up the empty place of the Stage ; and how, if they do, an Actor can fee another

P   place

Place at the other end of the Stage, beyond all thefe Houfes; and in a word, how this Stage, which is but an Image, reprefents a thing of which it has no refemblance?

Let it then be fetled for a conftant Maxim, That the *Profcenium*, or floor of the Stage, can reprefent nothing but fome open place of an ordinary extent, where thofe, that are reprefented by the Actors, might naturally be in the truth of the Action; and when we fee it written, The Scene is at *Aulis*, *Eleufis*, or *Argos*, 'tis not that the place, where the Actors appear, is all that Town or Province, but onely that all the Intrigues of the Play, as well what paffes out of the fight of the Spectators, as what they fee, are treated in that Town, of which the Stage takes up but the leaft part.

Thus in the Prologue of the laft Comedy of *Plautus*, the Poet, explaining the Place of the Scene, fays, that he begs of the *Romans* a little fpace in the middle of their noble Buildings to tranfport thither the Town of *Athens*, without the help of Architects; upon which *Samuel Petit* obferves, that we ought not to imagine that *Plautus* pretends to place all the City of *Athens* in that of *Rome*, but onely a fmall part of it, where the things reprefented in the Play did come to pafs, to wit, the Quarter of the *Plotæans*, and of all that Quarter only the place, where *Phronefion* liv'd, and he confirms this by the mending of two *Greek* words, of which he pretends one *Latin* one was made by a miftake, and by a Verfe, which he mends by fome Manufcripts which he had feen, making the Prologue then fpeak thus; *I abridge here the Town of Athens, upon this Stage, during this Play, and in this Houfe lives Phronefion.*

Thefe

(marginal notes, left column:)

Perparvam partem poftulat Plautus loci devoftris magnis atque amœnis manibus, Athenas quo fine Ar. chitectis conferat. Prolog Trucul.

Ibi Samuel Petit.

Non totas Athenas fed Athenarum regionem illam deformabat hæc Plauti fcena, in qua res iftæ quæ hoc Dramate repræfentace bantur geftæ dicebantur, &c. Et en fuite id eft Plotheenfium regionem, eamque non totam, fed extremam illius partem in qua habitare fingitur Phronefion meretrix.

Athenas arcto, ita ut hoc eft profcenium tantifper dum tranfigimus hanc Comediam, hic habitat mulier nomine quæ eft Phronefion &c. Prolog. Truc.

Thefe are the only Authorities of any either Ancient or Modern Authors, that I have found concerning the place of the Scene. *Caftelvetro* indeed fays, that Tragedy requires but a fmall fpace ; but fince he has not explain'd himfelf better, we are not bound to guefs in his favour.

Thefe things then once fetled for the Doctrine or Theory ; I have thought of what follows for the Practical part The Poet does not defire to reprefent to his Spectators all the particulars of his ftory, but the principal and moft moving circumftances, and thus he is oblig'd to fome part out of the fight of the Spectators; and indeed he ought not to do it, there being many things fitter to be hid then fhewed, he muft then firft of all confider exactly, what perfons he moft wants and cannot well be without, then let him chufe a place where they may probably meet ; for as there are places which certain perfons cannot leave without extroardinary motives ; fo there are others, where they cannot be without great Reafon.   A Nun cannot leave the place of her retreat but upon fome preffing motive, and a woman of Honour cannot accompany *Meffalina* to the place of her infamous debauches.

Paralipfis eft, cùm res omittitur, quæ adeò neceffaria eft, ut etiam non relata intelligatur : & per annos decem quæt partes quot arma mente reftituenda fint: fic non femper legimus quoties cibum capiant aliáque naturæ neceffaria expediant. Id quod fanè figura eft, nam plebeia oratio, nihil omittere. Scat. lib. 3. c. 77.

Befides, he muft obferve, whether or no in his Subject there be not fome Circumftances or notable Incident, which it will be neceffary to preferve for the beauty of his Play, and which cannot happen but in a certain place, for then he muft accommodate to that the reft of his parts ; fo he that would fhew *Celadon* half dead upon the Shore and found there by *Galatea,* muft of neceffity place his Scene upon the bank of a River, and accommodate to it the reft of the Theatral Action. *Plautus* followed

P 2

lowed this method in his *Rudens*, where he defir'd to
fhew the relicks of a Shipwrack, and therefore was
forc'd to place his Scene on the Sea fide, where all
the reft of his Adventures are very dexteroufly
brought to pafs.

The Poet, having chofen the place, muft examine
next, what things are fitteft to be fhewed with delight to the Spectators, and be fure to reprefent
them; as for the others not fo fit to be feen, they
muft be told fome way, that they may be fuppos'd
done, and that in places fo near the Stage, that the
Actor who tells them, may be fuppos'd to have been
there and back again, from the time he has been
abfent from the Stage, or elfe he muft be fuppos'd
gone before the Play began, for then he may come
as far off as you will. All which *Terence* hath obferv'd in his third Comedy, where the two Slaves, *Syrus*, and *Dromo*, had been fent a great while before
for *Clitophon's* Miftrefs; and by confequent, all that
Syrus tells of their Negotiation is very credible,
what time fo ever there needed for the dreffing of
the Lady, and the doing of all the reft.

And if the things or places to be fpoke of in
the Play, have been done too far from the Scene, or
*Nunc adeft ubi
opus eft Poetæ:
& vide hanc
caufam fuiffe
cur non ad vil-
lam diverterit,
omnes villas co-
micas fuburba-
nas effe, commo-
ditatem ipfam
nunc explicat
& oftendit. Do-
nat. in Euuuch.
Terent.*
are in themfelves too remote, one muft bring them
nearer in the Reprefentation; which may be done two
ways; either by fuppofing that they happened in other
places nearer, when 'tis all one to the Story, as *Donatus* obferves, that in Plays, Country Houfes are alwayes fuppos'd to be in the Suburbs : Or elfe by fuppofing the places nearer than they really are, when
'tis impoffible to change them, but in this laft, one
muft obferve not to bring known places fo near,
that the Spectator cannot follow the Poet in his
be-

belief: As for example, if a man should bring the
Alps, or *Pyrenæan* Mountains in the place of Mount
Valerian, that so he might bring an Incident to Play,
which else he could not; the Scene being at *Paris*;
truly the rigour of the Rule would be followed, as
to the Unity of the Scene and its Decencies, but
the Beauty of the Art, which is to please and per-
swade, would be lost: 'Tis therefore that I cannot
approve of this force upon Nature, as to the distance
of places, which we see done in the *Suppliants*, and
the *Andromache* of *Euripides*, in the *Captives* of *Plautus* and some other pieces of Antiquity. I speak not
here of our Modern Poets, for all the World knows,
there never was any thing so monstrous in this
point, as the Plays we have seen in *Italy*, *Spain*, and
France, and indeed except the *Horatius* of *Corneille*, I
doubt whether we have one Play, where the unity of
the Scene is rigorously observ'd, at least, I am sure I
have not seen any.

It is necessary to give one advertisement more to
the Poet in this place, which is, that none of his
Actors ought to come upon the Scene without some
apparent Reason, since else it is not probable they
should be there; and he must avoid to follow the Example of a Poet, who made a Princess come a purpose
out of her Tent upon the Stage which was before it,
to say some passionate complaints of a secret Misfortune of hers, for it was much more probable that she
should make them in her Tent: Therefore he ought
to have feign'd either that the Company of some people in the Tent, was importunate and troublesome
to her, and that to avoid them she came out, or else
he ought to have given her some sudden impatience
to look out, and then, as naturally upon reflexions
of our Misfortunes we are carried to expressions of
them,

them, he might have put in her mouth what words he had thought neceffary for his Subject. Thus when the paffion of fome perfon upon the Scene is to be fhew'd by fome Narration, which the Spectator has had already, and which cannot be repeated without difguft, one muft fuppofe the thing to have been told that Perfon in fome place near the Scene, and make him come in near towards the end of it with words in his mouth, expreffing the knowledg of the thing, and caufing the paffion he is to fhew afterwards upon the Stage. The Examples of this are frequent among the Ancients, and the imitation of them cannot but fucceed well.

CHAP.

CHAP. VII.

The Extent of the Theatral Action, or of the time fit to be allowed a Dramatick Poem.

THERE is no queftion more debated than This, which I am now treating. The Poets make it their difcourfe, and the Players fcarce talk of any thing elfe, as well as thofe who frequent the Theatres; nay, the Ladies in their *Ruelles* undertake to decide it, and all this while the thing is fo little underftood, that I have a great deal of Reafon to endeavour to explain it carefully. To talk with fome knowledge then of this Matter, one muft confider that a Dramatick Poem has two forts of Time, each of which has a different and proper lafting.

The firft is the true Time of the Reprefentation; for though this fort of Poem be but an Image and fo ought to be confider'd as having a reprefentative Being; neverthelefs one ought to confider, that there is a reality in the very Reprefentation, for realy the Actors are feen and heard, the Verfes are really pronounc'd, and one fuffers really either pleafure or pain in affifting at thefe Reprefentations, and there is a real time fpent in amufing the Audience,

dience, that is from the opening of the Stage to the end of the Play: This time is call'd the lasting of the Representation.

Of this time the measure can be no other, but so much time as will reasonably spend the patience of the Audience, for this sort of Poem being made for pleasure, it ought not to weary and fatigate the mind; and it must not likewise be so short, as that the Spectators go away with an opinion of not having been well nor enough diverted. In all this, Experience is the faithfullest Guide, and tells us most commonly, that a Play cannot last above three hours without wearying of us, nor less without coming short of pleasing us. I have seen a very learned Gentleman, who was present at the Representation of the *Pastor Fido* in *Italy*, who told me, that never was any thing so tedious, it having lasted too long, and that this Play, which ravishes the Reader, because he can lay it by when he will, had most horridly disgusted the Spectators.

There is another observation to be made here, which is, that the time, which we allow the Representation, may be spent many other wayes.

The Ancients had in their Tragedies many different mixtures, as *Mimes*, *Pantomimes*, and other Buffoons. These Diversions pleas'd the people, and yet I do not believe they made the Representations longer than those of our time; for besides that these Interludes were short, their Tragedies themselves were not of above a thousand Verses, and those Verses much shorter than our Heroick ones. Therefore the Poet must take great care, that if his Play be of the ordinary length, his Interludes be not too long, for let them be never so pleasing they will
dis-

difquiet the Spectator in the Impatience, which he will naturally have to know the Event and Succefs of the Story.

The other Time of the Dramatick Poem is that of the Action reprefented, fo ar as it is confidered as a true Action, and containing all that fpace which is neceffary to the performing of thofe things, which are to be expos'd to the knowledge of the Spectators, from the firft to the laft Act of the Play.

Now this Time is the chief Time, not only becaufe 'tis natural to the Poem, but becaufe alfo it all depends on the Poets Invention, and is made known by the Mouth of his Actors, according as his Ingenuity can fuggeft him the means of doing it, and this is the Time fo much talk'd of in our days. The three *Greek* Tragicks, *Æfchylus*, *Euripides*, and *Sophocles* allow but a few houres to the lafting of the Theatral Action in their Poems; but their Example was not followed by the Poets who fucceeded them; for *Ariftotle* blames thofe of his time, for giving too long an Extent to the lafting of their Plays, which makes him fet down the Rule, or rather renew it from the Model of the Ancients, faying, That Tragedy ought to be comprehended in the Revolution of one Sun. I do not know, whether this Rule was obferv'd by thofe that came after him, as by the Authors of thofe Tragedies which carry the Name of *Seneca*, which are regular enough in this Circumftance: But for all thofe that I have feen, which were made at the re-eftablifh-ment of Learning in *Spain* and *France*, they are not only irregular in this point, but in all the o-

Q

ther

ther moft fenfible Rules, infomuch that one would admire, that Men of Learning fhould be the Authors of them : When I firft had the Honour to be near Cardinal *Richelieu*, I found the Stage in great efteem, but loaded with all thefe Errors, and particularly with that, of exceeding the Time, fit to be allowed in Tragedy ; I fpoke of it in thofe Plays which were acted at Court; but I was generally oppos'd, and moft commonly turned into Ridicule both by the Poets, the Actors, and the Spectators ; and when I, to defend my felf, began to alledge the Ancients, I was paid with this Anfwer, That what they had done was well for their time, but now a days they would be laugh'd at, if they were here : As if the general Reafon of Mankind could grow old with time ; and accordingly we fee, that at laft it has prevailed over Prejudice and Ignorance, to make all the World confefs, that the Time of a Tragedy ought to be fhort and limited : But becaufe, even in this, there are different Interpretations given to *Ariftotle*, and that fome Poets do believe, to circumfcribe too narrowly the lafting of the Theatral Action would be to fpoil moft of the Incidents ; I will here give the true Explanation of the Rule, and ways of practifing it with Succefs. *Ariftotle* has faid, that one of the principal differences, which is between an Epick Poem and a Tragedy, is, That the Firft is not limited inany time, and that the Second is comprehended in the Revolution of one Sun. Now, though *Ariftotle* does exprefs himfelf in few words, yet I cannot underftand, how there was ground for fo much Difpute: For fince he fays, the Revolution of one Sun, it cannot be meant, the Annual Revolution, for that is the time generally allowed

to

to an Epick Poem, and there is none of the moſt Indulgent, that have offer'd to extend the Rule to that excels in Tragedy. It remains then to ſay, he means the Diurnal Revolution ; but as the day is conſidered two ways, the one with regard to the *Primum mobile*, which is call'd the Natural day, and is of twenty four Hours, and the other by the Suns preſence upon the Horizon, between his riſing and ſetting, which is call'd the Artificial Day. It is ne-ceſſary to obſerve, that *Ariſtotle* means only the Ar-tificial Day, in the extent of which, he makes the Theatral Action to be comprehended. *Caſtelvetro* and *Picolomini*, upon *Ariſtotles* Poetick, are of this Opinion againſt *Seigni*, who extends the Rule to the Natural day of 24 hours.

The Reaſon of this is certain, and founded upon the Nature of Dramatick Poems ; for this ſort of Poem ought to carry a ſenſible Image of the Actions of Humane Life ; now we do not ſee, that regu-larly men are buſie before day, nor much after night, and accordingly, in all well governed places, there are Magiſtrates to watch thoſe, who employ the night naturally deſign'd for reſt, in the Actions of the day.

Beſides, we have ſaid, and it cannot be called in queſtion ; that the Theatral Action ought to be one, and not comprehend any other Actions, which are not neceſſary to the Intrigue of the Stage. Now how can that be obſerved in a Play of 24 hours ? would it not be a neceſſity, that the Perſons Acting ſhould ſleep, and eat, and buſie themſelves in many things, which would not be of the Subject of the Play, and though the Poet ſhould ſay nothing of it, yet the Spectators muſt needs conceive it ſo.

Q 2   But

But befides, the Action of the Stage is to be continued, and not interrupted or broken. Now that could not be in a Play of twenty four hours; Nature could not, without fome reft, endure fo long an Action ; fince all that Men can commonly do, is to be in Action for the day time.

Moreover, we cannot omit a Reafon of the Ancients, which originally is Effential to Tragedy, which is, that the Choruſes, which they uſed, did not regularly uſe to ftir off the Stage for the whole Play, or at leaft from the time they firſt came on ; and I do not know with what appearance of Probability, the Spectators could have been perfwaded, that People, who were never out of their fight, ſhould have ſtaid twenty four hours in that place ; nor how in the truth of the Action, they could imagine, that thoſe, whom they repreſented, had paſs'd all that time without ſatisfying ſome neceffities of Nature.

After all, we can never better underſtand *Ariſtotle*, than by thoſe three Excellent Tragick Poets, whom he always propofes for Examples, who have regularly obferv'd, not to give above 12 hours to their Plays : And I do not think, that there are any of their Works which do comprehend the whole ſpace between the riſing and ſetting of the Sun.

It being moſt certain, that their Stage generally opens after Sun-rife, and is ſhut up before Sun-fet , as one may obferve in the Comedies of *Plautus* and *Terence.* 'Tis therefore that *Roffi*, an *Italian* , allows but eight or ten hours . And *Scaliger*, more rigorouſly but more reaſonably, would have the whole Action performed in ſix hours.

Scenicum ego-
tium totum ſex
ctove horis pe-
ragitur l. 3. c.
97. Poet.

hours. It were even to be wish'd, that the Action of the Poem did not take up more time , than that of the Reprefentation, but that being hard, and almoft impoffible, in certain occafions the Poet has the Liberty to fuppofe a longer time by fome hours, in which the Mufick that marks the Intervals of the Acts, and the Relations of the Actors upon the Stage, while the others are bufie off of it, with the natural defire of the Spectators to fee the Event, do all contribute very much, and help to deceive the Audience , fo as to make them think, there has paffed time enough for the performance of the things reprefented.

What we have faid hitherto of *Ariftotle's* Rule might fuffer fome difficulty in thofe Plays , which reprefent Actions that happened in the Night, if we did not own, that he has forefeen the Objection, when he fays, That *Tragedy endeavours to compre-* *hend its Action in the Revolution of one Sun,* *or in* *changing that time a little;* for by that means he lets us know, that the Poet is not always bound to place his Action between Sun-rifing and Sun-fetting, but may take a like time out of 24 hours, and place his Action in the night, as in the *Rhefus* of *Euripides*, and fome other Plays of the Ancients, of which we have nothing but Fragments in *Athenæus*. Nay, he may take fome of his time in the day , and the reft in the night, as *Euripides* has done in his *Electra,* and *Plautus* in his *Amphitryon ;* they that, upon this of *Ariftotle*, have faid, that he gave leave to exceed the Revolution of a Sun , and go fome hours beyond, did not well underftand him, having taken the word Changing for Exceeding.

ἢ μικρὸν
ἐξαλλάττειν.
Poet. c. 5. aut
parum variare.
Vict. p. 52.
Aut paulifper
variare. Ricco-
boni in Poët
Arift.

But

But without ftanding upon this fcrupulous nice-
nefs, I muft tell the Poet, that he need not fear to
fpoil his Play, by ftraitning his Incidents in fo fmall
a compafs of time; for quite contrary, 'tis that,
which fhall make his Play agreeable and wonderful;
'tis that, which will afford him the means of introducing extraordinary furprizes and paffions, which
he may carry, as far as he will; let him confider well
Horatius, *Cinna*, *Polyeuct*, and *Nicomedes*, the latter works of Mounfieur *Corneille*, and I believe,
he cannot but agree to it.

Now to contribute for my fhare to the neceffary
means of practifing this Rule, I here deliver my
thoughts.

Firft, Let the Poet be very careful in chufing the
day, in which he will comprehend all the Intrigues
of his Play, and that choice ought generally to be made
from the moft Noble Incident of the whole Story, that
is, from that Incident, which is to make the Cataftrophe, and to which all others do tend, like Lines to
their Center; and if he be free to take what day he
will, his beft will be to pitch upon that, which will
moft eafily bear the Affemblage and Concurrence of
all the Incidents of the Stage. So *Corneille*, being to
reprefent the Death of *Pompey*, took the laft day of
his Life, becaufe he could not do otherwife; but
when he was to make his *Cinna*, he chofe what day
he pleas'd for to facilitate the bringing in of the Con-
fpiration of *Cinna*, with the deliberation of *Auguftus*, whether he fhould forfake the Empire or no.

The choice being thus made, the next flight is, to
open your Stage, as near, as tis poffible, to the Cataftrophe, that you may employ lefs time in the negotiation part, and have more Liberty in extending
the Paffions and Difcourfes which may pleafe; but

to

to Execute this luckily, the Incidents muft be prepar'd by ingenious Contrivances, and that muft appear upon occafion in the whole Conduct of the
Action.

This we may obferve in the *Jon* of *Euripides,* the
Amphytrion of *Plautus ,* and the *Andria* of *Terence.* *Corneille* practifes it likewife well in *Horatius* and *Cinna.* The Stage in *Horatius* is opened
but a moment before the Combat of the three *Horatius's* againft the three *Curiatius's,* who are told of
their being chofen to fight againft each other, as
foon as they come upon the Stage. And *Cinna* had
already made his Confpiracy, before the opening of
the Stage, which opens juft before the Sacrifice, which
was to be the pretext of the Execution of it.

Things being thus difpos'd, the Poet muft next ftudy to bring together the Incidents all in one day, fo
Artfully, that there appear no Force nor Conftraint
in the effecting of it : And to fucceed in this, he muft
rectify the time of thofe things, that happened before
the opening of the Stage ; and fuppofe, fome of
them to come to pafs that day, though they really
happened before ; but he muft joyn them with fo
much Art, as they may feem to be naturally con-
nexed, and not put together by the Poets Invention.

Thus *Sophocles* makes, that *Creon,* who was fent to
Delphos to confult the Oracle, comes back juft at
the fame time that the news comes to *Thebes,* of the
Death of *Polybius* King of *Corinth,* though thefe two
things did not happen on the fame day. So *Plautus*
makes *Amphitryon* return victorious that very night
that *Alcmena* is brought to Bed of *Hercules.* But that
which one muft particularly have a care of, is how to
conjoyn the time of the Incidents

cipitation, that Probability be deftroyed by it , as in the *Suppliants* of *Euripides*, the *Captiv's* of *Plautus* and fome other pieces of the Ancients, which I cannot approve of, though for fome other Confiderations they are not unexcufable. They are indeed according to the Rule of time , but without any of the Graces of the Art. In a word, we muft ftill remember, that *Ariftotle* in giving his Rule of the confining Tragedy to the Revolution of one Sun, means, that the Poet ought fo to prefs his imagination, as to order a ll the Events of his Theatre in that time, but fo, as not to offend Probability, which is always the principal Rule , and without which all the others become no Rules at all.

C H A P.

C H A P. VIII.

Of the Preparation of the Incidents.

IT may be fome may Imagine, that the Inftruction we are going to give the Poet in this Difcourfe,
will be injurious to him, and, contrary to our pro-
mife, deftroy all the Graces of the Stage : for fay
they, if the Incidents muft be prepar'd fome time
before they happen, without doubt they will likewife be prevented, and fo be no longer furprizing,
in which confifts all their beauty, and without which
the Spectator has no pleafure, nor can the Poet
pretend to any glory in his Art.

To this I anfwer, That there is a great deal of
difference between preparing an Incident, and preventing it, for an Incident is then prevented, when
it is forefeen, but it ought not to be forefeen though
it be prepar'd.

To explain our felves better upon this matter,
we are to underftand that there are fome things in
the Compofition of a Theatral Action, which do
carry the minds of the Spectators naturally and almoft neceffarily, to the knowledge of fome others;
fo that as foon as the firft are either faid or done,
one may conclude eafily thofe that depend upon
                          R   them,

them, and that is call'd an Incident prevented; and we do allow all these Preventions to be faulty in a Dramatick Poem, because they spoil the Events, and make them of no effect in the Imagination of the Spectators, who most commonly expect things contrary to what they see, and seem to be promis'd.

But there are another sort of things, which are to be laid as a foundation to build others upon, according to the Rules of Probability, and yet nevertheless do not at all discover these second ones, which they are to produce; not only because there is no necessity they should come to pass in consequence of the first; but also because the first are shew'd with colours and pretexts so probable, according to the state of the Affairs of the Stage, that the Minds of the Spectators pass them over, not thinking that from thence there can spring any new Incident, so that the preparation of an Incident, is not to tell or do any thing that can discover it, but rather that may give occasion to it without discovering it; and all the Art of the Poet consists in finding Colours and Pretexts to settle these Preparations, so, that the Spectator may be convinc'd, that that is not thrown into the Body of the Play for any other design, than what appears to him. *Scaliger* has own'd this to be necessary, even in the Epick Poems, and calls it, *The Seeds of a future Harvest*: as if he would say, that just as the Grain or Seed contains in it self the force and virtue of producing in its time Flowers and Fruit; and yet Nature has so fram'd it, as that one cannot discover any likelihood of such a Production, by the sight of the Seed; so must the Discourses and other considerations to

prepare

Arist. c. x. poet.
In multis œ-
conomia Co-
micorum Poeta-
rum ita se habet,
ut casu putet
Spectator venis-
se quod consilio
Scriptorum fa-
ctum sit. Donat.
in Terent. Andr.
& in Eunuch.
Idem aliis ver-
bis.

Vbique verò
aliquid jacit se-
minum ad fu-
turam messem,
ut auditorem
quasi prægusta-
tione alliciat ad
epulas. Similis
præparatio in
primo, cum enim
recipiendus est
Æneas proponit
hoc intelligen-
dum ex pictura,
in ea namque ip-
se quoque pictus
erat. lib. 4. c.
26.

prepare an Incident, enclofe it fo fecretly, and hide it fo well, as nothing can be guefs'd of the Event from them. This Excellent Man brings divers Examples of this, and particularly, that taken from the *Æneid* of *Virgil:* For he obferves, that to make way for the kind reception, which *Dido* gives to *Æneas* and his *Trojans, Virgil* tells us, how Queen *Dido* had caus'd the Story of the War of *Troy* to be painted in a Temple, where *Æneas* himfelf was reprefented, fighting in the midft of the *Greeks*; for then this painting feems only an Object for the admiration of *Æneas*, to fee that the *Trojans* misfortunes were already known all the World over; but the fecret is, that it ferves to give a foundation in the Mind of *Dido* to the kind welcome fhe makes to thofe, to whofe ill fortune in all probability fhe had already given fome compaffion.

As for the Dramatick Poem, I have not met with any Examples in all the Authors that I have feen, except in one *Victorius* in his Commentaries upon *Ariftotles* Poetick; and neither there does he do it by way of Inftruction, but fimply by way of Remark upon the Tragedy of *Medea*, made by *Euripides*, of which he fays, that the Cataftrophe is defective, becaufe the Poet unfolds the Plot by the flight of *Medea* in an Enchanted Chariot, of which before hand he had not given the leaft hint or preparation, the preceding Events contributing no ways to this laft. Thefe two paffages of *Scaliger* and *Victorius* came not to my knowledge, till after I had made all the neceffary Obfervations upon this Subject; but as I never affected to be thought the Inventor of any thing, fo am I never better pleas'd, than when having by my Meditations

Reprehenfus eft Poeta, quia femina nulla hujus fabulæ exitus antea iacta erant, nec unquam ipfius adiuvant fuperio. res partes Tragœdiæ. Victor. in Arift. p. 149.

R 2 attain'd

attain'd to a certain knowledge, I difcover that o-
thers more able, and of greater reputation, had
faid the fame things before I thought them ; and
for that very reafon I have not diffembled thefe
two paffages which make to our Subject, and if
the efteem due to thefe Excellent Authors deprives
me of the honour of having faid the firft thing, of
which I thought I was the only Inventor, I fhall
draw that advantage at leaft from them, that they
give Authority to my thoughts ; and the Poet cannot refufe the Counfel I give him, of preparing ingenioufly his Incidents, when *Scaliger* efteems *Virgil* for having done it with prudence, and *Victorius*
condemns *Euripides* for having fail'd in it. I fhall
give two Examples of both thefe out of Monfieur
Corneille, the firft is in *Rhodogune*, and the other in
his *Theodora*.

In the firft Example, he kills *Cleopatra* by the
violence of a Poyfon, fo ftrong, that *Rhodogune* difcovers the effect of it, before *Antiochus* has pronounc'd ten Verfes. Indeed, that *Cleopatra* was
wicked and enrag'd enough to poifon her felf, that
fhe might poifon her Son and *Rhodogune*, That is
very well prepar'd in all the precedent Acts, where
her hatred, ambition, and fury appear to the height,
having kill'd her husband with her own hand,
and deftroyed one of her Sons to preferve her felf
upon the Throne ; but that the effect of the poyfon
fhould be fo fudden, as to be difcover'd in fo fmall a
fpace of time, That is not prepar'd enough, becaufe,
the thing being rare in it felf, *Cleopatra* fhould
have faid, when fhe hopes by it to deftroy *Antiochus*
and *Rhodogune*, how ftrong a Poyfon fhe had prepar'd, and how fudden its Effect would be, and
fhould

fhould have exprefs'd joy at it; by which means, fhe would have prepar'd the Incident, without preventing it.   The Event, I fay, would have been prepar'd ; for fo fudden a Poifon, as fhe had mention'd, would have been expected to work that Effect it did upon her felf ; but withall it would not have been prevented, becaufe the Audience would have thought, that fhe had faid it as defigning it for the deftruction of the Innocent, and fo there would not have been any means of forefeeing, that fhe fhould have fuffer'd by it her felf.

The other Example is in all the Exactnefs that a Dramatick Poem can wifh, which muft needs make us confefs, that when *Monfieur Corneille* has well meditated upon the conduct of an Incident, there is no Author, either among the Ancient or Modern Poets, that executes it better.

In his *Theodora*, there are five notable Incidents, to wit the death of *Flavia*; the deliverance of *Theodora* from that infamous place, to which fhe had been condemn'd; the death of *Didymus* and *Theodora* by the hands of *Marcella*; the death of *Marcella* by her own hand; and the wound of *Placidus* endeavouring to kill himfelf; all thefe Incidents are fo well prepar'd, that there is not one, which might not probably come to pafs in confequence of thofe things which preceded it.

That *Flavia* fhould dye that day, is not ftrange; fince 'tis often faid that fhe is defperately ill; but when that is faid, 'tis onely to give a pretext to the fury of *Marcella*, and to thofe violent means fhe ufes of being reveng'd of *Theodora*, without giving an Impreffion that her Daughter fhould really dye fo foon,

That

That *Didymus* ſhould expoſe himſelf ſave *Theodora*, in giving her his Clothes; that might well be, ſince he appears very paſſionately in love with her, and that *Theodora* did not reject his love but only out of Religion; but when this paſſion is talk'd of upon the Stage, it ſeems in appearance to be, to foment the Jealouſie of *Placidius*, without any likely-hood of foreſeeing ſo Extraordinary an Action.

That *Marcella* ſhould with her own hands kill *Didymus* and *Theodora*, that is probable, ſhe knew the love of *Placidius*, and the reſolution he had taken to ſave the two Lovers, ſhe ſaw him arm'd, and followed by a great number of his Friends, all theſe are preparations enough to make that Woman revenge the death of her Daughter, and all the injuries ſhe had receiv'd by one furious tranſport in an occaſion ſo precipitated; and neverthelefs, though one could not from all theſe things expect this Event, yet they have all their neceſſary Colours, when they appear upon the Stage.

The ſame happens in the death of *Marcella*; ſhe had perſecuted *Placidius*, and injur'd him in the perſon he moſt tenderly lov'd; ſhe ſees him with his Sword drawn, and being animated with nothing but furious Sentiments, ſhe was reſolv'd not to fall under the power of her Enemy, from theſe Circumſtances it follows, that probably ſhe might kill her ſelf, and that ſhe was preſs'd to make that deſperate end.

As for *Placidius*, who endeavours to kill himſelf, after having ſeen his Miſtreſs murder'd by the hand of his Enemy, 'tis an Incident well prepar'd, becauſe of the Exceſſive love he bore her, and

and by the difpofition he appears to be in, to forfake all the Grandeur of the World to poffefs
her, who was his Soveraign felicity ; and neverthelefs, of all thefe Confiderations one could pre-
fume naturally nothing more, than that he would
do all he could to fave her. Thus fo many different Events arife from one another, and without any precipitation in the Body of the Story.
I know not how Mr. *Corneille* may value this
Play, but I fay that in my mind it is his Mafter-
piece, for though in the Subject, the punifhment,
to which *Theodora* is condemn'd, does fomething
offend the modefty of the Spectators; yet all the
reft is in fo much regularity, and there is fo much
Art and Conduct fhewed by the Poet, that if the
choice of the Subject had anfwer'd the skill of the
Author, I believe we might propofe this Play as
a moft perfect Model.

He that would cite here all the Plays of the
Ancients, where the Incidents are well prepar'd,
would be oblig'd to copy whole Poems, for they
have always done it with great Art and Judgment.
See the *Curculion* of *Plautus*, there is a Ring, which
ferves to find out *Planafion*, to be a freeborn Woman and the Sifter of *Terapontigonus*, when 'twas
no ways poffible to forefee this Event; but it is
fo well prepar'd in all the Play, where this Ring
is employed in a great many other Intrigues,
that it is not at all forc'd, though much againft
the Expectation of the Spectators: And when this
Ring is ftol'n from the Souldier, and that from
thence it runs through a great many hands, 'tis for
fome prefent action, which has no regard to the
Cataftrophe, the event of which could not thence
be forefeen.   And

And when in the 4th Act, *Cappadore* says, that he had paid but ten Mines of Silver for that Maid, 'tis probably, onely to explain the profit he makes by selling her for thirty; but 'tis in effect to prepare the Narration which *Planesion* makes her self of her own Adventure.

So in his *Trinummus*, *Carmides* arrives at a nick of time, from a long Voyage, for a very diverting Incident, meeting with a Cheat which was suppos'd to come from him, but That is very well prepar'd by the discourse of *Calicles* in the first Act, and by that of his Slave in the second. And nevertheless when *Calicles* speaks of the absence of his Friend, 'tis onely to make known the fidelity he owes him; and that which the Slave says of his return, is onely to make his Son *Telesbonicus* be afraid of his Fathers just severity.

In a word, I deliver here all that I can say of this matter, which is, that the Events are always precipitated, when there has been nothing said before, from whence they might probably proceed, as when a man appears expresly in the end of the Play, of whom there has not been one word said all along, and yet this man comes to make the winding up of the Plot. Or when towards the end, there is some important Action done, which has no coherence with all that pass'd before; for though the Spectators love to be surpriz'd, yet 'tis still with probability; and they are not bound to suppose any thing, but what follows naturally these things which the Poet shews. The Theatre is a world by it self, where all is comprehended in the notions and extent of the Action represented, and has no communication with the great World, onely so far as the Poet him-

self

felf extends it, by the knowledge which with Art he difpenfes abroad. But the main thing to be remembred, is, that all that is faid or done as a Preparative or Seed for things to come, muſt have fo apparent a Reafon, and fo powerful a Colour to be faid and done in that place, that it may feem to have been introduc'd only for that, and that it never give a hint to prevent thofe Incidents, which it is to prepare.

S   CHAP.

CHAP. IX.

Of the Cataftrophe or Iffue of the Dramatick Poem.

I Do not think it neceffary here to trouble my felf much about the explication of this word *Cataftrophe*. 'Tis taken ordinarily, I know, for fome fad calamitous difafter, which terminates fome great defign, for my part I underftand by this word a fudden change of the firft Difpofitions of the Stage, and the return of Events, which change all the Appearances of the former Intrigues, quite contrary to the expectation of the Audience. Comedies have generally happy *Cataftrophes*, or at leaft they end in fome buffoonry or fooling, as the *Stichus* of *Plautus* ; but as for ferious Tragedies, they alwayes end either by the Misfortune of the Principal Actors, or by a Profperity fuch as they could wifh for ; we have Examples of both in the Poems of the Ancients, though that latter way, of terminating their Tragedies, was not fo common with them, as it has been in our time. But now, I come to the Obfervations, which may be ufeful in all forts of Poems, as they are common to all forts of *Cataftrophes*.

Cataftrophe converfio negotij exagitati in tranquillitatem non expectatam. Scal. l. 1. c. 9.

S 2　　　　　The

The principal Obſervation has a dependance on what has been ſaid in the laſt Chapter, which was, *that Incidents, not prepar'd, offended againſt Probability, by being too much baſtned at laſt :* For this fault appears no where ſo much as in the *Cataſtrophe.* Firſt, the *Cataſtrophe* is the term of all the Affairs of the Stage, by conſequent they muſt be diſpos'd by times, that they may arrive there eaſily. Secondly, 'tis the Center of the Poem, therefore all the other parts, like lines, cannot be drawn ſtraight to any other point. Thirdly, 'tis the laſt expeĉtation of the Audience therefore all things ought to be ſo well order'd, that when they fall out, it may not be ask'd, by which way they came to paſs, and therefore there needs for it, as for the moſt conſiderable Event, the greateſt and moſt judicious Preparations. *Ariſtotle,* and all his Followers, would have the *Cataſtrophe* drawn from the very middle of all the buſineſs of the Stage, and that the very knots, whith ſeem to embarraſs the whole Subjeĉt, ſhould at laſt ſerve for the opening of it, as if they were laid for that purpoſe. Therefore they always valued this way of ending a Tragedy, much more than That which was founded upon the preſence or favour of ſome God; and when they did make uſe of Gods in Machines, they always deſir'd, that in the Body of the Play, there ſhould be reaſonable Diſpoſitions for it, either by the particular care that That God took of that Hero, or by the intereſt the God might take in the Theatral Aĉtion, or by a natural and rational expeĉtation of the aſſiſtance of ſome God, or ſome ſuch Inventions.

Yet this firſt Rule may ſeem uſeleſs in thoſe Plays, where the *Cataſtrophe* is known either by the Story
ry

ry or Title, as the *Death of Cæfar*, and fuch like, Therefore in this Cafe, without omitting any of the neceffary preparations we have mention'd, one may do thus.

The Poet muft fo manage all the Affairs of the Stage, that the Spectators may be inwardly per-fwaded, that That perfon, whofe life and fortune are threatned, ought not to die: For by this Art he keeps them in fentiments of pity and commi-feration, which encreafe and become very tender at the laft point of his Misfortune, and the more one finds motives to believe, he fhould not die, the more one is concern'd, when one knows he muft, the injuftice of his Enemies raifes a ftronger averfi-on in us for them, and his difgrace is pitied even with tears. We have feen the Examples of this in *Mariamne*, and the Earl of *Effex*, though, in ma-ny other things, they were very defective Plays.

But if the *Cataftrophe* be not known, and that the Poet defigns, that, for the greater Ornament of his Play, it fhould unfold all the Intrigues of it by a fuprizing Novelty; he muft be very careful not to difcover it too foon, and particularly order it fo, that none of his preparations do prevent it, for not only then it would become ufelefs and difagreeable, but as foon as ever it fhould be known, the Theatre would grow dull, and be without Charms for the Au-dience: And we are not in this Circumftance to go-vern our felves by what happens in a Play, that we have feen, or of which the *Cataftrophe* is known; for they do ftill pleafe, becaufe the Spectators in that cafe confider things only as they pafs, and give them no greater extent, than the Poet would have them. They confine all their underftanding to

the

the pretexts and colours, which he advances, without going any further, and being all along fatisfied of the Motives of the chief Actions, they do not prevent thofe, which are not made known to them, fo that, their imagination being deceiv'd by the art of the Poet, their pleafure lafts ftill. Whereas in the other Cafe, when the *Cataftrophe* is prevented by the want of Art in the Poet, the Spectators are difgufted, not fo much that they know the thing, as becaufe they are perfwaded, that they ought not to know it, and their difcontent in thefe occafions proceeds lefs from their knowledge, though certain, than from the imprudence and ill conduct of the Poet.

The laft Rule is, that the *Cataftrophe* do entirely finifh the *Dramatick* Poem, that is, that there be nothing left of what the Spectators ought to know, for if they have reafon to ask, *What became of fuch a one concern'd in the Intrigues of the Stage?* or if they have juft Subject to enquire, *What are the Sentiments of one of the chief Actors, after the laft event which makes the Cataftrophe?* Then, I fay, the Play is not well finifh'd, and wanted yet a ftroke or two, and if the Spectators are not yet fully fatisfied, the Poet certainly has not done his duty. 'Twas a confiderable fault in *Panthea*, who by her death leaves a reafonable defire to the Spectators, to know what became of *Arafpes*, who was fo paffionately in love with her: Whereas on the contrary, in the Earl of *Effex*, Queen *Elizabeth* fpeaks as fhe ought, after the death of the Earl, and fo finifhes the *Cataftrophe* perfectly.

But to avoid this inconvenience, the Poet muft not fall into another, that is, to add to the *Cataftrophe* fuperfluous Difcourfes and Actions, of no ufe as

to

to the concluding the Play , which the Spectators neither look for, nor are willing to hear; such is the Complaint of the Wife of *Alexander*, Son of *Herod*, after the death of her Husband, of which I shall speak in the Chapter of Pathetick Discourses ; and such is likewise the Explication of the Oracle in *Horatius*, for that having had nothing to do with the Plot, the Spectators never think on't, nor care to have it interpreted.

I might lengthen this Discourse with many more Remarks, as well upon the Tragedies as the Comedies of the Ancients; but since all *Catastrophes* turn upon these Principles, which I have laid down, it will be easie in reading their Works to see which are well or ill finish'd. The Tragick Poets have generally taken more care than the Comick, and amongst the Comick, *Terence* is the most exact; for *Aristophanes* and *Plautus* have left the best part of theirs unfinish'd.   I leave our Modern Authors to themselves, they generally are willing to be believ'd infallible, and when any body shews them that they might have done better, they are so much the more angry, as they find themselves convinc'd, and not able to oppose the strength of reason.

The End of the second Book.

THE
ART
OF THE
STAGE.

Book the Third.

Chapter the First.

*Of the Actors or Persons to be brought upon the Stage,
and what the Poet is to observe about them.*

I Do not design here to instruct the Players,
but the Poet, who will find in this Chapter
some Observations for the better disposing of
the Drammatick Poem, as to the persons that
are to appear upon the Stage.
    But before we begin them, it will not be amiss to
[A] observe

obſerve to the Reader a thing which will make us make a wiſh in favour of our Stage, when we reflect upon the Magnificency of the Repreſentations of the Antients, which is, that in many places of their Poems, where we ſee but one Actor nam'd, he did not appear alone upon the Stage; but on the contrary, when it was a Prince, or Princeſs, or ſome Perſon of Eminent Quality, he was followed by a very great Retinue, ſuitable to his Dignity; ſometimes of Courtiers, ſometimes of Souldiers, and always of Perſons proper to the Subject of the Play: Nay, a rich Citizen appear'd with a great many Servants, and a publick Curtizan, if ſhe were of free condition, and Miſtreſs of her own actions, had always a great many Maids and Servants about her; and in ſhort, Perſons of Quality were always well accompanied, except ſome particular reaſon requir'd they ſhould be alone, which may be eaſily perceiv'd by the Verſes, or the Nature of the Action. So *Ajax* in *Sophocles* is alone when he kills himſelf; and this the Antients did for two Reaſons; firſt to fill their Stage, which was much bigger than ours, and the other to make their Repreſentation more magnificent; whereas now five or ſix People fill our Stage, and beſides, the Players cannot be at the charge of more for pure Ornament ſake.

The truth of this appears in moſt of the Antients Plays, but particularly in the ſeven before *Thebes*, where *Eteocles*, who opens the Scene, ſeems to be alone, becauſe there is no body ſpeaks but he, but it is clear that he was followed by a very great number of Perſons, to whom he addreſſes himſelf, and gives them different Orders for the Defence of the Town.

Oreſtes

Oreſtes ſeems to be alone in the *Electra* of *Euripides*, and yet one may ſee that he ſpeaks to a great many Servants who followed him, whom he commands to enter his Siſters houſe, who did not know him, and is angry with her Husband for letting ſo many People of Quality come into his houſe. I cannot omit here the miſtake that ſome Authors have made in interpreting *Euripides*; for having not obſerv'd that *Hyppolitus* is followed by a company of Hunters, with whom he comes back ſinging a Hymn in the honour of *Diana*, they have taken him to be alone, and that they who ſung were the *Chorus* of the Tragedy; whereas the *Chorus* in that Play is compos'd of Women, followers of *Phædra*, who only come upon the Stage after *Hyppolitus* and his Company have ſung their Hymn, and one of them Entertains him ſome time about the reſpect due to *Venus*; after which Dialogue *Hyppolitus* commands his People to go and prepare his Dinner at his own houſe, out of which they follow him again, when by his Fathers command he is forc'd to withdraw.

But *Plutarch* affords us a proof of the ſtate with which the chief Actors us'd to appear upon the Stage, in a pleaſant Story he tells in the life of *Phocion*; for a Player being to repreſent a Queen and his Attendance, which was to be numerous, not being ready, he refuſed to come upon the Stage, whereupon *Melanthius Choragus*, whoſe Office it was to ſee all things well in order, thruſt him by force upon the Stage, with theſe words, *Doeſt not thou ſee that* Phocion's *Wife, whoſe Husband governs us all, is ſeen every day in the Street attended but with one Maid*: At which all the People fell a laughing, and by that Railery he excus'd the defect of the Repreſentation; which by the by may ferve our Poets for an Advertifement, to Read carefully the Works of the Antients, and not truft to the Printed Gloffes or Interpreters; but now let us come to our other more neceffary Obfervations.

And to begin, it has been often ask'd how many Actors may be brought on at once, fpeaking and acting upon the Stage, in the fame Scene. Some have confin'd us to Three, taking their Rule from *Horace's* Art of Poetry; but Experience is the beft Judg in thefe Cafes; and *Horace*, I believe, is not fo well underftood as he fhould be. 'Tis true, that the Stage having attain'd to have Three Actors in the time of *Sophocles*, who brought Drammatick Poetry to its perfection; the *Greeks* feldom bring any more than Three Actors at a time upon the Stage, if there be a Fourth, he generally is filent; and indeed a Scene is not ill fill'd when Three chief Actors are difcourfing at once upon the Scene. But the Anfwer to this Queftion depends not fo much upon the number of Perfons, as upon the order or confufion that would follow if too many were fpeaking in the fame Scene; and therefore I am of Opinion, that the Poet may bring on as many as he pleafes, provided neither their number, nor their difcourfes do confound the Spectators Attention; and there will be no confufion if the Actors Names, and their Concerns be fo known as to give a true underftanding of what is in Action: Three Actors indeed feldom bring any confufion, becaufe there is no Spectator fo fimple, but he can eafily diftinguifh their words and defigns; but ftill the Poet muft confider what neceffity he lies under; for if his Subject requires that Four or Five fhould appear and difcourfe in the fame Scene, if he performs it with diftinction,
and

and without obfcurity, I don't believe any body will fay he goes againft the Rules, there being nothing there againft probability. The Examples of this are frequent in the Comick Poets, both Greek and Latine ; and as for *Horace*, his Advice is only that the Poet do not bring a Fourth Perfon upon the Stage *Ne quarta la-* fo as to embarafs or confound the bufinefs in hand, *boret.* or perplex the Difcourfe of the other Three.

Our fecond Obfervation is, that the Poet muft bring no Actor upon the Stage that is not known to the Spectators as foon as he appears, and that not only as to his Name and Perfon, but alfo as to the Sentiments he brings upon the Stage, elfe the Spectator will be puzzled, and the Poets fine Difcourfes will be loft, becaufe the Audience will not know how to apply them ; and I have feen often 20 or 30 noble Verfes thrown away becaufe the Spectator knew not him that fpoke them, nor how to apply them. The Antients never fail'd in this, to which the *Chorufes* were a great help to them ; for they never leaving the Stage, generally as foon as a new Actor came on, they nam'd him with fome expreffions of fear, aftonifhment or joy, according as the Subject requir'd ; but if he were a ftranger, and unknown to the *Chorus*, then he nam'd himfelf, giving fome account of his good or bad Fortune, or fome confident of his, declar'd it without affectation, either by pitying him, or feeming to be concern'd for the doubtful fuccefs of his Enterprize.

As for us who have no *Chorufes*, we muft, inftead of them, make fome of thofe Actors fpeak who are already upon the Stage, and known ; and if we open an Act with Perfons unknown, they muft themfelves declare their condition, or fome of their Followers
muft .

muſt by the by, and without affectation inſinuate it: But if it be neceſſary that an Actor ſhould be *incognito* both as to his Name and Quality, in order to his being known with more pleaſure towards the end of the Play, then the Spectators muſt at leaſt know that he is *incognito*; and in a word all confuſion muſt be avoided, and it will be well if the Spectators conceive ſomething in general concerning the Inteterefts of this new Actor; not indeed ſo far as to difcover or prevent an Incident, but ſo much as is neceſſary to facilitate their eaſier comprehending all that is to be ſaid afterwards.

The Third Obſervation is, That the Actors do always come on, and go off of the Scene with ſome probable reaſon, which makes it more proper for them to do ſo than otherwiſe, and yet that muſt not be done groſly, but by nice and natural pretexts. For any Art that difcovers it ſelf too much, loſes its grace; and yet it is not neceſſary that the reaſon which makes the Actors go on and off ſhould always take effect; quite contrary, the leſs things ſucceed according to their firſt appearance, the more pleaſing and ſurpriſing they are. 'Tis one of the beauties of the Stage, that things croſs one another, and ſo produce unforeſeen Events; and when an Actor is upon the Stage, his good or bad Fortune is in the Poets hands, though the reaſon that brought him on be not at all conformable to what he meets with there.

As for the Practice of this Rule, I muſt defire our Poets to have recourſe to the Antients, and to obferve with what Art they govern themſelves; for the Reading of one Poem of theirs, particularly of *Sophocles*, will give them more light in this matter,

than

than all the Allegations with which I might fwell this Treatife.

The Fourth Obfervation is about a Difpute which I have often been witnefs to, which is, Whether or no in the fame Act the fame Actor may appear more than once? Firft, To anfwer this Queftion right, it is neceffary to diftinguifh the Plays; for in a Comedy, the Subject whereof is taken from the meaner fort of People, it would not be amifs that the Perfons concern'd fhould appear more than once in an Act, becaufe they are People whofe bufinefs is not weighty, their actions quick, and the manner of their life unquiet, and their Intrigues, moft of them happening in the Neighbourhood, fo that they need but a little time to go and come; but in a Tragedy, where they are moft commonly Kings and Princes, where their manner of living is very different, their actions all full of gravity and weight, it does not appear eafie nor reafonable to make them appear more than once in an Act; for their Intrigues are generally with Perfons remote, their Defigns great, and which are not to be brought to pafs but by flow means, and with great circumfpection, fo that more time is regularly requir'd to move all the Springs of their Affairs.

Secondly, In both thefe forts of Poems, one muft confider the condition of the Perfon; for in a Slave or Servant it would be nothing to fee him often in an Act, but it would be fomething ftrange in a Man or Woman of Quality, if fome very extraordinary reafon did not oblige them to precipitate their Actions.

Thirdly, We are to confider how far an Actor went, and if the thing he went about requir'd much time; or if he had fome reafon to return fo foon;

for the place he went to being near, and having but a ſhort buſineſs, and being obliged to return immediately, all theſe are circumſtances which may bring an Actor upon the Stage twice in an Act, without offending againſt the Rules. *Plautus* does it very ingeniouſly in many of his Comedys, but I know no Example of it in any Tragedys of the Antients. *Monſieur Corneille* indeed in his *Horatius* brings his *Hero* twice on in the ſame Act, becauſe he went but from the Hall of his Pallace to his Fathers Chamber, to take his leave of him before he engaged in the Combate between the Six Brothers. But for my part, I ſhould counſel the Poet to do it as little as poſſible, and with great circumſpection; for, methinks, it is a little undecent to ſee a Perſon of Quality go and come ſo ſuddenly, and Act with ſo much appearance of precipitation.

The Fifth Obſervation is about a thing which the Antients never fail'd in, and the Modern Writers often have, which is, to bring their Principal Actors on, upon the opening of the Stage, and indeed with a great deal of reaſon, becauſe their Perſons being conſidered as the Principal Subject of all the Adventures of the Play, and as the Center to which all the other Lines are to be drawn, the Spectators deſire to ſee them at firſt, and all that is ſaid or done before their Arrival gives them more impatience than pleaſure, and is often reckoned for nothing: And beſides, they often take the firſt Actor of Quality for the *Hero* of the Play, and when they are undeceiv'd, find themſelves in confuſion and perplexed; therefore thoſe Authors who bring not on their Chief Actor till the Third or Fourth Act, are much to blame, for that cauſes in the Audience ſo

much

much impatience and uncertainty, that it is afterwards very hard to fatisfie them; not but that in
fome occafions one may luckily defer the bringing
on a chief Actor for a while, but then that muft give
fome extraordinary grace to the Play, and be order'd fo, as not to confound the Spectators Application.

The Sixth Obfervation is, That the chief Actors
ought to appear as often, and ftay as long as poffible upon the Stage; Firft, becaufe they are always
the beft Actors, and fo fatisfie moft; then they are
the beft cloth'd, and fo pleafe the Spectators, who
are taken with their Drefs: And laftly, becaufe they
have the fineft things to fay, and the nobleft paffions
to fhew; in which, to fay truth, confifts the greateft
charm of the Stage; and befides, the whole Event
being to turn upon them, the Spectator rejoyces
and grieves with them, fears and hopes as they do,
and always has fome inward concern according to
the prefent ftate of their Affairs. This makes me
not approve of *Seneca*, who in a Play where *Aga-*
memnon is the chief *Hero*, and is kill'd, makes him
fay not above two and twenty Verfes in all. The
beft Advice I can give the Poet in this matter, is not
to have any thing told by way of Narrative, which
may be any ways decently perform'd by the chief
Actors themfelves; but if the Subject cannot fuffer
that the chief Actors fhould appear every Act, he
muft endeavour that that Act where they do not
appear, be fill'd with fome great circumftance of the
Story, and that the fecond Parts may repair the
want of the firft by fome noble and majeftick Adventure, elfe it is certain the Play will pall and lan-
guifh.

The

The Seventh and laſt Obſervation of this Chapter is particular enough, and it may be at firſt will not be rellifhed by all our Poets; but I deſire them to examine it in the practice, before they judg of it here upon the Paper. To explain my ſelf rightly, we muſt obſerve, that where an Actor appears firſt upon the Stage, he may come on in one of theſe Three Diſpoſitions, either in a moderate, calm temper, or in a violent paſſion, or in a diſpoſition ſomething moved, but not rais'd to the high pitch of Tranſport; and that may be call'd a half-paſſion. Now in the firſt caſe an Actor may eaſily acquit himſelf, for it comes ſo near our natural temper, that few fail to perſonate it well. In the ſecond caſe likewiſe of violent Tranſport, good Actors ſeldom fail to repreſent it well, becauſe Experience has taught them how far their Voice and Action is to be ſtrain'd in ſuch a caſe; but as it is much eaſier to go from one Extremity to another, than to ſtop with diſcretion in the middle; ſo the Actors, though they can eaſily repreſent theſe two Sentiments directy oppoſite, they do not always ſucceed when they are to come upon the Stage with the Sentiment of a *half-paſſion,* which paſſes a little our natural Tranquillity, and yet riſes not to the extremeſt violence; and the reaſon is, that not being ſtirr'd of themſelves, and yet not daring to riſe to the higheſt pitch of violence, 'tis hard for them to find that juſt temper to enter into this half paſſion; from hence it comes, that they often provoke the laughter of the Audience, by delivering with an ill grace, and unconcernedly, that which requires ſome Emotion, or appearing over-allarm'd at that which does not in its nature ſo highly affect the Spectators. Therefore my Obſervation

tion to the Poet is, that he firſt put ſome more moderate words in his Actors mouth, before he raiſes
him to that half-paſſion, that he may grow warm
by little and little, and that his Voice may riſe by
degrees, and all his geſtures acquire more and more
motion with his Diſcourſe; and as for the Actor, I
will tell him what in this caſe I have ſeen *Mondory*, the
beſt Actor of our days do, which was, that in theſe
occaſions having taken a turn or two upon the Stage,
and with ſome poſture ſuitable to his Part, as lifting
up his Hands and Eyes, or the like; having begun
to move himſelf, he brought himſelf to the true
point of a half-paſſion, and ſo came ſenſibly out of
the natural ſtate of Indifferency in which he came
on upon the Stage; withal, retaining his motions ſo
as they ſhould not go too far.   All this will be better underſtood by both Poets and Actors, if they
pleaſe to make ſome Reflections at Reheaſals,
and have the Comedians own Opinions who are beſt
Judges, having often experienced this, and other
Methods of performing a half-paſſion.

Chapter the Second.

Of Diſcourſes in general.

IF we conſider Tragedy in its own nature, it im-
plies ſo much Action, that it ſeems not to have
any room left for Diſcourſe : 'Tis called a *Dramma*,
which ſignifies an Action, and the Perſons concern'd
are called Actors, as thoſe that are preſent are nam'd
Spectators, or Lookers on, not Hearers.   And indeed

all the Difcourfes of Tragedy ought to be as the Actions of thofe that appear upon the Stage; for there to fpeak, is to act, there being not there any Speeches invented by the Poet to fhew his Eloquence. So we fee that the Narration of the Death of *Hyppolitus* in *Seneca*, is rather the action of a Man frightned at the Monfter that he faw come out of the Sea, and at the fad Adventure which befel *Hyppolitus*. In a word, all Difcourfes upon the Stage are but the Acceffaries of Action, though the whole Play in its Reprefentation confifts in Difcourfes. 'Tis they that are the chief work of the Poet, and in which he Employs all the ftrength of his wit; all that he invents, is in order to have it well deliver'd upon the Stage, and he fuppofes many actions that they may ferve for Subject of thofe Difcourfes. Thus he feeks all ways to make love, joy, hatred, grief, and the reft of our paffions fpeak upon the Stage; and yet if we examine rightly this Poem, the beft part of the actions are but in the imagination of the Spectator, to whom the Poet by his Art makes them as it were vifible, though there be nothing fenfible but the Difcourfes. And we may obferve in two of the Greek Poets, that though *Euripides*'s Tragedys are fill'd with more Incidents and Actions than thofe of *Sophocles*, yet they had not fo good fuccefs upon the Stage of *Athens*; neither are they now fo pleafant to read; the reafon whereof is, that the Difcourfes of *Sophocles* are more Eloquent, and more Judicious than thofe of *Euripides*. Nay, thofe *Dramma's* which carry the name of *Seneca*, howfoever irregular and defective they are in other things, do neverthelefs pafs very well, by reafon of the fenfe and force of fome Difcourfes that are in them.

them. And we have ftill a greater proof of this in the Works of our *Corneille*; for that which has fo clearly fet him above all the Poets of his time has not been the Plot, or Regularity of his Plays, but the Difcourfes, and the noble ways of Expreffing thofe violent paffions which he introduces, even fo far, that we fee very irregular actions in them fo accompanied with ingenious and pathetick Expreffions, that the fault could not be perceiv'd but by the Learned Obfervers, the beauty of the Thoughts and Language dazling the underftanding of all the reft of the Audience, and taking away from them the liberty of judging of any thing elfe. For Example, it was not very probable that *Rodrigues*, all bloody with the Murder of his Miftrefs's Father, fhould go and make her a Vifit, nor that fhe fhould receive it, and yet their converfation is fo pleafing and full of fuch noble Sentiments, that few have obferv'd that Indecency, and they that did were willing to fuffer it. Again, when *Don Sanche* brings his Sword to *Chimene*, he ought not to let her run on in thofe miftaken Complaints, fince with one word he could undeceive her; but that which fhe fays is fo agreeable, that the Spectator cannot wifh *Don Sanche* had been more prudent.

All the Learned men in the Drammatick Art tell us, that thofe Plays which they call *Polymythes*, that is, loaded with many Incidents, either are bad, or at leaft none of the beft; but they have not given the reafon, which in my judgment is, becaufe they are all taken up in action, and fo leaving no room for Difcourfes, the Subject is as it were ftifl'd for want of Air; and on the contrary, a Play which has but few Incidents, and a fmall Intrigue, but fill'd with

Excellent

Excellent Language, and thought, can seldom fail of pleasing.

We must nevertheless observe some difference in this Point between *Comedy* and *Tragedy* ; for *Comedy*, whose business lies among the common sort of People, not so capable of gravity and thought, as the Tragick Actors, is much more in action than in Discourses ; there is required there little Eloquence, and much Intrigue. *Terence* is pleasanter to read than *Plautus*, because he is more Elegant, but *Plautus* took better with the *Romans*, because he is fuller of action. *Terence* has many serious Moral sayings, which is not the proper work of *Comedy*, where the Spectators design is to laugh. *Plautus* is full of Intrigues, from which many Jests, and ingenious Raileries are created, and that's the thing we wish for in Comedy.

I could wish therefore that our Poets would excel in the Art of Rhetorick, and study Oratory and Eloquence to the bottom ; for we are not to imagine, that it consists in some puns and quibbles, to make the Citizens and Country Gentlemen laugh, nor in some *Antitheses*, or other Figures often ill employ'd; no, the Poet ought to know all the passions, the springs, that bring them on, and the way of expressing them with Order, Energy, and Judgment.

He may see many Examples of this amongst the Antient Poets, who best can shew him the way of pleasing, and acquiring Reputation. I, for my part, pretend to nothing here, but to give him my particular Observations, which at least may serve him to make better of his own. But to do this with order, I consider there are generally in a Play Four sorts of Discourses, *Narrations, Deliberations, Didactick*
Discourses

Difcourfes or *Inftru&ions,* and *Pathetick Difcourfes,* or the motions of paffions. This is the Method which I eftablifh to explain my felf, to which any body may add what they think neceffary, and take away all that they fhall judg fuperfluous ; and in a word, change all that fhall not pleafe them, and have my free confent to do it.

Chapter the Third.

Of Narrations.

THefe Narrations which happen in a Drammatick Poem, do generally regard two forts of things ; either thofe which have happened before the opening of the Stage, wherefoever they came to pafs ; nay, though it be long before ; or elfe they regard thofe things which happen off of the Scene in the Contexture of the Theatral action, after once the Stage is open, and within the Extent of time that it requires. As to the firft fort which are brought into the body of the Poem, for the better under-ftanding of things which happened before the open-ing of the Stage, they may regularly be us'd in the beginning of the Play, that they may give a Foun-dation to the whole Action, and prepare the Inci-dents, and by that means facilitate to the Spectator the underftanding of all the reft ; or elfe they may be made ufe of toward the end of the Poem, and ferve to the *Cataftrophe,* or the untying and opening of all the Plot.

Not but that they may be made in other parts of
the

the Play, as we fee it done in a Play call'd *Virginia*, where the chiefeft Narration is in the Fourth Act, and is perform'd with great grace, and equal fuccefs; but in that part of the Play 'tis very dangerous to ufe them; for they run a hazard of either difcovering the *Cataftrophe*, which is near at hand, or elfe they leave the Stage in fome obfcurity, and the Specta- tors ill inform'd of many circumftances, for having too long delay'd the opening of them; fo that to avoid both thefe Inconveniences, the Poet muft have a very fteddy hand, fince he muft order it fo as his Narration do not in the leaft prevent the beauty of the *Cataftrophe*; nor his firft acts be lefs intelligible for having kept back his Narration.

As for thofe things which happen in the courfe of the Action, the recital of them is to be made as they happen; or if it be thought neceffary, or more pleafing to delay them, there muft be us'd fome Art to feed the Spectators defire of knowing them with- out impatience; or elfe you muft quite ftifle his Ex- pectation, that he may be the better furpriz'd when they come to pafs. But we muft remember befides, that thefe Recitals or Narrations are introduced only to inftruct the Spectator about what paffes off of the Scene; for to relate either thofe things that have been feen, or might have been feen, as being fuppos'd to have been done upon the Stage, would certainly be very ridiculous; and befides, thofe things that give ground to thefe Incident Narrations, ought to be very confiderable, or elfe they are to be avoid- ed, and the thing to be infinuated into the Audience by fome words fcattered here and there either before or after.

Now all thefe Narrations do enter into the Compofition

pofition of the Drammatick Poem, for two ends,
either to make it clear and intelligible, or to adorn
and fet it out; but againft both thefe ends the Poet
often falls into Errours, which deftroy his firft Intention.

The firft is, when his Narration is obfcure, and
loaded with circumftances hard for the Audience
to retain diftinctly; fuch are *Genealogical* ones (which
Scaliger blames in *Homer*; or a great number of
Names, with a Chain of actions embroyl'd one in
in another; for the Spectator will not give himfelf
the trouble to obferve and retain all thefe different
Idæa's, he coming to the Stage only for his pleafure,
and in the mean time for want of remembring all
this, he remains in the dark as to the reft of the Play,
and is difgufted for all the time he ftays.   Such a
Story might be that of the three Brothers, and three
Sifters, which is defcrib'd in *Aftræa*, and that of the
two Children born of two Women, who had each
of them married one anothers Sons; if any body
fhould upon fuch Stories found the whole Intrigue of
a Play, he might be fure no body would underftand
it, and by confequent it would have few Spectators.

The Second fault of Narrations is when they are
tædious, and they are always tædious when they do
not contain things neceffary or agreeable; as alfo
when they are made with weak and faint Expreffions,
fuch as do not captivate the Spectators favour or attention, which by confequent muft pall, and make
him give over minding the Play; and this happens
likewife when they are too long; for variety being
the life of the Stage, and that being wanting, the
beft things grow dull, and weigh upon the Spectator, who takes it ill to be fix'd to one Subject with-

[C]   out

out diverſity for ſo long a time ; and though it may be the capacity of ſome would carry them thorow to comprehend it all, yet being come for diverſion, they will not take the pains to do it, which joyn'd with the incapacity of others to hearken to ſo long a Story, cauſes at laſt a general diſguſt in the whole Audience.

We may moreover make this diſtinction upon the length of Narrations, for they may be ſo either for the matter, when they are fill'd with too great a number of Incidents, and Perſons, of Names and Places ; or they may be ſo out of the form for the many words they contain, as when the circumſtances of an Action are too much exaggerated and particulariz'd in minute and inſignificant things; and when the Expreſſions are too full of *Epithets*, Adverbs, or other unneceſſary terms, with Repetitions of the ſame thing, though in a different way.

And indeed, to examine the difference of theſe two ſorts of lengths in Narrations, we may ſay, that the firſt is vicious in any place of the Play whereſoever it is plac'd : For firſt, at the opening of the Stage, the Spectator, who thinks all that Recital neceſſary for the underſtanding of the Play, endeavours to retain it all in his memory ; but finding his Imagination confounded, and his Memory diſtracted with ſo many things, he is firſt vex'd with himſelf, and then with the Poet, and at laſt gives out, without minding any more of the whole Poem.

Theſe long Narrations are not better plac'd in the courſe of the Action, for thoſe things which come to paſs after the opening of the Stage, becauſe it will never be thought probable that ſo many things ſhould have come to paſs in ſo little a time; (as for
Example,

Example, the Interval of an Act seems to be) not but that it is ordinary to suppose in that time a Battle, a Conspiracy, or some such other Event ; but to do it with probability, the Poet deceives the Spectator, and busies him with something else that is agreeable, that so he may be insensibly persuaded that there has been time enough for all the rest ; but that which is particularly to be heeded in that place is, that at that time the Stage is in all the hurry of Action, and in the turns of Incidents, which these long Narrations do cool and pall, whereas a true Narration ought to quicken the Stage, and lay the foundation of some new passion, which to obtain, it must be short, pithy, and full of life and warmth. The contrary of this appears in that Narration, which the Rich in Imagination makes in the Play call'd the *Visionaires*.

When these long Narrations happen towards the *Catastrophe*, they are then absolutely insupportable ; for the Spectator, who is impatient to see which way the Intrigue turns, has all his pleasure spoil'd just in the time when he ought to receive the most, which is so much the more dangerous for the success of the Play, because the Audience is already tir'd and dispos'd to give out.

In a word, I think it may be a kind of General Rule, that Narrations may be longer at the opening of the Stage than any where else, because the Spectator is fresh, and willing to give attention, and his memory receives agreeably all those new *Idæa's*, in hopes they are to contribute to the pleasure which is prepar'd for him ; and also that they are as much to be avoided at the *Catastrophe*, where they do so chock the Audience, who is then impatient to know

[C 2]   the

the Event, that no Figures of Rhetorick can make him amends. See, amongſt others, how dexterous *Plautus* is in the Narration of the knowing of *Ia-neſia*, at the end of the *Curculio* ; 'tis one of the moſt regular Narrations that he has.

Beſides theſe Cautions, it will not be amiſs to obſerve, that theſe Narrations may be made in two manners; either all of a piece, where a Story is told that is to give a foundation to all the Plot of the Play ; (though they that among the Poets do it beſt, have ſome Pathetick or other ingenious Interruptions) as the *Oreſtes* of *Euripides*, and in the Comical kind, the *Hecyra* of *Terence*, and the *Pſeudolus* of *Plautus* in the firſt Acts do ſufficiently illuſtrate : Or elſe, theſe Narrations are made by piece-meals, according as the Poet thinks fit to hide or diſcover any part of his Subject, to frame the different Acts with more Ornament, as one may ſee in the *Sphigenia* of *Euripides*, and in the *Oedypus Tyrannus* of *Sophocles*, where the Story is told by different Perſons, and at different times; which may be perform'd, when he that makes part of a Narration knows not all the Story, or when for ſome other neceſſary reaſon which muſt appear ſo to the Audience, he will not tell all he knows; or when he is interrupted by ſome body elſe (which muſt be done with great Art, and not by bringing on a purpoſe a man who has nothing elſe to do in the reſt of the Play, but to interrupt that Actor;) Or laſtly, when thoſe things that are neceſſary to be known, are not yet come to paſs, as *Corneille* has moſt ingeniouſly practiſed in his *Horatius* ; for by opening his Stage after the Truce concluded, he has found a way to bring *Curiatius* to *Rome*, and there has reſerv'd to

himſelf

himfelf to make different Narrations of the Combate of the three Brothers in fuch places of his Play
as he thinks the fitteft to change the ftate of Affairs
upon his Stage.

I may affure our Poets, that a Narration thus ingenioufly divided, requires great Art and Medita-
tation to confider how far one may carry each part
of it, and to give all the neceffary grounds and colours to the Audience, for leaving off in fuch a place,
and beginning again in fuch another; and indeed
fuch a Narration well managed, produces an admirable Effect; for leaving the Spectator always in the
expectation of fome Novelty, it warms his defire,
and entertains his impatience; and then the new
difcoveries that are made in the reft of the Narration furnifh the Stage with Subjects to vary all the
Motions and Paffions of the Actors.

Narrations may befides be confidered as fimply
and plainly telling the Tale, or as exaggerating pa-
thetically the circumftances of the Adventure.   In
the firft cafe they ought to be fhort, becaufe they are
without motion or ornament, and yet they are often neceffary, as when fome important Advice is to
be given to obviate fome preffing mifchief.

Pathetick Narrations are always the fineft, and the
only indeed fit to come upon the Stage, when they
are contain'd within the bounds of a reafonable Ex-
aggeration; then the mixture of fear, aftonifhment,
imprecations, and the like, according to the circumftances of the Story is fit, and produces a good Effect.   But particularly, thefe paffions ought to be
mingled in the Narration, when the perfon to whom
it is made is not at all ignorant of the whole Story,
and yet there is a neceffity of informing the Audience

by

by him; and I believe that I firſt found out this ſleight, to avoid abſurdity in doing of it; for in this caſe it would be ridiculous to make to him a plain Story which he knows already; therefore to avoid that one muſt bring in natural paſſions growing from the Story it ſelf, and the preſent ſtate of the Affairs of the Stage, either by Complaints, or Sentiments of joy, or fear; for by this means the Story is told, and yet no affected cold Narration brought on againſt all the Rules of probability. Such is the Narration of the Death of *Clitemneſtra* in the *Electra* of *Euripides*, and ſuch is the diſcourſe of *Tecmeſſa* in *Sophocles* in his *Ajax*, where the Poet makes her make an ingenious Narration of all that the Spectators were ignorant of under pretext of complaining of her own misfortunes, and the Narration of *Soſias*. In *Amphytrio* is one of the moſt ingenious ones, where the Poet, that he may inſtruct the Audience about *Amphytrio*'s Voyage, and the War, makes that Slave meditate to himſelf what News he ſhall tell his Miſtreſs, for by that means, though the Narration be made to himſelf, and very pleaſant things in it, fit for a Slaves wit to ſay, yet at the ſame time the Spectator is informed of every thing, without any apparent affectation. But in theſe Narrations the Poet muſt be very careful to keep up the humour, ſo as nothing of a ſtudied Recital do appear, for then 'tis faulty, as done on purpoſe for the Spectators. Therefore I can never adviſe him to uſe a certain way, common enough now adays, which is when an Actor knows ſome part of the Story, though the Spectators are not informed of any part of it; in this caſe I ſay Poets do often make another Repeat that which the Actor knows already, ſaying only, *You know ſuch a thing,*
and

☞ p. 393. middle.

and then adding, *Now here is the reſt which you do not know.* To ſay truth, this appears to me ver grofs, and it were better to let that which the Acto knows already, be expreſſed to the Audience by ſome motions of paſſion, and then find ſome ingenious pretext to tell the reſt in an ordinary Narration.

That which remains now to be done upon this Subject, is to explain ſome Rules, from which, without abſurdity the Poet cannot depart.

The firſt is, that he who makes the Narration be rationally ſuppos'd to know perfectly the thing he tells, or elſe he cannot be thought to tell it with any probability.

Secondly, That on his ſide, there be ſome apparent and powerful reaſon for him to tell it, either by the neceſſity of giving notice to ſome other perſon, or by ſome well-grounded curioſity, or by the Authority he has over the perſon that ſpeaks with him, or ſome ſuch conſiderations.

Thirdly, He that hears him muſt have ſome juſt Subject to be inform'd of the thing that is told him, and I for my part cannot bear that a *Varlet* ſhould out of ſimple curioſity be entertain'd with the Adventures of a great Prince, as the Poet has done in *Rhodogune*; for Narrations are always flat that are not made to a perſon concern'd for want of paſſions to animate both the Audience, and the Man that makes the Recital.

Beſides, a Narration ought to be made in a fit place, where probably both he that hears, and he that ſpeaks, might be ſuppos'd to meet; wherefore I cannot approve that in the Hall of a Pallace, where probably People go and come continually, there ſhould be a long Narration made of ſecret Adventures,

tures which ought not to be difcover'd without great
precaution for the danger that attends their being re-
vealed ; and therefore I never could conceive how
Mr. *Corneille* can bring to pafs with decency that.
In the fame place *Cinna* tells *Æmilia* all the circumftances of a great Confpiracy againft *Auguftus*, and
yet in that very place *Auguftus* holds a fecret counfel
of his two intimate Favourites ; for if it be a publick
place, as it feems to be, fince *Auguftus* fends away all
his Courtiers and Attendance to talk alone with his
friends, what probability is there that *Cinna* fhould
there vifit *Æmilia*, with a Difcourfe of about 130
Verfes, and a difcovery of the moft dangerous Affairs in the World, which might be over-heard by
fome body going or coming ; and if the place be pri-
vate, and fuppos'd the Emperor's Clofet, who dif-
miffes thofe he would not have participant of his
fecret, how is it poffible that *Cinna* fhould come
there to talk all that to *Æmilia*? And how is it probable that *Æmilia* fhould break out into outragious
Complaints and Invectives againft *Auguftus* ? This
is my Objection, to which *Monfieur Corneille* may
be pleas'd to give an Anfwer when he thinks fit.

    'Tis not lefs neceffary to chufe a fit time to make
a Narration probable ; for there are fome times

☞ p. 398. which will not bear a long Difcourfe : 'Tis a fault
which *Scaliger* does not fcruple to charge *Homer*
himfelf with, when he makes his *Hero's* make long
Narrations in the middle of a Battel or Engagement.
A Poet of ours has committed the fame fault in the
Scipio, while in the midft of the ftorming of a
Town, a victorious Army is abandoned to all Licence,
and the People in the diforder of a place taken by
affault. A young Maid difguis'd, makes a long
Narration

Narration to difcover her felf, whereas in fuch a time fhe ought not at moft to have fpoke above four Verfes.

But I do not take heed that infenfibly I am difcovering the faults of our Modern Writers, who, it may be, will not allow them to be fo, or at leaft will not be pleas'd with the difcovery; let the Poet then feek out of himfelf Examples of ill Narrations, and not expect from me that I fhould difcredit the beft part of our Plays, many of which have been fo favourably receiv'd either by the too much complaifance, or the ignorance of thofe who did not underftand their faults.

Chapter the Fourth.

Of Deliberations.

MY defign is not here to teach that part of Rhetorick which they call the *genus deliberativum,* by which is fhew'd the Art of faying ones Opinion floridly in all matters, in which counfel is askt. Our Poet ought not to ftay till he be upon the Stage to be inftructed in thofe Principles which are all comprehended under the name of the *Theory of the Stage.*

Drammatick Poetry is a kind of Quinteffence of all the Precepts of Eloquence that are found in Authors, becaufe they muft be us'd in it, but with fo much Judgment and Art, and fo nicely, that it muft often feem that one has quite laid them afide, the genius of the Stage being fuch, that a thing that does

[D]   not

not appear, contains in it very often the greatest Artifice, and a Sentiment that shall imperceptibly have been conveyed into the mind of the Audience, an imperfect Narration, an Adventure, begun in appearance without design, are capable alone of making a Play take, by giving a foundation secretly to the strongest passions, and by that means preparing a noble *Catastrophe* ; and without doubt there is much skill requir'd for any body to perform this, without which one cannot pretend to true glory in the Art.

I begin therefore with this Advertisement, which I think very considerable in matter of Deliberations, which is, that they in their own nature are not fit for the Stage, because the *Theatre* being a place of Action, all things ought to be in agitation, either by Events which cross one another, or by Passions born out of those Incidents, as Lightning and Thunder from the Clouds. In a word, 'tis a place where every body is disquieted and in disorder ; and as soon as ever the calm and quiet succeed, the Play is at an end, or grows very dull all the while that the Action is suspended; how is it possible then that Deliberations should have any part in the business? They are sedate and quiet things where Moderation and Temper ought chiefly to appear. He that asks counsel does it with tranquillity, at least in appearance, and they that are called to counsel ought less to be troubled either with Passion or Interest, they must speak with all the clearness of Reason, and argue upon the discovery, and not in the Clouds, and darkness of Passion ; and if they grow but warm, they are presently suspected of some secret Interest ; so that without very great Art, it will be hard to reconcile them to the Scene, without making the Stage lose its grace, and grow dull.   It

It may be anfwered, that the Stage abounds in Deliberations, and that the Antients have them in moft Acts of their Plays ; and for the Moderns, *Monfieur Corneille* excels in them, and has fcarce any thing in his Poems fo moving, and fo much admir'd, witnefs his *Stanzas* in the mouth of *Rodrigues* in the *Cid*. *Æmilia* in *Cinna* deliberates pleafingly between the danger fhe expofes *Cinna* to, and the revenge fhe covets. *Cinna* deliberates between the Obligations he has to *Auguftus*, and the love he bears his Miftrefs ; and *Auguftus* deliberates what to do in this laft Conjuration, in which his Favourite was the chief man to murder him.

To all this I anfwer, That thefe are not the true fort of Deliberations which I am treating of, though they do fhew Irrefolution, and a difpute between oppofite Confiderations ; they are rather to be plac'd in the rank of Pathetick Difcourfes, which make the beft Actions of the Stage. You fee minds agitated by different Paffions, and ftill carryed into extremes, of which the Spectator cannot forefee the Event; all their Difcourfes have the true Theatral Character, they are impetuous and figurative, and fhew you rather the Image of a Soul tormented in the midft of his Executioners, than one confulting in the midft of his Friends.

'Tis not therefore this fort of Deliberations that I exclude ; on the contrary, I exhort all our Poets to bring them upon the Stage, as much as the Subject will afford, and to examine carefully with what variety and Art they are managed by the Antients, and in the Works of *Monfieur Corneille*, for if he be well confider'd, 'twill be found that 'tis in that principally that confifts that which in him is called *Admirable*,

rable, and the thing which has made him so famous.

I only speak then of those Deliberations which are made designedly, and are Representations of the like Consults made in Courts upon some important Affair. We have two Examples remarkable in *Corneille,* that in the Play called *Cinna,* where *Augustus* deliberates whether he shall leave the Empire or no; and the other in a Play called *The Death of* Pompey, where King *Ptolomeus* deliberates what he shall do with so great a Man, newly arrived in his Country; and these two Deliberations have succeeded likewise very differently, for that of *Augustus* pleas'd the Audience to a wonder, and the other of *Ptolomæus* passes for a very common, ordinary Discourse; and that very difference of the success of these two Deliberations, confirms me in my Opinion, that they are dangerous upon the Stage, and have afforded me likewise the occasion of making some Reflections which may contribute to make them please.

The first is, That the Subject of the Deliberation ought to be great, noble, and extraordinary, and not of such things as fall every day in debate in Princes Councils, and 'tis in this for one, that the Deliberation of *Augustus* carries it from that of *Ptolomæus,* for it is not ordinary that a Monarch should have the thought of laying down the Soveraignty, and bring so important a Point to be debated by two Friends. There was but one Example of such a thing before *Augustus's* time, and we have had but three since, of which the Queen of *Sweden* makes still an Illustrious Remembrance. But it was not a thing so rare to see *Ptolomæus* deliberate about the Life and Liberty of *Pompey;* 'twas an important Affair, but no extraor-

dinary

becaufe then there has not been any paffion agitated which might produce fuch a Deliberation; but I would place them in the beginning of the fecond or third Act, that they may have fome foundation upon what is already done, and fome influence upon what remains to do.

They ought likewife not to be made all of a breath, without interruption from fome of the Counfellors, for that gives at leaft a little warmth to the coolnefs of the Stage. But above all, I think they ought to be as fhort as poffible, for they cannot be long without being tedious in prolix reafonings void of figures, which neverthelefs I would have the Poet ftrive to bring in as *Apoftrophes, Profopopœas, Hypotypofes,* and fuch like ; in which much Art muft be ufed, becaufe regularly thefe figures do not enter into **Deli**berations.

But that which above all things I think neceffary is, that the Perfons advis'd with, be concern'd in the thing propos'd, becaufe then 'tis not a plain Advice, but it has fomething of the Theatral Action ; then the Spectator too is much more concern'd, as appears very well in the cafe of *Auguftus,* who being made to advife about the moft important thing of his Life, with two treacherous Friends, and the Audience being already inform'd of the hatred of *Æmilia,* and the love of *Cinna,* they are all attentive to what they fay, every Spectator having a curiofity to know how they will come off, fo that all that they fay is hearkened to, and not a word of it loft ; and when after all the Emperour is yet kind to both thefe Traitors, the Spectators begin to think they will relent of their Treafon, and particularly when they fee *Maximus* and *Cinna* afterwards a little in fufpenfe,

and

and then when at laſt they ſee them perſevere in their deſign, they cannot imagine how the thing will turn, nor what will be the Event; ſo that this Deliberation is upheld by the Intereſt of thoſe who adviſe, and does it ſelf influence all the other Affairs of the Stage.

I have nothing more upon this Subjeƈt, but one general Obſervation, which is, That few People that go to Plays do approve of the Examining and Condemning of Criminals upon the Stage, which neverthelefs we ſee frequently repreſented there, and the reaſon is, becauſe that when it comes to that formality, 'tis generally perform'd by the worſt Aƈtors, who being ſeated and out of aƈtion, and having a few ſcurvy Verſes (which in ſuch an occaſion can hardly be made better) to recite.   The Audience can hardly forbear laughing, ſo far are they from being concern'd.   I know no remedy for this but to endeavour to order the Story ſo, as it ſhall not require ſuch a dull piece of Pageantry, ſo little capable of deſerving any applauſe from the Audience.

Chapter the Fifth.

Of Didaƈtick Diſcourſes or Inſtruƈtions.

THis is a new Subjeƈt in our Drammatick Art, I not having found any thing in thoſe Authors who have compos'd great Volumes about it ; and I am the firſt that have made obſervations upon it, ſuch as I may boldly ſay ought not to be deſpiſed by our Poets.

I under·

I underſtand then by Didactick Diſcourſes thoſe Maxims and general Propoſitions which contain known Truths, and are only apply'd in the Play, according as the Subject will allow, tending more to inſtruct the Audience in the Rules of Morality, than to explain any part of the Intrigue a foot.   An Example may illuſtrate the thing better. Suppoſe then the Poet had a mind to treat this Propoſition.

*The Gods are juſt, and were they not ſo, they would
    ceaſe to be Gods.*
                    Or this ;
A general Inſtinct cannot be ſuſpected of Errour.
                    Or this ;
A Subject that Rebels againſt his Prince is Criminal.

I ſay, That a Poet often endeavours to ſet out ſome of theſe Maxims by a great number of Verſes, upon which he demurs a great while, leaving all that time his Subject, and the Intrigue of the Stage, and keeping himſelf ſtill upon general Notions.

Now as to theſe Didactick Diſcourſes, I diſtinguiſh them into two ſorts, ſome I call Phyſical, and the others Moral ones.

I call thoſe Phyſical or Natural, which make a deduction or deſcription of the Nature, Qualities, or Effects of any thing without diſtinction, whether it be in the rank of natural or ſupernatural things ; or of the number of Artificial Compounds.

Under the notion of Moral Diſcourſes, I comprehend all thoſe Inſtructions which contain any Maxim of Religion, or Politicks, or Oeconomicks, or that any ways regard humane Life

To come after this to my Obſervations, we muſt
                                            lay

lay it down as a Maxim, That all thefe Didactick Difcourfes are of their own nature unfit for the Stage, becaufe they are cold, and without motion, being general things which only tend to Inftruct the mind, but not to move the heart, fo that the action of the Stage, which ought to warm our affections, becomes by them dull and indifferent. Young People who come to read *Euripides* and *Sophocles*, admire the firft much more than the latter, and yet *Sophocles* almoft always carry'd the prize from *Euripides* upon the Stage, and that by the Judgment of all the *Athenians*. This miftake of the young Reader proceeds from this, that they being themfelves not throughly inftructed in thofe Maxims, and finding a great many of them in *Euripides*, as well about Religion, as Politicks and Moral ones, they are charm'd to fee fuch Truths fo nobly expreffed, and the things themfelves being new to them, pleafe them beyond meafure. 'Tis for this that *Quintilian* in his Precepts of Rhetorick advifes young People to the Lecture of *Euripides* before *Sophocles*. In all which they do not obferve that *Sophocles* makes the groundwork of his Plays, of thofe very Truths, as well as *Euripides*; but he does it with fo much Art, that he utters them in a Pathetick manner, as well as in a Didactick one, whereby the People of *Athens* departed almoft always pleafed and charm'd by the high paffions which *Sophocles* fills his Stage with, but were more us'd to *Euripides*'s Maxims, which he fo often beats over to them, and by that means did not confider them as any thing rare and extraordinary: And from thence it proceeds, that in our Modern Plays, thofe very places in which the Poets have labour'd by noble Verfes, and high words to exprefs,

[E] fome

fome great Maxim, have leaft fucceeded, becaufe that falling into the Didactick way, they forfake the bufinefs of the Stage, and let the action cool. From thence it comes likewife that all Actors that appear with the Pedantick Character of teaching, fuch as are the Governour of a young Prince, a Doctor, a Governefs, or the like, are ftill ill receiv'd by the Audience ; the very prefence of them difpleafes and imprints the Character of *Ridicule* upon the moft ferious Piece. I am confident that if the *Linco in Paftor fido* appear'd upon our Stage, he would be hifs'd off of it, notwithftanding all the good counfel he gives *Sylvio*; and that which makes me believe it the fooner, is that one of our beft Modern Plays loft half its due applaufe, by there being a Governour to a young Prince, who was giving him Advice in the midft of moft violent pafsions, with which he was tormented, that being neither the Time, nor the Stage the Place for fuch Inftructions.

We do not fee neither that either Aftrologers, Conjurers, High Priefts, or any of that Character, do much take, for the very reafon that they can hardly fpeak without pretending to teach, or elfe talk in generals of the power of the Gods, the wonderful Effects of Nature, and fuch things which cannot fail of being tedious, when they are prolixely exprefled. *Scaliger* will not allow them in the very *Epick* Poems, much lefs can they be receiv'd in the *Drammatick*, but ought to be quite banifh'd the Stage.

We muft obferve befides, that Phyfical Inftructions about Nature, and its Effects, are yet lefs welcom than Moral ones, becaufe that 'tis hard an Actor fhould fpeak fo long as to explain the nature of a
thing,

thing, without difgufting the Audience, which foon grows weary of being ill taught the thing the Poet would have him learn; which, together with the little concern the no paffion of the Stage raifes in him, makes the whole very difagreeable. We have a notable Example of this in *Mariamne*, where a long Difcourfe is made of the Nature of Dreams, the thing is very fine, and the nature of them well explain'd; but it interrupts an agitation of the Stage, begun by *Herode* s trouble at his waking; the Audience would fain know the caufe of his difturbance, and the particulars of his Dream: But inftead of that, there is a long Difcourfe of the Nature of Dreams in general, to which the Spectator gives but little attention, as being thereby difappointed of his chief expectation.

To all this it may be objected, That the Stage is a place of publick Inftruction, and that the Drammatick Poet is to inftruct, as well as pleafe; and therefore that Didactick Difcourfes may be proper enough, or at leaft ought not to be condemned.

I confefs that the Stage is a place of Inftruction, but we muft well underftand how that is meant. The Poet ought to bring his whole Action before the Spectator, which ought to be fo reprefented with all its circumftances, that the Audience be fully Inftructed; for as Drammatick Poetry does but imitate humane actions, it does it only to inftruct us by them, and that it does directly, and properly: But for Moral Maxims, which may incite us either to the love of Virtue, or ftir us up to hate Vice; it does it indirectly, and by the *Entermife* of the Actions themfelves; of which Sentiment *Scaliger* is fo much, as I dare quote him for my Warrantee in this Opinion. Now this may be done two ways; the firft, when

[E 2]   th.

the Action of the Stage is fo judicioufly managed, that it fhews the force of Vertue triumphing in the midft of Perfecutions, after which it is often happily rewarded; but if it is totally overwhelmed by them, it remains glorious even in its death. By this all the deformities of Vice are difcovered; it is often punifh'd, but when even it triumphs and overcomes, it is in abomination with the Audience, who thereupon are apt to conclude with themfelves, *That 'tis better to embrace Vertue through the hazard of Perfecution, than to follow Vice even with hopes of Impunity*

'Tis thus principally that the Stage ought to be Inftructive to the Publick by the knowledg of things reprefented; and I have always obferv'd, that it is not agreeable to the Audience, that a Man who fwerves from the way of Vertue, fhould be fet right, and repent, by the ftrength of Precepts and Sentences: We rather defire it fhould be by fome Adventure that preffes him, and forces him to take up reafonable and vertuous Sentiments. We fhould hardly endure that *Herode* fhould recal his Sentence againft *Mariamne,* upon a Remonftrance of one of the feven Wife Men of *Greece;* but we are pleas'd to fee, that after the Death of the Queen, his Love becomes his Tormentor; and having opened his Eyes, drives him into fo fincere a Repentance, that he is ready to facrifice his Life to the regret he has for his Crime.

As for the other way of Teaching Morality, it depends much on the ingenioufnefs of the Poet, when he ftrengthens his Theatral Action with divers pithy and bold Truths, which being imperceptibly work'd into his Play, are as it were the nerves and ftrength of it. For, in a word, that which I condemn in

common

common *Didacticks*, is their ſtile and manner of ex-
preſſion, not the things themſelves, ſince thoſe great
Truths which are as it were the foundation of the
conduct of humane actions, I am ſo far from baniſh-
ing them off the Stage, that quite contrary, I think
them very neceſſary and ornamental, which to attain,
I give theſe following Obſervations.

Firſt, Theſe general Maxims muſt be ſo faſtened to
the Subject, and link'd by many circumſtances with
the Perſons acting, that the Actor may ſeem to think
more of that concern of his, he is about, than of ſaying fine things, that is, to ſpeak in terms of Rhetorick,
he muſt reduce the *Theſis* to the *Hypotheſis*, and of
univerſal Propoſitions, make particular Applications ;
for by this means the Poet avoids the ſuſpicion of
aiming to Inſtruct pedantickly, ſince his Actors do
not leave their buſineſs which they are about.   For
Example, I would not have an Actor ſpend many
words to prove that,

Vertue is always perſecuted ; but he may ſay to the
Party concern'd,

*Do you think to have better meaſure than Vertue has
always had ? and can you expect to be priviledg'd from
Perſecution more than* Socrates *or* Cato ?

And ſo continue a little ſpeaking ſtill to the Party
preſent, and upon the Subject in hand, by which
means theſe Diſcourſes ſeem a little to keep off from
being too general Precepts, and ſo diſguſt the leſs.

Secondly, In all theſe occaſions the Poet muſt uſe
figurative Speech, either by Interrogation, Irony, or
others that his fancy ſhall ſuggeſt ; for theſe Figures,
by not circumſtancing minutely the general Propoſitions, make them more florid, and ſo by ornaments
free them from the Didactick Character.   As for example,

ample, if there be a defign of advifing a young Woman to obey her Parents; inftead of Preaching downright obedience to her, I think an Irony would do better As thus ;

That's a fine way indeed, for a vertuous young Lady to attain the reputation of a good Daughter, to be carryed away by her own paffions, and neglect not only the cenfure of the beft fort of People, but break through all the fences of duty and honour.

My third Obfervation is, That when any of thefe great Maxims are to be propos'd bluntly and in plain words, it be done in as few as may be ; by that means they do not cool the Stage, but add fomething to the variety of it; but there muft be care taken that this do not happen in the midft of a violent paffion ; for befides that in thofe cafes men do not naturally fpeak fentences, the Actour cannot then appear with that moderation which thofe reflections require. *Seneca* is very guilty of this fault in all his tragedies where moft commonly in the heat of paffion all his fine Common places are beftowed upon the Audience.

We have neverthelefs fome Examples of Didactick, Propofitions made in direct terms, and at length not without fome fuccefs in *Corneille*, which to attain as well as he, requires the fame Ingenuity and Art. The Expreffions muft be ftrong, and feem to have been faid only for that particular Subject to which they are applyed, and that requires a particular genius, and much ftudy to accomplifh.

I have obferv'd befides, that common Truths, though in a Didactick ftile, yet do very well upon the Stage in the mouth of a Rogue or a Cheat when his Character is known; for the Spectator is delighted

lighted to fee him cunningly ufe all the Maxims and Difcourfes of a good man to intents and purpofes quite contrary, fo that by that means 'tis all figurative, and moves the Attention of the Audience.

One may likewife fuccefsfully enough *burlesk* all thefe common Truths, but that can be perform'd no where but in Comedy, where by that means they forfake their natural ftate, and are difguiz'd under a new appearance, which caufes both variety and ornament. But Tragedy in its own nature is too grave to admit of any thing fo low and buffoon as this would be ; neither do I remember to have met with any thing of that kind in any ferious Tragedy; I fay *ferious Tragedy*, becaufe that in *Satyrical Tragedy* there was admitted a mixture of Heroick Actions, and low Buffooneries ; and therefore this difguizing of ferious Precepts might have room among the reft in them.

Chapter the Sixth.

Of Pathetick Difcourfes ; or of the Pafsions and Motions of the Mind.

I Do not undertake in this Chapter to teach the Nature of Paffions, nor their different Species, nor their extraordinary Effects; all Moral Authors do that fufficiently.   I do not think neither that it is neceffary to fhew here the Art of ufing them in order to perfuade, after all that *Ariftotle* has faid upon that Subject in his fecond Book of Rhetorick ; fo that I will avoid all Repetitions of that nature,
and

and not fo much as touch upon any thing that is contain'd in his Poeticks, or his Interpreters Commentaries, where may be feen which are the Paffions fitteft for the Stage, and how they are to be manag'd. *Monfieur de la Menardiere* has made two Chapters in his Poeticks on this Subject, fo learned and fo proper, that they alone would filence me, if I offer'd at this matter, they being able to fatisfie the moft curious in that Subject.

I confider therefore here the Paffions, as they are plac'd in Difcourfe, and thereupon I bring my Obfervations towards employing of them with conduct upon the Stage. In a word, I only intend to fhew with what Art a Pathetick or Moving Difcourfe ought to be regulated fo as to make it agreeable to the Spectators, by the impreffion it is to make on them.

Firft then, The Caufe which is to produce a Motion in the Actors themfelves, and then in the Audience, ought to be fomething true, or believ'd to be fo, not only by the Actor who fpeaks (who would be ridiculous to make a great Difcourfe of Grief or Joy for a thing he fhould know to be falfe) but alfo by the Spectators, who probably would not be concern'd if they knew that the Subject he had to complain or rejoyce were fictitious; and if it fo fall out, that by the reft of the Story, the Spectator muft know a thing contrary to the belief of the Actor: As for Example, that a Princefs is alive, though a Lover believe her dead : I fay, if in that cafe one would have the Paffion take with the Audience, there muft not be a long Complaint mingled with Sentiments of kindnefs and grief; but the Actor muft be prefently tranfported into Rage, that the Spectators may

be

be touched by his violent defpair, and feel a great
deal of compaffion, if in that Errour he happens to
kill himfelf, as we fee it falls out in *Pyramus* and
Thisbe in both kinds ; for the long Difcourfe he
makes upon the fufpicion he is in, that a Lion has
kill'd his Miftrefs, does not much affect the Audience; but when he draws his Sword to facrifice his
Life to the *Manes* of his dead Miftrefs, and fo expiate
his negligence in his own blood, there is hardly one
of the Audience that does not fhake with horrour ;
and upon this occafion I remember I faw a young
Lady, who had never been at a Play before, cry out
to her Mother, that *Pyramus* ought to be told
that his Miftrefs was not dead, which made me make
this Judgment, that the Poet ought not to have de-
ferr'd fo long bringing his Actor to the moving part ;
three or four Lines had been enough to have explain'd his belief of her death, and then all the reft
ought to have been pronounc'd, his Sword drawn,
and in the neareft difpofition to death, which would
certainly have produc'd immediate horrour and
compafsion in the Audience.

Not but that it happens often that the Actor may
lament or rejoyce at fomething he thinks true, while
the Audience neverthelefs muft know that it is falfe.
As for Example, if the Story requires that in the Perfon of that Actor there be feigned a Pafsion, of which
the Caufe is falfe, with a defign to have it believ'd
true by another, and by that means difcover fome
fecret ; 'tis good that the Spectators fhould be inform'd that he who feigns the Pafsion has no true
Subject for it, becaufe then they have the pleafure
of the Contrivance, to fee the Difguife well acted;
but he that is deceiv'd, ought not to make any long

Pathetick

Pathetick Difcourfes, becaufe that would not move the Spectators. It will fuffice that in few words he fhew the impreffion the fiction has made upon him, and what Event may be from thence expected. In a word, in all fuch cafes the Poet is to examine which of the two will beft pleafe the Audience to fee a circumventing defign well Executed, or to be concern'd for the Complaint made by an innocent, unwary perfon; for if they are pleas'd in the Cheat, they muft be inform'd of it, if in the Complaint, the falfenefs of the Grief muft be conceal'd from him, that they may believe as well as the Party grieved, that he has reafon to be afflicted.

Secondly, 'Tis not enough that the Caufe of fome extraordinary Motion of the Mind be true, but it muft alfo (to be agreeably reprefented upon the Stage) be reafonable and probable, according to the receiv'd Opinions of Mankind; for if any Actor fhould fly into a paffion of Anger, without reafon, he would be look'd upon as a Mad-man, inftead of being pitied; not but that there are fome paffions whofe Subject is falfe, which neverthelefs are very agreeable, though they are not reafonable in their grounds, for Example Jealoufie; but the nature of this paffion is to be without any foundation in truth or reafon, for elfe it would not be Jealoufie, but a juft Indignation which would infpire the Spectators with hatred againft the Woman, and compaffion for the Husband; whereas quite contrary, we have naturally averfion for a jealous Man, and compafsion for a poor Woman innocently perfecuted by him. The fame may be faid of Covetoufnefs, which will ftill be fo much the more diverting, if the cares and fears in keeping of a Treafure, with diftruft of all forts of People, be without grounds;

grounds; or rather, we may fay that the Difcourfes which are made to exprefs thefe pafsions, do not fo much pleafe the Spectator, by making him concern'd for thofe that fpeak, as they do it by giving him a fort of compafsion mingled with Sentiments of fcorn and derifion for the mifery and folly of thofe that are tyranniz'd over by them; at leaft thofe are the thoughts which I had in reading the fecond Comedy of *Plautus*, called *Aulularia*.

Thirdly, To make a Complaint that fhall touch and concern the Audience, the caufe of it muft be juft, for elfe no body will enter into the Sentiments of the grieved Perfon. For Example, if an Actor fhould exprefs great affliction for not having been able to Execute a Confpiracy againft a good Prince, or fome great piece of Treachery againft his Country, he would be look'd upon as a wicked, and not an unhappy Perfon, and all that he could fay would but encreafe the Peoples averfion to him.

Befides all thefe Confiderations, if the Pathetick Difcourfe be not neceffary, that is to fay, expected and defired by the Spectators, it will be very naufeous to them, let the Poets Art be what it will. That a Husband fhould be griev'd for the lofs of his Wife, is fo natural, that we need not be brought to the Stage to fee Examples of it; but that *Herode* fhould firft condemn his Wife in a tranfport of Rage, i͠ fpight of all the tender thoughts infpir'd by his love; it excites our curiofity to know what his thoughts are after fuch an Action. That *Mafiniffa*, forced by the *Romans*, fhould fend his Wife Poifon, though pafsionately in love with her, and fhe die of it, one cannot but defire to know what that unfortunate Prince can fay or do after fo defperate an Adventure. But that for Example. The Wife of *Alexander*, Son to *Mariamne*, fhould come and make great lamentations upon the Body of her Husband, whom *Herode* had put to death without any other motive, than becaufe fhe was his Wife, that was very fuperfluous, and did not prove very agreeable to the Audience, who knew well enough that fhe had reafon to grieve, but not upon the Stage, the Spectators knowing already all that fhe could fay upon that Subject ; and from thence we muft likewife infer, that all Confidents and Attendants of Princes, though they are very neceffary Perfons upon the Stage, for the union of all the Intrigues, yet they cannot be fuppos'd to carry their lamentations and reflections on their Mafters misfortunes very far, becaufe every body knows that they are things of courfe in true Friends, and faithful Servants, and fo not extraordinary enough for the Stage.

The fame thing may be faid of the chief Actors, when their Interefts are not grounded upon fenfible Motives. For Example ; If a Rival having fought his Miftrefs only for her Fortune, and not out of any Inclination from his heart, fhould complain of having loft her, it would produce no Effect in the Minds of the Audience, his lamentations having no ground in nature or reafon.

But one of the chiefeft Obfervations of all is this, That all pafsions that are not founded upon Opinions and Cuftoms conformable to thofe of the Spectators, are fure to be cold, and of no effect, becaufe they being already poffeffed with an Opinion contrary to the Action of the Player, cannot approve of any thing he fays or does in another fenfe. For Example; The grief of one who had undertaken to kill a Tyrant, a Tyrant, and fail'd in his defign, would not move us in *France*, fo much as it would have done the People at *Athens*, becaufe we living in a Monarchy, look upon the Perfons of Kings as Sacred, be they never fo unjuft; whereas the *Athenians*, bred up in a popular State, hated all Monarchs, and could not endure the name of them.

Thus, for the fame reafon, thofe Pathetick Dif-courfes, which we read in the Greek and Latine Comedys, will never take with us, as they did upon the Stages of the Antients, becaufe we have but little Conformity to the Rules of their Lives, in many things more abominably licentious than ours; and in others, their Cuftoms were fo various; as that which was a Jeft and a Concern to them, can be none to us, who have not fo much as the fame things, to wit, the Cheats of their Slaves, nor the Hunger of their Parafites; which made *Rotron*, one of our Poets, mifcarry in a Play of *Plautus's*, where his Parafite talks of nothing but eating, and is fo horrible a Glutton, that we could not bear him, having no fuch People among't us; all our *De-bauche* lying rather in drinking than eating; and in that too we mingle Songs and Catches.

'Tis for this reafon too I imagine that Tragedys taken out of the Stories of Scripture, are not fo agreeable, for all the Pathetick Motions are founded upon Vertues that have not much Conformity with the Rules of our Life, to which may be added, that be-ing fcarce pious enough to fuffer Devotion in the Chur-ches themfelves, it cannot be expected we fhould love it upon the Stage; and none do but thofe who are touch'd with a true Chriftian Piety, and they are in-finitely pleas'd at fuch Reprefentations.

Having

Having thus obferv'd what concerns the Caufe and Motive of Theatral Paffions, I have likewife made fome Reflections upon the manner of managing of them in a Pathetick Difcourfe.

The firft Obfervation is, That it is not enough to raife a pafsion upon a good Incident, and to begin with ftrong Lines, but it muft be carry'd to the point of its fulnefs. 'Tis not enough to have fhaken the Minds of the Audience, you muft ravifh them ; and to do it, you muft feek matter, either in the greatnefs of your Subject, or in the different Motives and Colours which environ it; but particularly in the ftrength and richnefs of your own Imagination, which ought to be warm'd, and elevated, and as it were, be in labour to bring forth fomething worthy of admiration. In this particularly *Monfieur Corneille* does excel, for he has a moft difcerning Judgment to diftinguifh between rich pafsions, and the common ones, and then he drives them to their juft period, with the greateft felicity imaginable, but which cannot be but the Effect of ftrong and lafting Meditations. The difficulty here lies in the exactnefs of meafure; for as you are not to ftarve your Hearers appetite, fo you muft have as great a care not to cloy him; you muft give him the height of fatisfaction, without over-powering him with fatiety. He that in this cafe will do more than he can, does often lefs than he fhould.

This is a fault obferv'd not only in *Lucan's Pharfalia*, but in moft of *Seneca*'s Tragedys, and particularly in his *Hercules Oeteus*, where the Author has given up himfelf to the fecundity of his own wit, not confidering that the excefs of it might fometimes be infupportable; and yet I could wifh our Poets rather

guilty

guilty of this noble fault, than of that mean one of sterility : For we have seen often upon our Stages, passions begun and forsaken half way, or at least pursued with so little Art and warmth, that they had been less defectuous if they had stop'd in the beginning of their career. To give this measure exactly, is impossible; the Poet must examine what his Subject, the force of his Discourse, and the beauty of the Passion will afford; let him consult his Friends, and use all his Judgment in so nice a point.

But he must be very careful not to spend all the strength of a passion at first ; he must reserve some thoughts for the continuation of it ; for the same passion continued and held up by divers Incidents, with a change of appearances, must certainly be much more agreeable than a new passion in every Scene ; and 'tis in that *Monsieur Corneille* is admirable in the *Cid*, for being to shew the state of a generous Mind distracted by the Sentiments of Honour, and the tendernesses of a violent Love, he produces the Monuments of these passions by degrees, keeping still, till the end many of his noblest Thoughts and Expressions, which if he had not been very judicious, he might have us'd at first ; he has done the same thing in *Horatius*, and most of his Plays. 'Tis true, that to imitate him requires a great deal of felicity and conduct ; but whosoever shall carefully study the Antient Drammaticks, and apply himself to a diligent understanding of the Morals of Life, will always be rich enough to answer these Intellectual Expences.

Secondly, To guide these Pathetick Motions to the point of their true Extent, it must be done with order, and by following the Motions of Nature, with a regard to the quality of the things that are said.

The

The order of Nature is very different, for fometimes the Mind breaks out into violent Tranfports, which not being able to hold, it returns to fome Moderation, or rather fome Relaxation of its own Excefs, the pafsion remaining ftill very fenfible at other times, the Soul moves flowly, and agitating it felf by degrees, arrives to the higheft Tranfport, even to founding away. Now to regulate a Pathetick Difcourfe upon thefe different orders, there is no Advice can be given, the Poets prudence muft guide him according to the Characters of the perfons, and the prefent ftate of the Stage.

Yet he muft always remember that Pathetick Difcourfes are not to end juft as they begin; but after the greateft violence he may bring the pafsion to fome moderation, fo far as to doubt and debate; and as thofe who underftand fuiting of Colours, never place two Extremes together, becaufe that would be too harfh. One muft not likewife in the pafsions of the Stage fall from one extremity to another; nor of a fudden calm into fome great agitation, without fome precedent reafon to arrive at that Tranquillity. Yet it may happen that even in thofe Extremes fome very ornamental paffage may be plac'd, but great circumfpection is requifite. As to the order of the nature of the things that are to be faid, the Mind is not to be hurried from one Motion to another, without connexion or dependance upon what has been faid; nor is it to leap from one confideration to another, and then back again to the firft; the Subject of which the Actor is to fpeak, ought to be carefully confidered; the place, time, and other particulars, which may contribute to the pafsion, and then of all that make up the moft judicious and moving

Difcourfe

difcourfe that may be : For Example, if an Actour is to make imprecations againft any one, he ought to obferve the order in which they naturally may happen, for it would be abfurd to fee him wifh to his Enemy at laft a curfe which would be but the confequent of his firft imprecation.

To order muft be added Figures, I mean thofe great Figures which exprefs the things themfelves, not thofe little boyifh ones which play in words, fuch as Antithefes, which always fpoil a pathetick difcourfe becaufe they feem affected and Scholar like, fhewing rather a quiet then a troubled mind.

The Figures too ought to be very various, and not ftaid too long upon, becaufe a mind that is in agitation cannot talk long the fame way; the Figures of tendernefs and grief ought to be mingled with thofe of fury and rage: a man is to complain and figh, and not to roar or fcold, and he is feldom to break out into the higheft violence, but when there is enough to make him rave, for that agitation of the mind has no limits and goes much further, then the motions of grief, anger or defpair.

To all this may be objected, that a pathetick difcourfe thus managed and governed by rules cannot fail of appearing affected, and fhew the very art it is made by not reprefenting naturally by confequent the ftate of the humane mind, which acts according to its Idea's and motives without any rule but confufion and diforder. To Anfwer this we muft fay, that this diforder in the words of a man is a fault which weakens even the impreffion which elfe his paffion would make, and therefore ought to be reform'd upon the Stage, which fuffers nothing imperfect; but in doing of it there ought to be a mixture of the greateft

[G]   figures,

figures, that ftill the Image of the Motions of a troubled Mind may remain. Thus by an orderly Method one reforms the defect of Nature in her Tranfports, and by a fenfible variety of figures, one keeps fome refemblance of the diforder of Nature. This is all that I can fay, that is any ways fingular upon fo common a Subject.

Chapter the Seventh.

Of the Figures.

ALL thofe ingenious Varieties of Speech which the Learned have invented, whereby to exprefs their thoughts in a nobler way than the vulgar, and which are call'd Figures of Rhetorick, are without doubt the moft notable ornaments of Difcourfe ; for by them every thing appears to a greater advantage : 'Tis they that give the grace to Narrations, probability to all other reafonings, and ftrength to the paffions, and without them all our Difcourfes are low, mean, and popular, difagreeable, and without effect. Therefore the beft Advice one can give to a Poet, is, that he fhould be perfect in the knowledg of the Figures, by ftudying carefully what the Profeffors of Rhetorick have writ on that Subject, and which we fhall not here repeat : Yet let him remember, that 'tis not enough to read and know their names and diftinctions, but let him diligently examine their Energy, and what Effect they are like to produce upon the Stage : Neither ought that to fuffice without knowing, and that particularly, how to

apply

apply them, and vary them, to produce the Effect we have obferv'd in the precedent Chapter ; he muft know when to ufe the impetuous ones, and when to employ the milder, fuch as Ironies, according to the diverfity of his Subject, and the Effect he defires they fhould produce. For Example ; If it be neceffary that an Actor fhould leave the Stage in a great rage, then he muft be mov'd by degrees, beginning by the fofter Figures, and at laft be raifed to the higheft Tranfports a Soul is capable of; but if on the contrary an Actor is to grow calm before he goes off, then 'tis beft beginning with violent Figures, and fuch as moft exprefs the impetuofity of a difturb'd Mind, till by little and little he becomes more moderate, and gives room to ufe gentler Expreffions. To make our Poet expert in this, he ought, befides reading of the Antients, to frequent the Stage much ; for there, much better than in Books, he may obferve good or ill Figures, and when they are well or ill plac'd, and to help him a little, I will communicate thofe Obfervations I my felf have made.

Firft, He will difcover that which I have faid elfewhere, which is, that nothing is to be expreffed without Figures upon the Stage : And if the fimpleft Shepherds are clothed in Silk, and wear Silver Sheephooks, every thing they fay ought likewife to be adorn'd, and have its grace, even fo much, that thofe very things which feem leaft capable of that Imbellifhment, muft be order'd with fo much imperceptible Art, that no Figures appear, and yet be there fecretly and nicely applyed ; for if Poetry is the Kingdom of Figures, the Stage is its Throne, from whence it conveys by appearances well managed by him that fpeaks, Sentiments into the Soul of the hearers, which are not really in his.   [G 2]   But

But let him obferve likewife, that as there is great difference between Tragedy and Comedy, they have alfo their different Figures. Tragedy, as it is always ferious and great, employs none but noble Figures, which draw their force from the Sentiments of the Stage, and when we mingle Allufions, or Antithefes, or Equivocal, Proverbial ways of fpeaking, it degenerates immediately, and lofes all its Majefty. 'Tis quite otherwife with Comedy, which having none but vulgar Sentiments, it rejects not *Proverbs*, nor any thing that may contribute to make a Jeft, that being its Character, and the beft part of its Ornaments; nay, 'tis hard *Comedy* fhould rife without a fall, for no fooner does it aim at folid Difcourfes, or Figures fit for Tragedy, but we laugh it out of doors, as we would do a Chambermaid that fhould talk nothing but Romance; therefore 'tis hard that the Figures for one of thefe Poems fhould be aptly ufed in the other without great warinefs, and that *Plautus* has done in fome of his Plays with fuccefs.

Befides, among thofe Figures which are great and ferious, the Poet may obferve fome to be fitter for the Stage than others. For Example, *Apoftrophes*, which I have always obferv'd to do very well; for they fuppofe either a true perfon who is abfent to be prefent, or fome feigned perfon which is but in the Idæa of Fiction, fuch as *Vertue*, ones *Country*; and thereupon the Actor talks to them as prefent, which is extremely Theatral, becaufe it makes two perfons where there is but one; and though the deceit is vifible enough, yet being an effect of the paffion of the Actor, it carrys along with it the Imagination of the Audience, and that particularly when he that fpeaks is alone; for then there can be no miftake in
the

the Mind of the Spectators ; for 'tis plain, that the
perfon to whom the Actor fpeaks, is a Fiction of his
own brain, his Difcourfe not being applicable to any
other. *Monfieur Corneille* ufes this Figure frequently,
and *Stiblinus* efteems extremely the complaints of
Hecuba in the *Troades* of *Euripides*, by reafon of
this Figure, which is there frequently and beautifully
made ufe of. But in the practice of this there are
two faults to be avoided ; the firft is not to have it
too often, for then, befides the want of variety, which
argues want of Invention to pleafe ; it grows likewife troublefom, by making too many imaginary
perfons, and in this kind one of our Authors was
faulty, who in the fame Play, and that a piece of no
great length made an Actor fpeak at leaft a dozen
times to Heaven. The other fault to be avoided is,
that an Actor fpeaking to a King, a Father, a Judge, or
fome perfon to whom refpect is due, ought not to
fall into a long *Apoftrophe* to an Imaginary perfon, becaufe it is againft the Rules of decency, that a man
fhould leave addreffing to a perfon of Authority, to
talk to a thing abfent, or a Chymera of his own brain;
not but that if it were extreme fhort, and the Difcourfe prefently continued to the perfon prefent, it
might very well pafs ; as in this Example.

*Q Nature! who knoweft how true I have always
been to thy Sentiments, fpeak here in my defence.*

And then continuing and addreffing to his Father,
fay,

*'Tis fhe, O my Father, that muft juftifie what I have
done,* &c.

By this flight the Figure brings force and variety
to the Difcourfe, and yet does nothing againft the
Laws of Refpect, fo fmall a Tranfport being very
allowable

allowable to a man paffionate and innocent, and the quick return brings all things in order again.

Profopopæa's quite contrary are very unlucky upon the Stage ; for though, as well as *Apoftrophes*, that Figure fuppofes perfons that are not,and makes dumb things fpeak, yet it generally creates confufion, becaufe the Actor already reprefents a perfon that is not, and this perfon reprefented makes another feign'd perfon fpeak by his mouth, which makes a double Fiction, and much obfcurity ; for very few of the Audience are either able, or attentive enough to obferve the Actors pafsing from his own Difcourfe, to that of the fuppos'd perfon in this Figure, the leaft noife, or other diverfion at that time being enough to make them lofe the Chain, and fo confound the Difcourfes attributed to the feign'd perfon by *Profopopæa,* with thofe that the Actor makes in his own perfon.

I dare affirm befides, that to the people the beauty of this Figure is not fenfible upon the Stage, but rather troublefom, becaufe of their want of skill and application to diftinguifh things. For Example ; They fee an Actor who acts the King, and are poffeft that all that he fays is the Difcourfe of the King he reprefents ; fo that if he comes to make a *Profopopæa,* by fuppofing that either Vertue, or Love, or fuch like things fpeak to him, they are mightily puzzled; for, though they have fenfe enough to know that this fpeech of Love or Vertue does not properly belong to the King, yet they penetrate not the Myftery of that double Fiction of a King reprefented, and fpeaking by the mouth of an Actor, and of Vertue likewife fpeaking by the mouth of the fame King; therefore this Figure is to be avoided, and cannot well be brought upon the Stage, or if it is fometimes, it muft

be

be in Narrations, and then it muſt be very ſhort, or in *Soliloques*, otherwiſe called *Monologues*, where the Poet muſt uſe much Induſtry to ſhew what the thing is he feigns, and makes ſpeak in the *Proſopopœa*, that ſo there may be no obſcurity nor room for miſtake, neither is he to judge of the uſe of this Figure by its being employed in Epick Poems and Orations ; for they being generally deſign'd to be read at leiſure, it is eaſie upon any obſcurity to look back and diſcover where the difficulty lyes ; but in the Stage where the beſt part of the Audience is made up of the unlearned, and where the thing paſſes in Diſcourſe of a ſudden without repeal, there is no remedy for thoſe who are once fallen into obſcurity, but to remain in it ; and in Orations, the obſcurity cannot be ſo great, becauſe there the perſon that ſpeaks makes no double Fiction, and ſo is eaſily underſtood.

Irony is a Drammatick Figure, and of its own nature very Theatral ; for by ſaying in jeſt or ſcorn the contrary of that which it really means, it carrys a kind of diſguiſe, and makes an agreeable Effect.

Exclamations are extreme proper for the Stage, as being the marks of a Mind much mov'd with paſſion.

Hyperbole is of the ſame rank, becauſe the words there carrying ones Imagination further than their natural ſenſe, it is fitteſt for the Stage where all things are to be magnified, as if it were continual Inchantment and Illuſion.

Interrogation, which *Scaliger* ſays is only a Figure by uſe, and not of its own nature, is likewiſe the mark of an agitated Mind, and by conſequent Theatral.

And amongſt them all, certainly *Imprecation* will be judg'd Theatral, as being the Effect of a violent
Tranſport,

Transport, and its Discourse ought to be impetuous, with bold expressions, and words full of Extremes.

This I think may suffice for our Poet, without making an unnecessary repetition of what the Rhetoricians may have taught him, and which he may read with great profit in *Scaliger's* Poeticks.

Chapter the Eighth.

Of Monologues, or Discourses made by a single Person.

THough I have not met with the word *Monologue* amongst Antient Authors, who have treated of the Stage ; and that *Scaliger* himself, who has not forgot any curiosity upon this Subject, has nothing of it ; I shall not nevertheless forbear to say something of it according to the meaning of our Modern Poets.

To begin therefore by a necessary Observation we must not confound the *Monodia* of the Antients with that which we call now *Monologue*; for though the first is some piece of Poetry, sung or recited by one man alone, yet custom has fixt its signification to those Funeral Songs which were sung by one of the Quire, in honour of the Dead ; and 'tis thought that the Musician *Olympus* was the first that us'd it, in memory and favour of *Python*, as *Aristoxenes* affirms ; which makes me wonder at one of our Modern Authors, who says, that the *Monodia* was a Poem compos'd under the name of one person, such as the *Cassandra* of *Lycophron*.

Besides, there are among the Learned some who
will

will not receive the Greek word for a Difcourfe made by one man by himfelf, but fay it means a Difcourfe in every thing one and like its felf without variety.

For my part I believe that in our time we have call'd *Monologues* that which the Antients call'd the Difcourfe of a fingle perfon *Monoprofopon*, as many Eclogues both Greek and Latine, and many Difcour-fes of the *Chorus*'s in Plays, which *Stillinus* calls *Monodias*, as the Difcourfe of *Electra* alone in *Euri-pides*, and another of the fame in *Sophocles*, though fhe fpeaks in the prefence of the Quire.

I confefs that it is fometimes very pleafant to fee a man upon the Stage lay open his heart, and fpeak boldly of his moft fecret thoughts, explain his de-figns, and give a vent to all that his paffion fuggefts ; but without doubt it is very hard to make an Actor do it with probability.

The Antients could not bring in thefe *Monologues,* becaufe of the *Chorus*, which never, or very feldom left the Stage ; and except that *Monologue* which *Ajax* in *Sophocles* makes at the corner of a Wood up-on the point of killing himfelf while the *Chorus* was gone out to look for him ; I do not believe there is any other in the Five and thirty Greek Tragedies which are left. I know very well that in many Scenes there is but one Actor nam'd ; but if we obferve nar-rowly, we fhall always find that he is not alone up-on the Stage, and that his Difcourfe is directed to fome that follow him, though they are not fet down at the beginning of the Scenes.

As for *Prologues*, they are indeed made by one fingle Actor, but not in the nature of *Monologues* ; 'tis a thing by it felf, which indeed among the Antients was one part of the Dramniatick Poem, but not of

[H]   the

the Theatral Action; 'tis a Difcourfe made to the Spectators, to inftruct them of the Story which begun amongft the Antients as foon as the *Chorus* came on.

The two Latine Comick Poets have many *Monologues* in all their Plays, fome of them are brought in properly and according to reafon, others not. I fhall not here make any Criticifm upon them, but give my Opinion what Rules are to be obferv'd to make a *Monologue* with probability.

Firft of all, an Actor muft never make a *Monologue*, while he addreffes himfelf to the Audience, with a defign to inform them of fomething they are to know; but there muft be found out fomething in the Truth of the Action that may be colourable to make him fpeak in that manner. Elfe 'Tis a fault in the Reprefentation, of which both *Plautus* and *Terence* are guilty.

Secondly, When he that thinks he fpeaks alone is over heard by chance, by fome other he muft then be reputed to fpeak foftly, becaufe it is not probable that a man by himfelf fhould fpeak fo loud as Players muft do to be heard by the Audience. I confefs indeed with *Scaliger*, that this is one of the faults of the Stage, which muft be excus'd only by the neceffity of Reprefentation, it being impoffible to reprefent the thoughts of a man otherwife than by his words; but that which makes this fault the more apparent, is, when another Actor hears all that that man fays, who fpeaks alone; and though it may happen that a man may fpeak aloud of that which he ought only to think, and which he intends only to fay to himfelf, yet that being a grofs Imprudence, ought not to be reprefented upon the Stage.

Therefore

Therefore in thefe Cafes one muft either find out a probable reafon to make the Actor fpeak aloud, which is very hard to do, or elfe the Poet ought to ufe fuch Art in the Compofition of the *Monologue*, as that the Actor fhould fometimes raife his voice in faying certain words only, and fpeak with a low voice in others, that fo the Actor who is within hearing might be fuppos'd to hear fome fpoke with paffion, and not the others, as being fpoke foftly, and in the mean time the other Actor upon what he does hear might make fome Exclamations, and feem concern'd that he could not hear the reft. Nay, when the Actor, who fhould fpeak the *Monologue*, fhould fpeak foftly, then the other Actor fhould obferve all his Actions, as of a man much taken up with his own thoughts, and in a deep ftudy; and it may be this way the probability of the Stage might be preferv'd with fome addition of ornament to the Scene in hand; but to execute this well, one muft not meet with proud, impertinent Players, who taking no Advice but from their own Ignorance and prefumption, think they perform all things admirably well; for a Scene of this nature would hardly fucceed, except as docile Actors as thofe of the new Company of the *Mareft* were wont to be, undertook it.

The third Obfervation about *Monologues*, is to make them fo, as not to chock the probability of the circumftances of time & place: For Example; It would be abfurd to put a *Monologue* in the mouth of a General of an Army, who fhould be in the middle of a Town juft ftorm'd by his Army. There would be likewife little probability if a Lover fhould hear of fome great danger his Miftrefs were in, and inftead of running to her relief, fhould ftand ftill and make

a long

a long complaint againſt the Stars, he would be as little forgiven in the Repreſentation, as in the Reality; ſo that in a word, all that can be done, is ſtill to keep to the Rules of probability and decency as the only Guide of the Stage.

Chapter the Ninth.

Of a Partes, *or Diſcourſes made to ones ſelf in the preſence of others.*

IT often happens upon the Stage, that one Party ſpeaks in the preſence of another who hears and ſees him, and that neverthelefs his words repreſent ſome thought known to no body but himſelf.

There are very few of thoſe to be met with in the Greek Poets, and except a Verſe or two that the *Chorus* ſpeaks after ſome long Diſcourſe of an Actor; or when a new Actor comes upon the Stage, I do not know of any other Example, and this may ſerve to give us a hint how cautious we are to be in obſerving the probability of the Stage, ſince in a matter of forty Poems they have ſo rarely taken the liberty of repreſenting a man's ſecret thoughts by words ſpoke aloud.

The *Romans* have taken much more licence in this kind; *Terence* not quite ſo much as *Plautus*, who makes *a partes* very frequently, and often intollerably abſurd. *Seneca* the Tragedian is not more regular in this, than in any other of the Rules of the Stage; for in his *Agamemnon, Clytemneſtra* makes an *a parte* of ſeventeen Verſes. Our Moderns, who have imitated

ted the Antients much more in their faults, than in their Excellencies, make likewife fuch abfurd *a partes*, that the moft grofs among the common people can hardly bear them.

I know that thofe *a partes* do fometimes make very good fport upon the Stage, and 'tis often necef-fary to introduce them to make known to the Spe-ctators fome fecret thought of fome Actor, without which they would be in the dark : As for Example ; When an Actor diffembles, but at the fame time it feems a little hard to conceive (though *Scaliger* by a great Indulgence for the Stage allows it) that an Actor fhall fpeak loud enough to be heard by the Audience, and yet not be over-heard by another Actor who ftands by him ; and that which is worfe is, that to feign he does not hear him, he is forc'd to make twenty ridiculous *Grimaces.* Let us fee therefore if by Art we can any ways render thefe *a partes*, if not entirely probable, at leaft fupportable to the Stage.

In order to this I divide them into three forts; the firft, when two Actors, each of them at one corner of the Stage fpeak as it were to themfelves of their own concerns, making as if they did neither fee nor hear one another.

The fecond fort is, when one Actor fpeaks, fup-pofing the other Actor whom he fees and hears, not to fee nor hear him.

The third fort is, when both Actors hearing and feeing one another, one of them for fome fudden confideration, fpeaks as if he were not heard by the other.

Now, to order it fo in all thefe occafions, that the Spectators Judgment fhall not be chock'd by any im-
pro-

probability, I have bethought my self what might be done.

First then, an *a parte* ought to be very short, and contain very few words; particularly, when in all the rest of the Action both Actors see and hear one another; and indeed about half a score, or a dozen words, or one Verse, are the measure of a just *a parte*; the best of all is an *a parte* of one word, because even in the nature of things, one word may slip from us, and not be over-heard by him that speaks to us: But long *a partes*, such as *Plautus* makes, are unexcusable, because they put the other Actor quite out of countenance, and make him, that he knows not at last what posture to be in, to make the Audience believe he does not hear the other, who speaks aloud so long, and so near him.

Besides, one must take ones time very well to make an *a parte*. An Actor who is serious in talking, not being lightly to be interrupted by another, without some probable colour for his stopping in the middle of a Discourse, which must give the other who is to make the *a parte*, an opportunity to make it handsomly; and if he that is speaking does as it were interrupt himself, by saying something softly, which ought not to be over-heard, he that hearkens must wonder at his ceasing to speak, and either know or think he ghesses the true reason of it, for else it would be unnatural that a man should speak and be silent by fits, and they that stand by, neither be surpriz'd at it, nor ghefs at the cause. The Poet therefore must take either the time of an Exclamation, or some such other Figure, whereby an Actor may be suppos'd to be in a condition not to speak for some moments, nor to hearken to what

another

another fays, and at that time a few words, or half
a Verfe may be put in another Actors mouth, to
make a reafonable *a parte*. If it happens fo that the
time in which one Actor makes his *a parte*, is fenfible to the other, he muft fay fome word that
marks his aftonifhment of the others diftractfulnefs,
either feigning that he did not hear him well, or
miftook him, or fo. We have an Example of this in
Plautus's Moftellaria, where *Tranion* having made
an *a parte*, *Theuropides* asks him what it is he
mumbles to himfelf, which fhews the Slave to have
fpoke foftly. The fame Poet does the like in his *Aulularia*, where *Staphila* having faid afide, that fhe
had rather be hang'd than ferve any longer fuch a covetous, mad Fellow as Euclio : *Euclio* anfwers, *See how
this Jade murmurs fomething to her felf.*

☞ p. 337.

When two Actors fee not one another, and each
of them make an *a parte*, one of them muft ftill be
fuppos'd to be fometimes filent. For Example ; If a
Lover be to make a complaint in fome folitary place,
where another Lady comes to look fomething fhe
has loft, I think the Lover ought to be in fome great
Extacy of grief to give the Lady time to fpeak, and
then the Lady ought to be employ'd in looking what
fhe came for, to give the Lover time to continue his
complaint, and then thefe *a partes* may be longer
than the ordinary ones.

There are fome occafions where they may be
yet longer ; as if one of the Actors does not fee the
other, and is doing fomething which requires fome
time, he that fees him, without being feen, may
make a Difcourfe that fhall laft as long as his Action.
For Example ; If a covetous man tell his money, the
Thief that fees him may make an *a parte*, that fhall
laft

laft all that time; nay it is neceffary there fhould be one then, there being no greater fault upon the Stage than to have it filent; and whatfoever is doing, fome body or other muft fpeak, and there is to be no ceffation of that, but in the Intervals of the Acts; nay, if fomething falls out in the Play, that may feem naturally to ftrike them all dumb, yet one Actor ought to be kept on purpofe to fay fomething of their filence, left the Action fhould ceafe in the middle of an Act or Scene.

From thefe general Obfervations, the Poet may eafily govern himfelf fo as to make a judicious *a parte* ; but if he defires more light upon this Subject, let him read *Monfieur de la Menardiere*, in his fixth Chapter of his Poeticks, where he makes many judicious Remarks ; only I cannot agree to two Obfervations he makes ; the firft is, when he fays that Poets might make more reafonable *a partes*, if it were written on one fide of the Stage. For Example ; *This is the Louvre*, and on the other fide, *This is the Palace Royal*; for the Stage cannot comprehend two places fo far diftant from one another. I thought at my firft reading him, that it was a raillery he made upon our Modern Poets abfurdities, but having afterwards obferv'd that in the eighth Chapter he makes his Stage contain a whole City, I faw he was in earneft. The other thing in which we difagree is, that he cites *Scaliger* in the one and twentieth Book of his Poeticks, to fhew that he condemns all *a partes* upon the Stage ; for *Scaliger* in that place does not fay one word of it; he defcribes in that Chapter the *Theatre* of the Antients, and having fpoke of the *Scene*, which reprefented the Actors Houfes, and of the Profcenion, or *Forefcene*, where they appear'd;

and

and of the *Orcheſtra* deſign'd for the Muſick and Dancers, he reproaches the *French* Nation with ſo groſs an Ignorance in his time, that they had not ſo much as a Painted Cloth or Hanging to hide thoſe Things and Actors which were not to be ſeen : And theſe are his Words.

In France, ſays he, *they Act Plays ſo, that all things are expos'd to the Eyes of the Spectators ; all the Decorations appear upon the Stage, the Actors never diſappear ; onely thoſe that are ſilent, are reputed abſent : But certainly it muſt be very ridiculous, that the Spectators ſhould know that you hear and ſee, and yet you your ſelf ſhould not hear nor ſee what is ſaid of you in your own preſence, as if you were not where you are : Whereas the true Art of the Poet is to ſuſpend the Attention of the Audience, and make them always expect ſome Novelty ; but there, far from that, Satiety is upon one, before ones Appetite is rais'd.*

Thus it is that *Scaliger* deſcribes the old *French* Stage ; which I have alledg'd elſewhere, to prove the difference between that and our Stage, as it is brought to Perfection at this time, and to what Splendour it might be brought, by following the Example of the Ancients. But *Scaliger*'s Deſign, as it appears, was not here to ſpeak of ill *Apartes*, as may appear to any who ſhall carefully read what he writes there of the Fabrick of the Ancient Theatres.

Nunc in Galliâ ita agunt fabulas, ut omnia in conſpectu ſint, univerſus apparatus diſpoſitis ſublimibus ſedibus ; Perſonæ ipſæ nunquam diſcedunt, qui ſilent pro abſentibus habentur. At enim verò perridiculum ibi ſpectatorem videre te audire, & te videre, teipſum non audire quæ alius coram te de te loquatur : quaſi ibi non ſis ubi es. Cùm tamen maxima Poetæ vis ſit ſuſpendere animos, atque eos facere ſemper expectantes. At hic tibi novum fit nihil, ut priùs ſatietas ſubrepat, quàm obrepat fames.
Scal. l.1. c.21.
Poet.

Chapter the Tenth.

Of the Acts.

WE call *Act* that Fifth part of a Drammatick Poem which is begun and ended with Mufick, and confifts, in our Plays, of about Three hundred Verfes, or thereabouts. The ancient *Greek* Poets knew not the Name, though they had the Thing; for their *Epifodes* (which, according to *Ariftotle*, were that which was contained between two Singings of the *Chorus*) was the fame thing, and our Mufick anfwers their *Chorus*. The *Romans* have had the Word, (as we from them) but not, I believe, always; for at firft it fignified a whole Play, as the Word *Dramma* did among the *Greeks*: but, I believe, when Comedy came to lofe its *Chorufes*, and had nothing left but Dancing, Mufick, and Buffooning, for Interludes, then the Poets bethought themfelves to diftinguifh their Plays by Acts, for to take off the Confufion that muft elfe have been in reading of them. And this, I think, hapned but late neither; for we fee nothing of it in thofe who were Contemporaries with *Terence*. *Horace* is, I think, the firft that has given us any Precepts about it, as well for the Diftinction as Number; and 'tis wonderful that *Athenæus*, who cites fo many *Greek* Drammatick Poets, does not give us the leaft hint, from which we might conjecture, that this Diftinction was known in his time. But fince the *Greeks* have had the Thing, I will treat of it under the name of Acts, without examining in what time, or how it came by that Name.

Neve minor, neve fit quinto productior actu Fabula, quæ pofci vult & fpectata reponi.

Firft

First then, we must know, that Poets have generally agreed, that all *Drammas* regularly should have
neither more nor less than Five Acts: And the Proof
of this is in the general Observation of it ; but for
the Reason, I do not know whether there be any
founded in Nature.   Rhetorick has this advantage
over Poetry in the Parts of Oration, that the *Exord,*
Narration, Confirmation, and *Peroration,* are founded
upon a way of Discoursing natural to all Men ; for
every one always makes some little Preface, then
passes to the thing he has to say, which he confirms
by Reason, and, as he makes an end, endeavours to
gain the Favour of those that hear him. But for the Five
Acts of the Drammatick Poem, they have not been
fram'd upon any such ground ; only they owe their
being to the many Observations of the Poets, who
have studied to find out what would be most agreeable to their Spectators.   First then, having per-
ceived that it was not possible for their Spectators to
have a continued Attention to the Reciting of Fifteen
or Sixteen hundred Verses, without interruption,
they used *Choruses* , whose Singing and Dancing
eas'd the Impatience of the Spectators , and put
them in good humour to hear the Remainder of the
Dramma : and for the same reason they divided it
into Five Parts, which hapned so well, that whether
it be that that is a Proportion that just hits the Weak-
ness of the Audience, or that by Custom we are
made Friends to it, 'tis certain, that we do not naturally like a Play that has more or less than Five
Acts, which divide the Time of so many Hours as
we can well spare to a Diversion, without making
it a Toil.   We see by experience, that the *Italian*
Comedians, who fail in this, by making only Three

Acts, according to their ill-received Custom, make the First Act so very long, that it is most importunately tedious. I should therefore advise the Poet to make Five Acts, and each of them of about Three hundred Verses, or little more, having always observ'd, that the Patience of the Audience seldom reaches beyond Sixteen hundred Verses; and every body knows, that two of the most Ingenious and Magnificent of our Plays have miscarried for having been too long: For 'tis an ordinary thing to see the Spectators applaud a Play of a good just Length, though with some Faults, rather than admire an exact accomplish'd one, that is too long. We can find Excuses for the Poet in any thing else; but Weariness and Satiety have that particular to them, that they make even the best things insupportable to us.

Let the Poet then seek among the Ancients the Observation of this Rule. The *Greeks* have both known and practised this Division of the Drammatick Poem, but not all alike. It is pretty apparent in *Sophocles*: *Æschylus* had not attain'd in his time the exactness of the Rules; and as for *Euripides*, he always does so embarass himself with Prologues, that his Plays seem often to have Six Acts, and sometimes Seven. Besides, it seems that in some Plays the *Chorus* sings in the middle of an Act, and so interrupts the Sequel; which is confirm'd by *Horace*, who gives it for a Rule, That the *Chorus* shou'd sing nothing in the middle of the Acts, that is not proper to the Subject. But this regards a Criticism not useful in our days, by which perhaps we might doubt of the *Choruses* singing in the middle of an Act: For either the *Chorus* did not

sing,

fing, or the Verſes are ill placed in our Impreſſions, as we can make appear by divers Plays of *Ariſto-phanes,* and in the *Bacchants* of *Euripides.*

As for the *Latin* Tragedies, which we have under the Name of *Seneca,* I think our Poet may forbear imitating them in the Structure, as in all the reſt, except in the Refinedneſs of the Thoughts ? for to me nothing ſeems ſo ridiculous, and withal ſo tedious, as to ſee one Man alone make an Act, without any Variety; and that a Ghoſt, a God, or ſome Heroe, ſhall make at the ſame time the *Prologue,* and, according to *Euripides,* an *Act* too.

It is not ſo eaſie to give Advice about *Ariſtopha-nes*'s Comedies; for they have all of them a Prologue, after the way of the *Greek* Tragedy; but the Plays are not all alike: ſome of them are very regular, and others ſo full of confuſion, that it is very hard to name the Acts diſtinctly; as in that called *The Birds,* where it is hard to ſay which is the firſt Singing of the *Chorus,* nor how many Acts there is, nor where the Second begins: And we ſee that the Interpreters have not marked the Acts in our Impreſſions, finding them too much out of order to be eaſily methodiz'd. Though, I think, the greateſt difficulty has been, either out of the Licence of old or middle Comedy, or by the Corruption of the Copies, which Time partly diſperſed, and the Ignorance of the Compilers and Printers has ill re-eſtabliſh'd.

Plautus's Comedies have been liable to the ſame Misfortunes in many places, where there are whole Scenes loſt, others added, and Acts confounded, as in the *Moſtellaria,* of which the Scene which is reckoned the Third of the Firſt Act, ought to be the Firſt of the Fourth: For after the Second Scene of

the

the Third Act, the Stage is empty, and without Action, *Theuropides* and *Tranion* entring into *Simon*'s Houfe to vifit him, and no other Actor remains upon the Stage ; fo that the Mufick or the *Mimes* ought to have mark'd the Interval of an Act in this place : but the Scene which is counted for the Second of the Fourth Act, ought to be added to this, which is put for the Firft of the Third Act ; for there is no diftinction neither of Time nor Action between them, the Stage having ftill the fame Perfons prefent, and the fame Difcourfes going on ; and fo thefe two together muft make the Firft of the Fourth Act, fince between that which is put for the laft of the Third Act, and thefe two, there is no feparation ; for *Theuropides* is ftill upon the Stage, being neither gone off, nor come on again : fo that the Interludes have no time wherein they may be inferted to diftinguifh the Acts.

As for *Terence*'s Comedies, they may be a Model for a great many things, to thofe who have a mind to gain Reputation, and excel in this Art.

It has been ask'd fometimes, When one may fay properly, that an Act is finifhed ? And it has been anfwered by *Donatus*, That it is when the Stage is empty, and without any Actor. But if it were fo, we might object, That it would be in the power of the Players to fhorten or lengthen any Act at their pleafure ; for if they did but take away the Mufick, they might appear one after another, without ever leaving the Stage empty : And befides, when the Scenes are broken, as they are frequently enough in our Plays, the Mufick might play, fince the Stage would be empty. Therefore, I think, that the Act ends not when the Stage is without an Actor, but

Eft igitur attente animadvertendum, U-bi, & quando Scena vacua fit ab omnibus perfonis ut in eâ Chorus vel tibicen audiri poffit, quod cum viderimus, ibi actum finitum effe debemus agnofcere, &c. Donat. in Andr. Terent.

when

when it is without Action. And that which makes
me fay fo, is, that I have obferv'd, that among the
Ancients the *Chorus* does both fing and dance, and
the Mufick play, though there be an Actor upon the
Stage , which happens two ways ; the one, when
an Actor remains upon the Stage, but incapable of
Action, as *Hecuba* in *Euripides*, who falls in a fwoon
between the Firft and Second Act ; and the *Amphytrio* of *Plautus*, furpriz'd by a Thunderbolt, between
the Fourth and Fifth Act.   The other Cafe is, when
the Actor which appears at the end of an Act does
mingle with the *Chorus*, as *Electra* in the Intervals
of the Acts of the *Oreftes* of *Euripides*; and other
Actors in the fecond *Iphigenia*, and in the *Bacchan-
tes* ; this being common enough to Tragedy,   Now
in the firft Cafe, the Actor which remain'd upon
the Stage without Action, ftopp'd the Courfe of the
Theatral Action, and fo finifh'd the Act : And in
the fecond Cafe, the Actor making part of the *Chorus*, gave eafily to underftand, that the Theatral
Action was ceas'd, and by confequent the Act ended. Therefore I am not of *Donatus's* Opinion, when
he writes, *That the Reafon which oblig'd* Menander
to take away the Chorus *from Comedy, and likewife
forc'd Poets to confound their Acts, fo as no body could
diftinguifh them, was, that the Spectators were grown
fo impatient, that they withdrew as foon as the Actors
difappear'd from off the Stage, to make room for the
Mufick, which was to mark the Interval of the Acts.*
For, I think, he fpoke as a Man not thorowly inftructed in the Matters of the Stage. For the Impatience of the Spectators muft needs be greater, if
their Attention had no eafe ; and ftill more, if the
Acts were not broken, nor diftinguifh'd, as that
                                                    muft

muſt be, if the laſt Scene of an Act was immediately rack'd to the firſt of the next ; for then the Theatre being never without Actor or Action, you could
not naturally part that, which was not ſeparated by
any Interval of Time. Beſides, the Muſick among
the Ancients was very agreeable, and did not, as
now a days, conſiſt of two or three ſcurvy Violins,
but was one of the greateſt Diverſions of their Comedies ; and the Maſters of thoſe Muſical Compo-
ſitions had their Names graven in all Publick Inſcriptions, with thoſe of the Poet, and Chief *Hiſtrio*
or Player.

To which, if we add the other Interludes, of
Mimes, Dances, and Buffooning, we may eaſily
judge, that there was leſs reaſon to be impatient in
the Intervals of the Acts, than in the Acts themſelves ; particularly, if ſome ſcurvy Actor were to
come on to ſpoil a Part, ſuch as formerly was *Pellio*,
who acted ſo ill in *Plautus*'s *Epidicus*, that the Poet
affronted him publickly the next day, when the
Bacchides was repreſented.

Beſides, we do not ſee any where but in *Plautus*,
that the Acts are not well diſtinguiſh'd ; (and in him
too 'tis the fault of the Printers.) Neither do I think
that his Plays were ſo little diverting, as to need ſuch
a ſcurvy Contrivance to fix the Spectators Attention;
for his Plays have more Action, and are not ſo ſerious as *Terence*'s, and always ſucceeded better in the
Repreſentation, though *Terence*'s pleas'd the Reader
better, as having Paſſions better govern'd, more
elegant Expreſſions, and modeſter Characters. But
to come to *Donatus* ; he ſhews himſelf that he was
not very ſure of what he writ, when he adds, *That
the Learned were not all agreed, that it was for this
reaſon*

reafon that Menander *took away the* Chorus *from* Comedy, *and confounded the Acts*. Befides, that which makes me think that he fpeaks as a man that did not very well underftand the Stage, is what he fays of *Terences Eunuchus, That the Acts are there more confounded, than in any other of his Plays, and that none but the Learned can diftinguifh them well. In which* (fays he) *the Poet has made but one Act of all five, that the Spectator might fcarce have the time to breathe, and to hinder him by the continuation of the Events from rifing before the Scenes were taken away :* For 'tis moft certain, that this Comedy is one of thofe in which the Acts are beft diftinguifh'd, though the Scenes are alfo beft knit together ; for at the end of every Act the Actors fay precifely where they are going, and what they are going to do; and they that begin the next Act tell whence they come, and why they come on upon the Stage; fo that there is not the leaft fufpicion of that imaginary confufion, of which *Donatus* fpeaks.   Nay, the Latines are generally fo careful to make the diftinction remarkable, that *Plautus* having made *Pfeudolus* go out the laft man in the firft Act, and come in the firft man in the fecond, becaufe that is againft the Rules, and that it might caufe fome confufion, he makes him fay thefe words as he goes out ; *While I retire to my houfe there to call the great Council of all my Cheats, the Mufick will divert you.* And for this reafon in the *Heautontimorumenos* of *Terence, Menedemus,* who makes an end of the fourth Act, and begins the fifth, fays precifely, *That he had been fome time abfent, that he had been in the remoteft part of his houfe, where he had feen* Clitipho *fhut himfelf up with* Bacchide ; fo that there is no room to believe that confufion of Acts, as *Donatus*

[K]   would

Would have it, and indeed may fay, that in moſt of the Latine Comicks, it is only by the ignorance of thoſe who have marked the Acts, that there is any confuſion, as in the *Amphytrio* of *Plautus,* where the fourth Act ought to begin by that Scene which is put for the laſt of the third Act; and in the *Heautonti-morumenos* of *Terence,* where the fourth Act ſhould begin at the Scene cited for the ſecond, that which is mark'd for the firſt belonging properly to the third Act, it is then much more reaſonable to believe what we have ſaid, which is, that the Actor in theſe occaſions where he ſeems to continue an Act, did mingle with the *Mimes,* and other Interlude Actors, as in *Tragedy* with the *Chorus,* or that the Copys are corrupted, and Scenes loſt; or at leaſt ſome Verſes which might have juſtified the Poets Art; as it has happened to *Plautus* in many places, of which I ſpeak more at length in my Obſervations. But let us come now to the Inſtruction of the Poet about the diviſion and ſtructure of his Acts.

Having then choſen his Subject, he muſt remember to take the Action he has a mind to repreſent in its laſt point, and he muſt believe, if he be not very ſterile indeed, that the leſs matter he ſhall borrow, the more liberty he ſhall have for agreeable Invention; therefore let him ſo ſtrengthen himſelf, as in appearance not to have wherewithal to make above one Act; things paſs'd will furniſh him with matter to fill up the others, either by bringing the Events of the Story ſomewhat nearer, or by *Recitals,* or other ingenious Inventions. Thus *Euripides* in his *Oreſtes* opens his Stage with the very moment in which thoſe that were guilty of *Clitemneſtra*'s death, were to be judg'd. One would think that there were

not

Perſpecto argumento, ſcire debemus hanc eſſe virtutem poëticam ut à noviſſimis argumenti rebus incipiens, &c. Donat. in Terent. And.

not matter for one Act, and that the *Cataſtrophe* muſt preſently follow; but he prepares all ſo dextrouſly by the coming of *Menelaus*, and *Hermiones* abſenting her ſelf from the Pallace, that this Tragedy is one of the moſt Noble and Excellent ones of all Antiquity. *Corneille* does ſo in his *Horatius* ; he begins his Story juſt after the Truce agreed upon by both Armies, and the Combat of the three againſt three reſolv'd upon for the deciſion of the Cauſe; then he furniſhes his Stage with thoſe paſſions which he draws from *Sabina*'s Marriage.

After this, he muſt conſider that which *Ariſtotle* ſays of *Epiſodes* ; for the Drammatick Poem has three things differing from each other, which are the *Conſtitution of the Fable or Story, the Compoſition of the Tragedy*, which is properly, the diſpoſing of the Acts and Scenes, and the *verſification* or Poetry.

The conſtitution of the Fable is the Invention and Order of the Subject, whether from Story, or receiv'd Fables, or the Imagination of the Poet. *Ariſtotle*, by the Conſtitution of the Fable, means only that part of the Story or Subject which comprehends the Theatral Action, that is, which happens after the opening of the Stage, and is of Opinion, that all that is done before, is out of the Conſtitution of the Fable ; and for this reaſon, ſpeaking of probability, he ſays, *That it is lawful for the Poet to ſuppoſe ſomething againſt probability, provided it be without the Fable*, that is, in thoſe things which are done before the opening of the Stage, and are to be made known afterwards by ſome Actor; and he brings for Example *Sophocles* in his *Oedipus*, in which he ſuppoſes in the part which happens before the overture of the Stage, that *Oedipus* did not know how

King *Laius* died, which was not at all probable.

But for my part, I am of Opinion that the Conftitu-tion of the Fable ought to comprehend the whole Story of the Stage; for that which happens before the opening, is as much of the Subject, as that which happens when the Stage is open; and I cannot con-fent that the Poet fhould fuppofe any Incidents againft probability in thofe Adventures which precede the Action reprefented, becaufe that they being a foun-dation for things which happen afterwards upon the Stage, it breaks all the Chain of Events, it being a-gainft all order that a thing probable fhould be built upon an improbable one; and the Poet is lefs to be excus'd in this, than in any thing; for the Incidents which are before the opening of the Stage, are in his power, whereas often in the fequel of the Play the Events conftrain each other, and take away fome of the Author's liberty.

The Compofition of the Tragedy is the difpofition of the Acts and Scenes, that is, of the *Epifodes*, which are to be added to the Conftitution of the Fable, **to** give it its juft proportion, in which often confifts the greateft beauty of the Poem, as it is the greateft Art of the Poet; for the fame Subject, that is, the fame Conftitution of Fable, without altering the Fund or the Events, may have a Difpofition of Acts and Scenes fo differing, that is, the *Epifodes* fo di-verfly order'd, that there may be a very good, and a very bad Tragedy made of it. For Example, that *Cinna* had refolv'd to kill *Auguftus*, and engaged di-vers of his Friends in the Defign, is of the Conftitu-tion of the Fable, but that he comes and tells the De-fign to *Emilia*, repeating to her the very words he had us'd to excite the Confpirators, that is of the

Com-

Compofition of the Tragedy, or Difpofition of the
Acts ; for without changing either the Fund of the
Events of the Fable, another befides *Cinna* might have
related the Confpiracy, and to another perfon than
Emilia ; but fuch a Narration would not have had
the fame Effect ; and 'tis in that that Mr. *Corneille*
does particularly excel ; for he has an Art of placing
in his diftribution of the Acts and Scenes, fuch Incidents as afford him moft lively, moving paffions, and
another man, without changing any thing in the Subject, would place the fame Incidents fo as to draw
little of beauty from them.   This has made me often wonder at fome Learned men, and well read in
Ariftotle, who have confounded the Conftitution of
the Fable with the Difpofition of the Tragedy.   For
the *Philofopher* fays in exprefs words, *That after ha-*
ving conftituted the Fable, you muft infert the Epifodes,
that is, all the Pathetick Difcourfes, Narrations, Defcriptions, *&c.* and take care that they naturally flow
from the Fable or Subject.   As to the verfification,
which is the laft part, that depends upon the Talent
the Poet has receiv'd, and his ftudy in the Art, which
will help him to cultivate and polifh Nature.   To
come then again to our Subject, the Poet muft examine if the Conftitution of his Fable can fuffer *Epi-*
fodes ; and if fo, of what kind, which will be the
moft taking, and in what place they will appear,
and have their beft Effect ; and after this he muft
divide his Acts fo, as if poffible, they may not be
very unequal, and that the laft Acts have ftill fomething of ftrength and ornament more than the firft;
either by the greatnefs of the Paffions, the fingularity
of the Events, or the rarity of the Show and Decoration.

To

To do this well, we muſt have a full Idæa or Pro-
ſpect of his whole Subject, and have it entire before
him ; for he that comprehends the whole, can eaſily examine the parts, and range them; but he that
knows his Subject only as he divides it, runs the hazard of dividing it very unequally.

Some have maintain'd, that every Act is to be
opened by a new Actor that has not appear'd before. I ſhould not diſlike this if it could be done
ſo as that the new Actor brought no confuſion upon
the Stage, and that his coming on be ſo prepar'd, as
that this variety may ſeem natural to the Subject,
and not appear to be the bare Invention of the Poet,
*for Art that diſcovers it ſelf, is againſt the Rules of
Art upon the Stage.* Yet I do not think it neceſſary
to be always thus practiſed, the Poet having other
ways of diverſifying his Acts by Incidents, Paſſions,
or ſome ſuch thing; not that I would confine the
Poet neither to one *Epiſode* in an Act, but if he produce more, he muſt be careful that they do naturally,
and without affectation, create one another; and one of
our beſt Plays was condemn'd for being too richly
various in this kind, ſo as the Audience had not time
to breathe after the impreſſion of a moving Paſſion ;
the Graces of the Stage muſt have time to be relliſh'd,
and like other humane pleaſures, we loſe the Enjoy-
ment of them, if we are either cloy'd with them, or
have not the leiſure to taſt them thoroughly.

Sometimes it happens that there are in a Story
ſuch circumſtances, that they are not agreeable, nor
decent in the Repreſentation, and yet they might
give riſe to noble Narrations, and produce Sentiments, of which the Expreſſions would be admirable.
In theſe occaſions there is nothing to be done, but to
uſe

ufe the Antients Artifice, which is to fuppofe the things done. For Example; It would have been hard and ridiculous to reprefent *Ajax* upon the Stage killing of Sheep, which he miftook for the Greeks in his rage, and whipping a great Ram whom he thought to be *Ulyffes*, and yet it was fitting to give fome Image of this to the Spectators ; therefore *Sophocles* does not only make the recital of it, but fuppofing this Maffacre, arriv'd in the night, he opens *Ajax*'s Tent, where appear thefe creatures flaughter'd, and that poor Prince overwhelm'd with grief and madnefs. Where we may take notice, that the Poet avoided to open the Stage by the beginning of *Ajax*'s fury ; for he could not fo well have govern'd his Subject, neither would he let it quite pafs over, becaufe then he fhould not have rais'd compaffion in the minds of his Spectators. *Euripides* likewife is very ingenious, when he avoids making *Phædras* Nurfe corrupt *Hyppolitus* upon the Stage (as *Seneca* and our French Poet *Garnier* have done) becaufe he muft either have made her fay things weak, and of no effect to her defign, or have made her ufe expreffions againft the Decency and Majefty of Tragedy ; therefore by making that young Prince appear angry at the old Womans Difcourfe to him, he preferves to the Stage all its Sentiments of Vertue, and yet informs the Audience of the thing that was neceffary for them to know.

In a word, the moft general Precept is fo to caft your Subiect, as to throw between the Acts all that can be troublefom to the Poet, or difagreeable to the Spectators. That which I have faid before, that the fame Actor ought not to finifh one Act, and begin the next, in ftrict regularity is true, becaufe that

the

the Actor that goes off, is suppos'd to do it upon some important busines, which requires some reasonable time, for the Execution of it ; and if he come in immediately upon the playing of a Tune or two, the Spectators are surpriz'd to see him come back so soon ; but yet there are some Exceptions ; for if the Actor have but little to do, or go but a little way, he may begin the next Act ; and 'tis ordinary for *Plautus* so to do ; and *Terence* does it sometimes : But Comedy suffers this better than Tragedy, because that the Actors in the first being but of mean condition, they may do any thing hastily, without indecency ; but in *Tragedy*, the persons being all Ladys, and great Men, their Actions must be more grave and serious. If the Antient Tragick Poets begun an Act by the Actor, that had just ended the preceding Act, it was when he stay'd upon the Scene, being mingled with the *Chorus*; a thing pretty ordinary with the Women, and of which the Examples are frequent.

Above all things, methinks the first opening of the Stage ought to be magnificent, either by the number, the Majesty of the Actors, or by the Pomp of the Decoration.

The Greek Tragedys begun generally by a Machine, which brought on a God or Goddess ; that is very noble, but must be but seldom practis'd amongst us, they had a veneration for their Gods, and Plays were a part of their Religion ; but we are ignorant of those Mysteries, and despise them ; and I for my part should rather approve of any other Invention or Contrivance, which should raise some great Expectation, or a strong desire of knowing something that were past.

The

Principium debet esse illustre.
Voss. lib. 1. cap. 7. Poet.
Sumendum principium ex illustri re, eaque .tùm cognata, tùm proxima.
Scal. lib. 3. cap. 95. Poet.

The *Oreſtes* of *Euripides* begins very finely, by
expoſing that unhappy Prince lying upon a Couch,
wrapp'd up in his Cloke, ſleeping with diſquiet and
ſtarts ; his Siſter at his Feet weeping, the *Chorus*
ſcarce daring to tread for fear of waking him, and ſo
raiſe his Fury : all that is pleaſing, and raiſes an expectation of ſomething extraordinary. The waking
of *Herode* in the *Mariamne*, is a fine opening of the
Stage.   Theſe are things not to be neglected; for
they are to the Poet what an *Exordium* is to the
Orator, to gain the Attention of the Audience, and
the Good-will of his Judges.

Chapter the Eleventh.

Of the Intervals of the Acts.

PAinting and Drammatick Poeſie, beſides many
other Points that they meet in, do alſo agree
in this, that they cannot poſſibly give the entire
Image of that which they deſign to repreſent, and
can comprehend but the leaſt part of their Deſign.
A Picture cannot ſhew any Perſon entire, nor any
Story but by halves, and by the viſible Parts onely.
So the Stage cannot repreſent an Action in all its
Circumſtances : Battels of Armies muſt be ſuppos'd,
which cannot be ſeen ; and many other things, either undecent, or frightful.   But likewiſe as the Excellence of the Painter conſiſts in finiſhing ſo rarely
well all that he does ſhew, that by that the Spectator may judge of what he hides ; ſo the Poet muſt
work with ſo much Induſtry, that thoſe things which
[L]   he

he ſhews upon the Stage, may lead the Spectator to an eaſie comprehending of thoſe which he either cannot or ought not to ſhew. 'Tis for this reaſon that the Drammatick Poets have made uſe of the *Intervals* of the *Acts*, to perform thoſe things which could not ſo well be done upon the Stage : And the Ancients fill'd up that ſpace of time with *Choruſes*, and other Interludes, as we do now with Muſick. Some may ſay, perhaps, That theſe Intervals are not ſo very neceſſary, becauſe one might ſo continue the Scenes of a Play without Interludes or Muſick, that the Actors who ſhould diſappear, ſhould be reputed to do off of the Stage, all that either could not, or ought not to be done there, while other Actors ſhould appear and act their Parts. This in it ſelf may be true ; but Experience teaches, that Mankind has not Attention enough to ſupport the reading of one entire Play, without interruption : for even one Act too long is a moſt inſupportable trouble ; and, as *Cicero* ſays, That *no Man would make an Oration of one Period, though he had Breath enough to recite it* ; ſo no Auditor would be content with a *Dramma* without any pauſe or ſtop, though he had an Attention ſtrong enough to mind it. Variety is our greateſt Charm ; and by that means Beauties will paſs upon us more agreeably, than a great and excellent one, always the ſame. But beſides, it happens ſometimes, that all the Actors are to be buſied for ſome time off of the Stage, which then remains empty ; and ſo that time muſt be fill'd up, that the Audience may not expect with diſguſt and tedIouſneſs. Moreover, if there were always ſome Actor preſent upon the Stage, the Spectators could not naturally imagine that an Actor had employ'd

ploy'd any more time in what he had been about,
than while the other Actor was fpeaking ; and yet,
it may be, that firſt Actor muſt be ſuppos'd to need
two or three Hours to do his buſineſs in, which cannot be thought to have paſs'd away in half a quarter
of an Hours Talking by another, whom the Audience has feen all the while. But the *Intervals* make
this probable enough ; for the abfence of all the
Actors, with the Muficks playing, and the ceſſation
of the Audiences attention, do all contribute to deceive the Imagination ; ſo as we may take a few
Moments for whole Hours : and then when the
Actors return, and ſay what they have been doing,
we do not wonder that they have perform'd ſo
much in ſo little a time. Befides, the impatience
we are in to fee the Continuation of the Story, makes
us think we have ſtaid a great while, and ſo give the
more allowance for the things we hear have been
done in that time.

The Poet then muſt confider well in his Subject
what things cannot well be expos'd to view, and
throw them in the Intervals ; but if they are to afford Matter to any great Paſſion or Narration, there
the Poet's whole Art will be neceſſary, and the
Reading of the Ancients to boot, who will afford
him great light in managing thofe Contrivances.

Sometimes the Beauty of an Action lies in its beginning onely, and then you muſt ſhew the firſt
Strokes and Preparations of it, and finiſh it in the
Intervals, and behind the Stage : So we fee that
Eteocles and *Polinices* difpute their Pretenſions before their Mother ; but they do not fight and kill
one another before her. Otherwhile it happens, that
an action has nothing but the latter part of it fit for

[L 2]   Repre-

Reprefentation, and then the beginning muft be fuppos'd to be done in the Intervals, and the laft Touch-
es onely made fenfible, and prefent to the Spectators.
Sophocles,as we have obferv'd in the preceding Chapter, has done this in his *Ajax* ; not that the Poet is
bound to do this always at the end of an Act ; for
fometimes the thing may come to pafs fomewhere
further than the Place reprefented by the Stage,
and then the Bufinefs may be related in the next
Scene.

The greateft Advantage the Poet has from the Intervals of the Acts, is, that by that means he can
throw off all the troublefom Superfluities of his Subject.   But he muft have a care not to fall into one
Errour, common enough among our Poets, which
is to fuppofe a thing done in the Interval of an Act,
which in all probability could not have been done
without having been feen by the Audience . And this
muft happen when it is fuppos'd to have come to
pafs upon the Place reprefented by the Stage ; for
that being open, and expos'd to the Spectators Eyes,
nothing can probably be perform'd there, that fhall
not be feen.   I remember, upon this Subject, that I
was once at a Play,which otherwife was no ill Drammatick Poem, in which there was a Baftion of a be-
fieg'd Town, upon which were armed Men for its defence ; and then in the Interval of an Act this Town
was fuppos'd to be taken by Affault, and yet this Baftion was neither attack'd nor defended upon the
Stage ; and fo the Spectators remain'd with an imagination that the Town was not taken.   Whereas
the Poet might at leaft have faid fomthing of the probability, if he had found a way to let the Audience
know that the Town had been carried by an Affault
in

in another Place, and fo there had been no need of defending it there.

I fhall not here enter into a particular deduction of the Kinds of Interludes with which the *Romans* mark'd the Intervals of the Acts in new Comedy, after having taken away the *Chorus's.* I fhall not neither fay at what time it was that the *Mimes* and the *Embolarii* took poffeffion of the Stage, nor what their Dancing, Mufick, and Buffooning was; why they made ufe of *Flutes*, and of what fort they were that are nam'd in ancient Infcriptions of Comedy *equal* and *unequal*, right or left : all that concerns onely the underftanding the Stage of the Ancients, and not the Art of making a Drammatick Poem. I had undertaken to treat of all this in a Book which I fhould have called *The Reftoring of the Theatre in France,* to fhew what Ornaments might be added to ours from Antiquity ; but I fhould here go too far from my Subject, if I fhould lanch into this Matter. I will onely fay, That much of it may be learn'd out of *Scaliger, Vitruvius, Julius Pollux, Voffius,* and others, though they fpeak of thefe Matters with ill Methods, and not much Application.

Chapter the Twelfth.

Of the Scenes.

I Was in fome doubt whether I fhould explain here all the different Significations of the Word Scene, becaufe the Learned will meet with nothing but what they know already ; however, having con-

fider'd,

fider'd, that others may have by it fome Inftruction about the Matters of the Stage, I thought it not amifs to do it,

Firft then, the Word *Scene*, in its original and proper Signification, is taken for a Covering of Boughs made by Art, from whence the Feaft of the Tabernacles of the *Jews* was call'd *Scenopegia*; and from thence too fome People of *Arabia* were call'd *Scenites*. Sometimes too it fignifies a natural Shade of fome **Grotto**, or folitary place; fo *Virgil* has it,

Tum Sylvis Scena corufcis--------
Defuper horrentique atrum nemus imminet umbra.

But becaufe the firft Comedies, or rather the firft Buffooning, was under fome green Shade, the name of *Scene* was given to all Places where Comedy was reprefented; and Tragedy too, though transferr'd into great Cities, yet preferv'd the name of *Scene*, with that of *Theatre*, which fignifies a place for Spectacles. But then the Word *Scene*, even in Drammatick Poetry, was taken in different Significations; for fometimes it fignified the Place of Acting, as we fay, to be upon the *Scene*; and *Pliny* has it, That *Lucia, an old buffooning Woman, recited upon the Scene at the Age of a hundred years.*

Sometimes it fignifies that which we call the Decoration of the Stage; that is, all the Ornaments of painted Cloth which reprefent the Place where the thing is acted; and according to the three kinds of Drammatick Poetry, *Vitruvius* teaches how to make three forts of Scenes or Decorations of the Stage, fit for *Tragedy*, *Comedy*, and *Paftoral*; and from this Signification is come the Word *Profcenion*, or Fore-

fcene,

scene, attributed by the *Greeks* to that part of the Stage where the *Hiſtrions* or Actors did both act and ſpeak. At laſt its Signification became ſo extended, as to expreſs at once the Place where the Actors acted, and that where the Spectators were. And it is in this ſenſe that the Juriſconſult *Labeo* defines the Scene, according to *Ulpian.* Sometimes likewiſe it ſignified all that pompous Structure of Buildings, Galleries, Walks, Seats, and other places, where the *Romans* us'd to repreſent their Games.

From theſe different Significations have proceeded many Miſtakes amongſt the Modern Writers, becauſe they did not rightly underſtand the Ancients, and ſo have confounded the *Proſcenion* with the Decoration, and that again with the whole Building.

The laſt ſenſe in which the Word *Scene* has been taken, and which we particularly need here, is, when it ſignifies that part of an Act which brings any Change upon the Stage, by the change of Actors.

The *Greeks* never us'd it in this Signification, tho they had the ſame diſtinction of Acts which we have. The *Latins* firſt brought it in uſe, with the Word *Act*, in *New Comedy*, having taken away the *Choruſes.* I do not find any thing about this, in any Author ancienter than *Donatus*; but ſince we have receiv'd it, it will not be amiſs to put here ſome Inſtructions to correct the Irregularities of Scenes.

Fabulæ quidem in Actus diviſio vetus eſt & à Poetis ipſis: Actus autem in Scenas diſtributio eſt à Grammaticis & à vet. Terentii & Plauti cod. abeſt. Voſſius, l 2. c. 5. Poet.

The Ancients, who had no Diviſion of their *Acts* into Parts, have always very exactly obſerv'd the Union or Dependance of *Scenes* upon one another; for knowing that the whole *Act* could not contain above one ſenſible Action upon the Stage, they judg'd very reaſonably, that there was no need of

ſeparating

separating the Parts that should compose it. But when our Poets begun to write for the Stage, they hardly knew what an *Act* or a *Scene* was; they plac'd a Man upon the Stage, to recite there what they had compos'd for him, and they took him away again when the *Capricio* of their Muse pleas'd, and then brought on one or more, which went off too with as little reason; so that one might have transpos'd any of their *Scenes*, without any injury to the *Play*, every one of them making as it were an *Act* by it self. We have seen upon our Stage a Captain, a Poet, and a Visionary Lover, all without having any thing to do with one another; and what they said, was more like so many Scholars Declamations, without any dependency upon each other.

Now I have obfrv'd, that there are four ways of uniting the Scenes together; to wit, an Union of *Presence*, another of *Seeking*, a third of *Noise*, and a fourth of *Time*.

The Union of *Presence* is, when in the following Scene there remains upon the Stage an Actor of the preceding Scene; which may be done three ways: Either by bringing on at once all those that are to be employ'd in that Act, and make them retire one after another, according to the diversity of their Interests; for still those who remain make a new Scene, which is united to the precedent Scenes by the Presence of those who rest. And this is a noble manner for a First Act. The second is, when the Actors come upon the Stage one after another, and none of the first go off; for then all the new Actors make new Scenes, which are united to the preceding ones by the Presence of those who were already upon the Stage. And this manner is very

good

good for a laſt Act.   The Third Way is, when the
Actors go and come according to their Intereſts and
Buſineſs: As when two Actors meet upon the Stage,
if there goes off but one, the ſecond who remains
makes a new Scene, and knits it with the firſt, by
other Actors who are to appear; and this way is
capable of as much variety as the Poet pleaſes.

The Second Way of uniting the Scenes is, by ſeek-
ing when an Actor who comes upon the Stage, looks
for him who went off; and the Examples are very
frequent among the Latine Comick Poets ; but one
muſt be very careful that the reaſon for which one
Actor looks after the other, be a reaſon taken from
the Subject in hand, and ſenſible to the Spectators,
or elſe it would be a falſe Colour affected, and of no
effect; and we muſt remember beſides, that if the
Actor who was upon the Stage goes off, for fear of
being ſeen by him that comes on, that does not make
an union of Scenes, except he that comes on, comes
with an Intention to look for him that goes off. Some
of our *Moderns* have fail'd in this, in withdrawing
their Actors for fear of being ſeen by the comers on,
when the New Actor had no Intention to look for
him that went off; for in this, far from being an union
of *Seeking*, it is rather one of *avoiding*, and ſo the
Scenes would be united by the very Actor who
broke them.

The Union of *Noiſe* is, when upon ſome Noiſe
which is made upon the Stage, an Actor, who probably might hear it, comes to know the cauſe, and
finds no body upon the Stage, that Scene made by
him is very well united to that which was made by
thoſe who went off, ſince the Stage does not remain
without Action, and that a *Chorus* or Muſick could

[M]   not

not be brought in without interrupting the Sequel of the Story. *Plautus* has many Examples of that.

As for the laſt which is made by *Time*, 'tis when an Actor, who has nothing to do with thoſe who go off the Stage, comes on, but in ſuch a nick of time, that he could not reaſonably be ſuppos'd to do it ſooner or later. We have a preciſe Example of this in the *Eunuchus* of *Terence*, in the third Act where *Antipho*, who has nothing to do with *Chremes*, nor thoſe who go off the Stage, ſays, *That he is in much trouble not to find* Chærea, *who was that day to take care of the Dinner for a Club of young men, that the hour of the Aſſignation was paſs'd, and that he is going to look him,* and ſo popt upon him. Now 'tis moſt certain *Antipho* comes on naturally at the due time, and that *Chærea* had fail'd by being taken up in the Intrigue, in which *Parmeno* had ingag'd him by making him paſs for an Eunuch, with a young Woman that he was in love with. Yet I muſt ſay this, that this Union of Scenes, except it be done with very natural Colours, and great Exactneſs, is not to be much practis'd.

Some have put the Queſtion, What ought to be the number of Scenes in each Act? The Poet muſt uſe in that his own Judgment; if there be very few, the Act will want variety; if there be many, and ſhort, the Act will be perplex'd; there will be little ſaid, and much confuſion. But we muſt obſerve that Comedy endures many more Scenes than Tragedy, as being more active, and leſs engaged in great paſſions which take up time. The Antients have ſometimes made up an Act of one ſingle Scene, but I do think that tædious, and much more when as in *Seneca* there is but one Actor for that Scene. I think in Tragedy
there

there ought to be at leaft three Scenes in an Act, and that if there be above eight, it cannot pleafe; I believe experience will juftifie this ghefs of mine.

I fhall now add here a thing, which it would be difficult for me to place any where elfe with more order, which is a difficulty which has often puzzled our beft Poets; and I fhall at the fame time fhew them how to avoid it. It happens then very ordinarily in Drammatick Poems, that to give a foundation to fome things which are to be fpoke, or to clear fome others which have been faid already, there is a neceffity of doing it in a *Theatral* way, and by confequent by an Actor, but as often fome other of the Actors are not to know or hear of it; it is then neceffary to make a new Scene, to drive off thofe who are to be ignorant of the thing, and to bring on others who may fpeak of it; and this I call a Scene of *Neceffity*, when it precedes what is to be done; and a Scene of *Efclairciffement*, or clearing, when it follows, and takes away any miftake or confufion that might have been: But it is good to obferve, that fuch Scenes, being as it were independent and loofe, they break the Union of the others, and often make the Stage dull; both which to avoid, I think we may take this Method.

Firft, To chufe the perfon that is to fpeak upon this occafion, and the place where the Speech fhall be; all that depends on the Poets Judgment, who to gain Obfervations, may read *Plautus* and *Terence*; both which have many of thefe *Scenes*; and for thofe of Neceffity, fometimes they are in the beginning of the Play, as *Sofia* in *Andria*, and *Geta* in *Hecyra*, where both thefe Slaves are of thofe Actors whom we call *Protatick*, who appear only at the

[M 2]　　　　　opening

opening of the Stage, to give intelligence about the Subject of the Play; and this way is not to be us'd without great dexterity.

As for that dulness which such Scenes bring along with them when they are not in the beginning, but in the body of the Poem, it must be corrected, by making the Discourse of him that speaks eager and quick, which cannot be done but by great Figures, such as *Admiration, Exclamation,* &c. or by some motions of fear or joy strongly expressed; for else, though the thing which is expressed be necessary, yet it will be cold and dull, without any grace, because there will be a plain affectation, which is the greatest fault a Poet can fall into. As for the coming off of such Scenes, which is often very troublesom, he may avoid it by introducing in the beginning of an Act the person whom he intends to employ in any such Scene, provided that may appear probable, and consist with the following Scenes; or else he may retain at the end of an Act one or two persons to this end. But the most refin'd way of performing this is, to do it in the middle of an Act by some body retain'd on purpose to unite the following Scene; and who in that interval of time makes alone a Scene of Necessity, or of *Esclaircissement,* by taking occasion to speak of the different concerns of the Actors, who are gone off, or of those who are to come on; for this way neither the person, nor the thing, are affected, and the Scenes are not broken, and the Stage being warm'd by the passions of those who are gone off, is kept so easily by those who are to come on next. In all this nevertheless I leave the Judicious Poet his liberty, only I have thought fit to warn him of these Inconveniencies.

Chapter

Chapter the Thirteenth.

*Of SpeEtacles, Machines, and Decorations of the
    Stage.*

HAving treated at length in my *Terence* juſtified
about the conſtruction of the Theatres of the
Antients ; together with the *Decorations*, *Ornaments*
and *Machines*, which were employed in the Repreſentation of their Drammatick Poems, I can ſay
little here that's new upon that Subject ; therefore I
ſhall not repeat any of it here, my deſign being only to inſtruct the Poet, and not the *Decorator* ; but
ſome Advertiſements may not be amiſs to the firſt, to
teach him ſome ways how to add ſome external
Ornaments to the Inventions of his Brain, to make
them appear with more grace and perfection.

'Tis certain that the Ornaments of the Stage with
the Scenes, Machines, and Decorations, make the
moſt ſenſible delight of that ingenious Magick which
ſeems to make *Hero's* live again in the world after ſo
many Ages ; it ſets before us a new Heaven, and a
new Earth, and many other wonderful appearances
of things which we imagine preſent, though we
know at the ſame time that they are not ſo, and that
we are agreeably deceiv'd : Theſe Ornaments make
the Poems themſelves more illuſtrious ; the people
takes them for Enchantments, and the men of underſtanding are pleas'd to ſee the dexterity of the
Artiſts (who deſervedly attract admiration) with the
concurrence of ſo many Arts and Profeſſions employed in the Execution of theſe contrivances, to
                                              which

which all run with joy and delight. It was for this that the People of *Greece* and *Rome*, though as Martial as Learned and Ingenious, did bestow the richest Decorations upon their *Theatres*; there one might see the Heavens open, where appear'd their Imaginary Gods descending to converse with Men; the Air was often full of the noise of Thunder and Lightning; the Sea shew'd Tempests, Shipwracks, Men of War, Gallys, and Battles: The Earth did not only produce Gardens, Deserts, and Forrests, with magnificent Temples and Pallaces, but it often opened, and shew'd flaming *Abyssus*'s, Mountains came out of its bosom, Furies, Dæmons, and all the Prodigies of their fabulous Hell: In a word, the Objects of the diversion of these People were taken from all the supernatural Effects of the Divinity, the Miracles of Nature, the Master-pieces of Art, and all the beautiful contrivances that Imagination could form for the adorning their Theatre. Their Magistrates always strove to surpass one another in these magnificencies, and the People gave the highest dignities of their Government at this price: therefore the Poets, who saw that in the fortune of great Men there always was, and would be a fund for these Illustrious Expences, did not spare to fill their Poems with Incidents, where the richest Artifices were employed; and the Workmen were pleas'd in adding their labour and contrivance to acquire those riches and fame which certainly attended the success of their undertakings.

But for our times, though the Court does not dislike these Ornaments, and that the People crowd to see them, yet I would not advise our Poet to busy himself much in these *machine* Plays; our Players are neither Rich, nor Generous enough to make the Expence

pence of them, and their Decorators want ability in the performance ; I muſt add that our Authors them-ſelv's have been ſo negligent in acquiring the know-ledge of the Ancients ways in this matter, and in their means of Execution, that we need not wonder if we ſee ſo many ill Invented Embelliſhments of this kind.   Yet one would think that our Age, as ſoon as any might recover the priſtine glory of the *Theatre,* conſidering the Liberality of our Princes, the Application of our Poets, the Ingenuity of our Work-men, and the Care of our Comedians, and that which we have ſeen already perform'd in this Kingdom, is, it may be, but a pattern of what we may expect in the plenty of Peace.   Therefore that we may not be wanting to any thing that may contribute to the accompliſhment of ſo great a work, I ſhall here com-municate ſome Obſervations upon publick *Spectacles* and *Machines,* which I hope will be of ſome uſe.   I conſider all publick Spectacles and Decorations of the Scene three ways.

Some are of *things*; when the Spectacles are per-manent and immovable; as a Heaven open, a ſtormy Sea, a Pallace, or the like Ornaments.

Others are of *Actions*; when the Spectacle depends principally upon ſome extraordinary Fact ; as that one ſhould throw himſelf headlong from a Tower, or from a Rock in the Sea.

The Third ſort is of thoſe that are mingled with *Things* and *Actions,* as a Sea-fight, where at the ſame time is the Sea and Ships, and Men acting upon it.

Theſe may be all further diſtinguiſhed into natural, artificial, and marvellous.

The Natural ones are thoſe which repreſent the moſt agreeable things in Nature, as a Deſert, a Moun-tain on fire, *&c.*   The

The Artificial are thofe which fhew us the moſt magnificent works of Art, as a Temple, a Pallace.

The Marvellous are thofe which fuppofe fome Divine Power or Magick Production, as the defcent of fome God from Heaven, or the rifing of fome Fury from Hell.

And of all thefe, the leaft confiderable are the laſt, becaufe there goes little contrivance to the inventing of them, there being hardly any wit fo mean, who by this may not bring in, or carry off a great Intrigue. I faw once a Play, in which the Author having brought on a Rival, and concern'd him fo deeply in his Subiect, that he did not well know how to bring him off, bethought himfelf to kill him with a Thunderbolt ; the contrivance was pretty fure; but if this fort of Invention be admitted in *Dramma's*, we need not much trouble our felves to wind up the Plot any other way ; therefore all thefe Machines of Gods and Devils are to be us'd with great difcretion, and great care to be taken that in the Execution they play eafily, for elfe the people are apt to laugh, and make Railleries of a God hanging in the Air, or coming down too faſt.

I fhould not likewife advife our Poet to ufe frequently thofe, where Actions are to make the greateſt Effect, becaufe that all the fuccefs depends upon the Exactnefs of the *Comedians*, who are often fo negligent in the performance, that they will neither ftudy the manner, nor time neceffary ; or elfe they are fo poffeffed with an Opinion of their Abilities, that they think it beneath them to be inform'd ; fo that either their Idlenefs, or their Vanity, moſt commonly fpoils that which was well invented, and ought to have made the beauty of the Play. That which

remains

remains then is the permanent Decorations, of what nature foever they are; and to thefe I would confine the Poet, but ftill with many Precautions: For,

Firft, They are to be neceffary, infomuch as the Play cannot be acted without thefe Ornaments; or elfe they will not take, though never fo ingenious. And in this, I think, our *Andromeda* has not all its Regularity; for in the Firft and Fourth Act there are two noble Buildings, of different Architecture, and no mention made of them in the Play; fince thefe two Acts might be reprefented with any of the Decorations of the other three, without offending the Poet, or fpoiling any Incident of his *Dramma.*

Secondly, Thefe Ornaments muft be agreeable to the Sight; for 'tis for that, that the People flock to them. Not that I would abfolutely forbid the Poet to put in things monftrous or horrible; but at leaft then the Painting muft be exquifite, that the Art may be admir'd.

They muft likewife be modeft, and not againft that Pudour which the moft diffolute love the appearances of. I believe that the fhewing of *Mars* and *Venus* furpris'd in a Net by *Vulcan,* would not be allowed for a fine Decoration.

They muft, befides, be eafie to put in execution; that is, that the *Machinifts* do difpofe their *Machins* to play fo well, that there may be no need of great numbers of Hands, but they do of themfelves perform to a Minute; for the People cannot endure to expect long the Effect of a *Machin,* and when they do not hit the Minute, they do not agree with the Motion and Pretence of the Actor upon the Stage, and fo fpoil his Part.

It will likewife be reafonable to confider, whether

[N]   the

the Place reprefented by the Scene, will bear in truth that which is to be fhewed in Image ; for elfe it would be a grofs Fault againft Probability : For example, If the place of the Scene were a Palace, and that clofe to it were a Prifon, or fome noifom place; for Princes and Great People do not live near fuch places.

There muft not likewife be any Decorations made which are not agreeable to the Unity of Place ; as to fuppofe the Scene the Palace or Chamber of a Prince, out of which there fhould be an immediate Paffage to a great Foreft : For all thefe Fictions, though pleafing to the Eye, yet are otherwife, to our Reafon, which knows them to be falfe, impoffible, and ridiculous.

But particularly, the Poet muft fo order it, as that out of this Shew and Decoration fome notable Event may refult in the Body of the Play ; that is, fomething that may contribute either to the perplexing of the Plot, or the eafier unweaving of it ; for if all this Shew is onely for fhew, and not of the Effence of the Piece, the Men of Underftanding will value the *Decorator* for executing, but not the *Poet* for inventing fo ufelefs an Ornament. In the *Rudens* of *Plautus*, the Shipwrack that is there reprefented, makes both the Knot and the Unweaving of the Intrigue. The *Frogs* of *Ariftophanes* have a vaft Decoration, which ferves to all the Acts, and almoft to all the Scenes. And we fhall find few among the Ancients, but what agree with our Rules.

I cannot omit here to advertife the Poet of two important Confiderations : The firft that regards himfelf, which is, That when the Spectacles are of *Things*, that is, of Permanent Objects, they muft,

if

if poffible, appear at the firft opening of the Stage, to the end that the Surprife and Applaufe of the People, which generally attends fuch Sights, may be over, before the Actors begin to fpeak : or, that if there be any neceffity of changing the Decorations, let it be done in the Interval of an Act, that the Workmen may have the time neceffary for their Machins moving, and the Actor that is to appear, that of dreffing himfelf at leifure.   But if, by the neceffity of his Subject, fome great Change is to be in the middle of an Act, let him contrive his Actors Part fo, as he have but little to fay at that time, and thofe too Words of Admiration, Grief, or Aftonifh-ment, to give fome time to the Murmur of the Spectators, which is always rais'd upon fome fuch new Appearance.

The other Confideration regards the *Comedians* ; which is, when the Spectacles confift of Actions : that is, when the Actors are to be in fome pofture extraordinary : The Actor, I fay, muft ftudy this Pofture with care, before he comes to act it upon the Stage ; or elfe 'tis odds but he performs it very ill and not without danger fometimes to himfelf : all which does not a little trouble the Beauty of the whole Piece.

THE
A R T
OF THE
S T A G E.

Book the Fourth.

Chapter the Firſt.

Of the Quantitative Parts of the Drammatick Poem, and particularly of the Prologue.

THE Drammatiek Poem is ſo chang'd ſince the time of *Ariſtotle*, that though we ſhould make an Allowance for his Tranſlators and Intepreters Errours, yet we think we have great reaſon not to be altogether of his mind, particularly in the Matter of which we are going to treat.				He

He writes, That Tragedy has Four parts of Quantity, to wit, the *Prologue*, the *Chorus*, the *Episode*, and the *Exode*; and to make them the more intelligible, he defines three of them thus. *The* Prologue (fays he) *is that part of the* Tragedy *which is before the Entrance of the* Chorus. *The* Episode *is all that is between the two Cantos of the* Chorus. *And the* Exode *is that part after which the* Chorus *sings no more.* This I cannot conceive to be true, according to the present state of the *Greek* Tragedies; neither can I allow, that *Aristotle* has well distinguish'd the parts of Tragedy as it was in his time, at least according to the Works of those three excellent Tragick Poets which have been transmitted to us.

To understand this aright, let us begin with the *Prologue*, and consider how many sorts of *Prologues* there were among the Ancients.

The first sort was of those which were made for the Interest of the Poet, either in answering the Invectives of his Adversaries, or in expounding his Proceeding in the Play. Many of this kind are to be found in *Plautus* and *Terence*, particularly in the last; which made some say, as he himself relates, *That without the Reproaches and Cavils of the old Poet, the new one would not have known what Subject to have taken for his Prologues.*

Vetus si Poeta non lacessisset prior, nullum invenire Prologum potuisset novus. Prolog. in Phorm.

There were other *Prologues* that regarded the Interest of the *Comedians*, either to obtain the Judges or the Peoples Favour, or to bespeak their Attention. Such is that of the *Pseudolus* of *Plautus*, and some others.

There are some likewise which make a Mixture of the Subject of the Play, with the Poets or Comedians Interest; and this was indeed the most ordinary

dinary

dinary one with *Plautus*, as appears in his *Captives,* his *Pænulus,* and his *Menechmes.*

Now thefe three forts of *Prologues* were particular to *Comedy*; for we meet with none fuch among the Tragick Poets; neither do I think, that if they had us'd them, that *Ariftotle* would have reckon'd thefe fort of *Prologues* amongft the Parts of Quantity of a Tragedy; for they are things by themfelves which may be omitted, without injuring the Poem, or otherwife leffening its true Proportion. 'Tis for this reafon that the Learned *Voffius* fays, *That the Prologues of Comedy and Tragedy are very different, becaufe in Comedy the Prologue is as it were alien to the Subject; but in Tragedy it is incorporated with it, and makes a part of it.* And yet I muft fay, That I think he is miftaken in both; for fometimes in Comedy the *Prologue* is fix'd to the Body of the Poem, as in the *Ciftellaria* of *Plautus,* where it contains three Scenes: and, on the other fide, the Tragedian *Prologues* are not always fo twifted with the Subject, as to make a part of it.

The firft and moft ordinary *Prologues* of the *Greek* Tragedies were made by one of the Chief Actors, who came and explain'd to the Spectators all that had paffed in the Story before the opening of the Stage. We have of this fort divers in *Euripides,* where the Actor having done this, ends with fome Verfes which give a beginning to the Action of the Poem.

But it cannot be faid, that thefe *Prologues* make a part of the *Tragedy*; firft, becaufe they are Difcourfes made to the Spectators, and by confequent, faulty, by mingling the Reprefentation with the Theatral Action: Neither are they neceffary, becaufe thofe things which precede the beginning of the

Play,

Play, ought to be dexterously told in the Play, in different parts of it; and this *Æschylus* and *Sophocles* always obferve. So that it is moft certain, that thefe *Prologues*, which contain the Argument of the Play, are ufelefs, defective, and may be eafily feparated from it. And therefore we do not fee that Monfieur *Corneille*, whom I always cite as a great Mafter for the Stage, has ever us'd fo ill an Artifice; and I cannot but condemn thofe *French* and *Italians* who have had recourfe to it.

Euripides makes another fort of *Prologue*, more faulty and defective ftill; to wit, when he employs fome of the Gods to explain, by his Omnifcience, not onely all that was pafs'd, but things to come in the Play, even to the *Cataftrophe*; by which means all the Events were foreftall'd, than which there could not be a greater Fault, fince it deftroys all that Expectation and Sufpenfion which makes the Surprife and Novelty of the Play. Now I do not think that *Ariftotle* means this fort of *Prologue* neither, when he fays 'tis a Quantitative part of the *Dramma*.

The two forts of *Prologue* which remain for us to confider, feem to agree better with *Ariftotle's* Definition: *The* Prologue, fays he, *is that part of the* Tragedy *which precedes the arrival of the* Chorus *upon the Stage:* By which he feems rather to teach us the Place of the *Prologue*, than its Nature: And according to this Definition, thofe *Tragedies* that begin with the *Chorus*, have no *Prologue*: Such are the *Rhæfas*, the *Perfians*, and the *Suppliants* of *Euripides*; and by confequent, according to this Doctrine, they have not their due Proportion, being depriv'd of their firft Quantitative part: (And by the by, we may by this difcover the Miftakes of thofe

who

who have given us Arguments and Preambles upon thefe Greek Tragedies) for they fay at the begin-ning of thefe three Plays which I now mention'd, *That the Chorus makes the Prologue*; for fince the Prologue, according to *Ariftotle*, ought to contain all that is faid before the *Chorus* comes on; 'tis im-poffible for the *Chorus* to make the Prologue; or if the *Chorus* could make the Prologue, then *Ariftotles* definition is good for nothing: But now let us come to thefe two laft forts of Prologues.

One of them did ufe to contain in three or four Scenes made before the coming on of the *Chorus*, fome things which concern'd the Theatral Action, but which in truth were not neceffary parts of the Poem. We have two Examples of this in the *Phœ-nicians*, and in the *Medæa* of *Euripides*. In the firft *Antigone* appears upon the Walls of *Thebes*, with her Governour, who fhews her the Army of the be-fieging Princes, with fome Difcourfes about the Commanders of it, and this in fome fort does regard the *Dramma*, but does not in rigour make a part of it; and the Author of the Argument fays exprefly, that all that *Antigonus* does upon the Walls of the Town, is abfolutely out of the Theatral Action.

In the other Tragedy *Medæa*'s Children appear with their Governour, to whom *Medæa*'s Nurfe re-commends them, expreffing fome fear for them in the fury and rage of *Medæa* againft *Jafon* their Fa-ther; and this at firft feems to belong to the Sub-ject, but yet it makes no part of the *Dramma*; for if you begin the Play juft after the firft *Chorus*, you will not mifs any thing in it; and therefore in both thefe Plays the Prologues are not infeparable from the body of the *Dramma*; and that which may ftill

[O] contri-

contribute to convince us of this is, that in thefe Prologues the Poets often put things which were incon-
fiftent with the Rules of the Stage; as in the *Agamemnon* of *Æfchylus*, where one of the Guard that
fpeaks the Prologue feems to fee things which could
not come to pafs in the time prefcrib'd by the Drammatick Poem ; and if this Prologue were to be fuppos'd part of the Play, it would make it defective,
and againft all the Rules.

The other fort of *Prologue* plac'd before the *Chorus*, contain'd not only fuch things as regarded the
Poem, but fuch alfo as were proper, and incorporated with its Subject, making a true part of it; as in
the *Sphigenia* in *Aulide*, where the difquiet of *Agamemnon*, and the Narration he makes to an old Man,
whom he fends his Letters by, to his Wife, do certainly begin the Play, and make an infeparable part
of the Subject; and if the definition that *Ariftotle*
gives of Prologues can be reduc'd to any rational
meaning, it muft be to this fort of Prologue ; but
yet I cannot underftand neither why this muft be
call'd a Prologue fooner than any other part of the
Play; 'tis properly an *Epifode*, and its being before
or after the *Chorus* changes nothing in its nature, but
only alters its place ; and this, in my Judgment, is
not enough to make a juft and true diftinction of the
parts of a *Dramma*, who ought to have more Effential differences between each other. My Conclufion
then is, that that which is properly Prologue, cannot
be reckon'd a part of the Play ; and that which is a
part of the Play can no more be nam'd a Prologue,
than the other *Epifodes* that compofe the Play.

If in oppofition to this any one fhall fay, that in
the beginning of all the Tragedys of *Sophocles* and
Æfchylus,

Æfchylus, we meet with the fame word that is in
Euripides (and which fignifies to fpeak a Prologue)
though neither of thefe Poets defign'd a Prologue,
except *Sophocles* in his *Electra*, and *Æfchylus* in his
Agamemnon) I fay, that is not fo much to be minded,
becaufe the words fignifie likewife to *fpeak firft*, and
are fo tranflated in the Latine Verfion; and this may
ferve to avoid a miftake upon this Subject.

As for the *Chorus*, of which *Ariftotle* makes the
fecond part of Tragedy, it muft be confider'd in
two different ftates; the firft is, when the *Chorus*
fpeaks with the other Actors in an *Epifode*, or the
continuation of an Act, for then the *Chorus* is perfectly an Actor concern'd, and working in the Intrigues of the Stage, according to the Doctrine of
Ariftotle and *Horace*; and in this fenfe the *Chorus*
can in no wife be counted a diftinct part of the
Play.

The other ftate in which we are to confider the
Chorus is, when it fings to mark the Intervals of the
Acts, and therefore is defin'd by *Voffius* a part of the
Fable after an Act, or between two Acts.   Now I
will not deny but *Chorus*'s may have been true parts
of Tragedy, as long as they fung things concerning
the true Subject of the Poem upon the *Theatre*; but
they were not neceffary parts, fince they have been
fo eafily omitted, no more than our Mufick that plays
between the Acts can be faid to be an Effential part
of our Plays.

Chorus pars fabulæ poft actum vel inter actum & actum. Voff. l. 2. c. 5. Inft. Poet.

Ariftotles Exodus, or laft part of Tragedy, is not,
in my Opinion, any whit better diftinguifh'd; for if
the *Exodus* contains all that is faid after the *Chorus*
gives over, it is no more than our fifth Act; and
therefore *Voffius* would have the *Cataftrophe* and the

L. 2. cap. 5. Inft. Poet.

[O 2]   *Exodus*

Exodus to be the fame thing; but in that he does not agree with *Ariftotle*, for according to him the *Cataftrophe* often begins towards the end of the fourth Act, and fometimes it does not begin till towards the middle of the fifth Act, fo that then you would be ob-lig'd to cut off from the *Exodus* all that fhould be faid after the *Chorus* gives over, or elfe according to *Voffius* it would be cut in two by a *Chorus*; both which are againft *Ariftotle*'s Doctrine. But befides, what will become of this *Exodus* in thofe Tragedys that end with a *Chorus*, as all *Euripides*'s, and the beft of *Sophocles* and *Æfchylus*'s do ; for the laft Verfes of their Tragedys were according to the moft receiv'd Opinion fung by the *Chorus*, and fo there could be no *Exodus* in thofe Plays, who by confequence, accord-ing to *Ariftotle*, muft want that part of quantity. It will not be amifs to obferve here by the by, that *Exodus*, and *Exodion* are not the fame things ; for the *Exodus* is the laft part of the Play, and the *Exo-dion* was a piece of *Buffoonery*, as the *Mimes* and *Embolimes* were, and were acted when the Play was done, by thofe they called *Exodiarii*, which may prevent a miftake, apt elfe to be made in reading the Antients.

From all this that we have faid, it appears that either *Ariftotle* did not explain himfelf well in his Definitions, or that thofe Plays which we have of the Greek Poets, did not ferve him for the Rules of his Poeticks; fo that of thofe four parts of quantity of Tragedy, of which *Ariftotle* makes mention, we have but one left, which alone makes up our whole Tragedy, and that is the *Epifode*; for fince the *Epi-fode* contain'd all that was between the Antient *Cho-rus*'s, and that our mufick with which we begin and

end

end our plays is to us in the place of the Ancient *Chorus's,*it is manifeft,that five*Epifodes* make our five *Acts* ; but becaufe we divide our *Acts* into *Scenes,* and that we feparate our Acts by a confiderable diftance of time, neceffary to the Theatral Action, I therefore think that a Drammatick Poem can be properly faid to have but two parts of quantity, to wit, *Five Acts fubdivided into Scenes, without any limited number ;* and the *four Intervals* of thofe Acts. If any one elfe has more light to fhew us other parts, I fhall eafily fubfcribe to his Opinion.

Chapter the Second.

Of Epifodes *according to the Doctrine of* Ariftotle.

TO underftand this matter well, we muft look back to fome things that have been faid already,and know thatTragedy &Comedy begun thus.

Hygin. l. 2.
Aftronom. in Actoph. Ex Eratoftene.
*Virg.Georg.*2.

Bacchus having found out the Art of cultivating the Vine, and making Wine, taught it *Icarius,* who then was Mafter of a little Territory in *Attica,* to which he gave his name. *Icarius* having prefently put his Skill to tryal, met with a Goat in the Vintage time, that was eating his Grapes, therefore looking upon him as an Enemy to *Bacchus,* facrificed him to him ; and having call'd his neighbours to this Sacrifice, they all together fell a dancing and finging fomething in the honour of *Bacchus,* whom they had thus reveng'd of his Foe. This appear'd to them both fo religious, and fo pleafant, that they continu'd it every year at the fame time,and call'd it *Tragœdia,* that is, a Vintage-fong.

*Caffiod. li.*4.
Var.Varr.l. 1.
*de vit. pop. Rom. Plutar. Sympofion.*19.
qu. 1.

The

The *Athenians* having in procefs of time tranf-
ferr'd this Ceremony to their Town; their beft Poets
began to be concern'd in the Hymn to *Bacchus*, and
to ftrive with one another for the honour of excel-
ling in it. They brought in befides great *Chorus*'s of
Mufick and Dances, with many turnings and wind-
ings, and fo transferr'd it from the Temples to the
Theatres, without any irreverence; neverthelefs, becaufe thofe very Theaters were dedicated to *Bacchus*,
and the Victim that was facrificed to him, was a
Goat, as deftructor of the Vine; from whence this
Hymn was called *Tragedy*, as who fhould fay, the
Goat-Song, and fo much of it as remain d among the
Country people in Villages, was called *Comedy*, as
who fhould fay a *Country-Song* : All this appears
clearly from many famous Authors of Antiquity.

Athen. l. 2.
Caffiodor. l. 1.
Plut. Sympof.
l. 1. q. 1. Suidas.
Initium Tra-
gædiæ & Co-
medi e à rebus
Divinis Incenfis Altaribus, & admoto hirco id genus carminis quod facer Chorus libero patri red-
debat Tragedia dicebatur. Donat. in Terentium.

Thus were diftinguifh'd thefe two Poems, though
they had the fame beginning in the fame Country
of *Icaria*, and by the fame adventure, according to
Athenæus, of whofe Opinion are *Donatus Maximus*
of *Tyr*, and *Euftathius*.

Now it happening that by little and little the Subjects that the Poets took to praife *Bacchus*, being ex-
haufted, they were forc'd to add little Stories or
Fables, which they handled merrily at firft, in honour of *Bacchus*. To confirm this, *Ariftotle* writes,
that *from little Fables made with mirth and fooling,*
Tragedy rofe by degrees to that perfection it acquir'd in
Sophocles *time.* Some are of Opinion that *Epigenes*
the *Sycionian* was the Author of Tragedy, whether
it were that he firft brought the Song from the Vintage

tage to the Town, or that he firſt inſtituted the Diſpute between the Poets, in which the Conquerour
receiv'd for reward the *Goat* that was ſacrific'd to
Bacchus, after a formal Proceſſion; the Ceremony of
which deſcrib'd by *Plutarch,* was ſimple enough at
firſt, though much alter'd in his time : However,
Tragedy remain'd a great while in the ſame ſtate ;
for between this *Epigenes* and *Theſpis,* who firſt
added an Act to this Hymn, there are reckon'd four-
teen famous Tragick Poets, almoſt all Succeſſors to
one another; and 'tis of the Tragedies of that time
that *Diogenes Laertius* is to be underſtood, when he
writes in the Life of *Plato,* that the *Chorus formerly
acted the whole Tragedy.* Theſe words at firſt did extremely puzzle me, becauſe the neglect of *Chorus's*
in our days, hinder'd me from penetrating the true
ſenſe of the Author. I conſider'd Tragedy as I found
it in *Sophocles,* and there I could not ſee any conformity with *Laertius's* mind ; and all I could then
imagine in order to make ſomething of it was, that
they that made the *Chorus* were likewiſe the Hiſtrions and Actors of the Tragedy : But beſides that
thereby I made no diſtinction between the Hiſtrions who were Actors, and the *Thymelicks,* who
were Muſicians, againſt all truth of Antiquity. I
found the difficulty ſtill grow upon me, when I read
in *Athenæus, That antiently all ſort of Tragedy was
compos'd only of the Chorus, and had no Hiſtrions or
Actors at all :* For theſe laſt words did entirely deſtroy all my firſt thought, neither could I any ways
relieve my ſelf by any of the Interpreters of theſe
two Authors, though ſo many Learned men have
commented them, without ſaying one word of this ;
therefore I began to go back to the firſt Original of
things,

things, and confidering that Tragedy at firſt was nothing but an Hymn of the Pagan Religion, danc'd and ſung by *Chorus*'s of Muſick, I eaſily found the ſolution of all my difficulties; for 'tis moſt certain, that in that time, and for almoſt ſix hundred years after Tragedy was repreſented only by the *Chorus*, as *Laertius* has it, and had no Actors, as *Athenæus* truly affirms.

At laſt *Theſpis* bethought himſelf of putting in an Actor, who ſhould recite without ſinging, that the *Chorus* might take breath, and reſt themſelves ; not that I think that Actor ſpoke alone, but he made a Dialogue with the *Coryphæus*, or ſome other perſon of the *Chorus*, who anſwer'd him ſomething to the purpoſe, to give him Subject to continue his Diſcourſe, as we may yet ſee in ſome fragments of *Epicharmus*, who liv'd in that time. We muſt not think neverthelefs, that *Theſpis* was the Inventor of Tragedy, as *Horace* ſeems to believe, but only that he introduc'd the firſt Actor without ſinging. And *Plato* tells us, that Tragedy was in great credit in *Athens* long before *Theſpis*'s time. And as for what is ſaid alſo of him, *That he carryed his Actors about in a Cart, from whence they ſpoke many Railleries and witty Jeſts againſt paſſengers*, that muſt not be underſtood of ſerious Tragedy, for which there were already publick Theaters, but of *Satyrical Tragedy*, in which they repreſented the Dances, and groſſeſt poſtures of *Satyrs* and *Silenes*, who were ſuppos'd to have accompany'd *Bacchus* in his Voyages, (for this Satyrical Tragedy was at firſt without Actors, as well as the ſerious one, according to *Athenæus*) and came at laſt to that perfection, that it was one of the four Poems which made the *Tetralogy* of *Dramma*'s, in which

which the Poets of *Athens* difputed the Prize at their four great Holidays.

Thefpis likewife added to his Jefts and Railleries the dawbing of his Actors with Lees of Wine, as *Horace* has it; or with Cerufe and Vermillion, as *Suidas* reports: And this was done to imitate fo much the better the Satyrs, who were always repre- fented with red Faces, as *Virgil* paints *Silenus's*, dawb'd with the Juyce of Elder berries and Mulber ries.

Quæ canerent agerentque per- uncti fæcibus ora. Horat. de art. Poet. Virgil in Silen. Sanguineis frontem moris & tempora pingit.

At laft Tragedy having receiv'd a total alteration, by Recitals in the Intervals of the Mufick, it acquir'd fhortly after its utmoft Perfection; for *Æfchylus*, who liv'd fifty years, or thereabouts, after *Thefpis*, added one Actor more, and fo made up two Actors: and indeed we never fee more than two, in any Scene of his, talking together, except it be for a word or two put in by a third, and that too very feldom, whatever *Scaliger* fays to the contrary; he invented likewife a convenient Drefs for his Actors with Co- thurnes, or High Shoes to make them appear tall like *Heroes*. *Sophocles* who was born Ten or Twelve years after the Death of *Æfchylus*, encreas'd the number of the Chief Actors to Three, and caus'd the Scenes to be painted with Decorations fitting for his Subiect. So that in lefs than Fourfcore years Tragedy attain'd to its higheft perfection, with all the Glory of which it was capable.

Diogen.in Plat. & Philoft. in Sophift. Et de vit. Apollon. l. 6. c.6.

As for Comedy, *Donatus* feems to think it was invented by Shepherds and Country People, who us'd to dance about the Altars of *Apollo* firnamed *Nomian*, and fing at the fame time fome Hymns in honour of him; but I had rather believe *Athenæus*, who makes it take its rife with Tragedy, and they

[P] were

were both confecrated to *Bacchus*, and not to *Apollo*: Except *Donatus* would judge of all Theatral Actions by the *Apollinary* Games, which indeed were *Scenick*, and celebrated in the Honour of *Apollo*.

I fay then, That Comedy and Tragedy were born together ; and accordingly we find in *Clemens Alexandrinus*, that the Invention of Comedy was attributed to one *Sifarion* of *Icaria* ; it may be, becaufe he was the firft that compos'd the Hymns of *Bacchus*, after the Sacrifice of the Goat by *Icarius*. And this may fuffice to appeafe the Quarrels of the Learned upon the Origine of Comedy , fince they are not agreed neither in Times, Places, nor Perfons.

Clem. Alexand.
Stromat. lib. I.
Σιοαείων ὁ
Ἰκάρευς.

But Comedy had not the fame progrefs with Tragedy, it being long detain'd in Confufion and Diforder : Nay, even in *Ariftophanes*'s time, which was after *Sophocles* and *Euripides*, it was full of fatyrical Reflections and fcandalous Slanders.   It will be hard for us to mark the degrees of its progrefs, from the time that it was a Rural Hymn, to that of its perfection upon the Stage ; becaufe, as *Ariftotle* fays, *it being not fo noble as Tragedy, there has been lefs care to make Obfervations upon it ; and the Magiftrates were a great while before they concern'd themfelves in giving the* Chorufes, *but us'd to leave them to the Difcretion of thofe who made the* Comedy.   Neverthelefs, if I may venture to bring to light things buried in fo long an Obfcurity, I think that it begun to have Actors about the fame time as Tragedy did, that is, under *Epicharmus* the *Sicilian*, the Contemporary of *Thefpis* ; and before that time I have not obferv'd any Speakers.   And 'tis from this, that the *Sicilians* do maintain, That Comedy was invented at *Syracufa*, becaufe *Epicharmus* was that Countryman ;

tryman : not that they can pretend that there was
no Comedy before him, (for we have yet the Fragments of *Alcæa*, a Comedy two hundred years before his time) but becaufe he firft introduc'd an
Actor with the *Chorus*. We may fay as much of
Sannyrion, who was the firft that added Masks and
Buffoons, according to *Athenæus* ; and the fame of
Cratinus, who fetled three Actors, and made the
whole Compofition regular ; the fame of *Ariftophanes*, who gave Comedy a further perfection ; and fo
of all thofe whom *Diomedes* calls the firft Comick
Poets, though they came a great while after Comedy was invented.

Now we are to take notice, that the Recital of
that Actor or Player introduc'd by *Thefpis* in Tragedy, and the number of which was fince encreas'd
by other Poets, receiv'd the name of *Epifode*, as who
fhould fay, an additional Difcourfe, thrown as it
were acrofs another ; therefore *Suidas* fays exprefly,
that *Epifode* fignifies a thing which is befides the
Subject of another, and to which neverthelefs it is
joyn'd. So when *Æfchylus* and others did infert into their Tragedies Actors that recited a Story which
was nothing to the Praifes of *Bacchus*, the Priefts
of *Bacchus* began to complain of that neglect, and
faid, that in thofe *Epifodes* there was nothing that
was proper either to the Actions or Myfteries of
their God ; which gave occafion to that *Greek* Proverb, ʼΟυδὲν προς τον Διονυσιον, *Nothing to Bacchus.*
And this Explication of the Proverb, which is according to all the Ancients, feems moft reafonable :
For to think, as fome do, that in Drammatick Poetry they call'd *Epifodes* all the Defcriptions, Narrations, and pathetick Difcourfes, as things not belong-

[P 2]   ing

ing to the Subject, seems very absurd, since without those things the *Episodes* themselves could not be.

These Complaints of *Bacchus*'s Priests did not at all stop the Progress of Tragedy, which by little and little went its Course, and at last grew to such a distance from its Originals, as that the *Episodes* became the Tragedy it self. Therefore now all the Doctrine and Precepts of *Aristotle* about the *Episodes*, how to make them successfully, is no more than the Art how to make a *Drammatick Poem* ; for we have neither *Prologue, Chorus,* nor *Exode* to make the Parts of our Tragedy : so that having none but the *Episode* left, that alone must be called the *Dramma* ; and when we read in *Athenæus, That* Alexander, *at the last Feast he made before his death, recited an* Episode *of the* Andromeda *of* Euripides, we must not understand it as *Natalis Comes* does in his Marginal Note, calling it *a Piece added to make Mirth* ; but rather in the sense of *Aristotle*, that it was some part of that Tragedy, either a fine Description, or some pathetick Expression in some Act of the Play.

It being then agreed, that the *Episodes* contain all that is between the *Choruses*, that is to say, Five Acts, distinguish'd by five Concerts of Musick, *Aristotle* gives three principal Instructions in composing of these *Episodes*.

The first is, *That having chosen your Story, and resolv'd how much of it you will bring upon the Stage, you must then cast your* Episodes, that is, the Descriptions, Discourses, Passions, and other things that are to entertain the Stage. And this is one of the greatest Dexterities of the Poet.

The second is, *That the* Episodes *be proper and na-*

tural

tural to the Story or Fable ; that is to fay, drawn from the very Eſſence of the Subject, and ſo fit, as to ſeem to jump naturally, and of themſelves, with the whole Concourſe of other Events.   And 'tis out of the ſecret Knowledge Men have of this Precept, that we have often ſeen them blame upon the Stage Narrations that were not neceſſary, ſuperfluous and vain Deſcriptions, Complaints, and other Paſſions, introduc'd out of order, and without which the *Dramma* might not onely have been, but have been better.

The third Rule is, *That the* Epiſodes *ought not to be too long.*   And that is it which even the Common people every day condemn upon our Stages ; for the fineſt Diſcourſes, and the moſt neceſſary ones, have a Meaſure, after which they become tedious.

To theſe three Precepts of *Ariſtotle*, I add two Obſervations of my own; That the Drammatick Poet muſt have a care in theſe *Epiſodes* not to enter too much and too ſtrongly into the particular of things; but he muſt onely touch the beautiful places of his Subject, by ſome ſtrong Thoughts ; becauſe elſe there will appear an Affectation, and be too un-like a Natural Diſcourſe, which in all things he is to imitate.

The other Obſervation is, That often the Buſineſs of the Stage does not ſuffer that the Actors ſhould make long Diſcourſes, not even of a thing neceſſa-ry ; as if they were to go in haſte to ſuccour ſome afflicted Perſon, or to avoid their Enemies.   I ſhould therefore adviſe the Poet, in ſuch occaſions, to uſe ſome other Means to inſtruct the Spectators of that which they are not to be ignorant of, or to do it at leaſt in very few Words, ſo as to keep the Rules of
                                                    Probability.

Probability. One great flight in thefe fudden Occafions, is to explain fome Circumftance of the Story, which may ferve for the underftanding of the
neareft Events, and fo referve to ones felf the Liberty of explaining the reft at leifure.

As for the other general Inftructions that *Ariftotle*
gives about the *Epifodes*, they are to be found in his
Interpreters ; but the Poet muft ftill remember, that
they are to be applied to the Acts and Difpofition
of Tragedy, as it is now treated amongft us ; it
being moft certain, that Drammatick Poems which
comprehend the Events of two Stories in the unity
of one Theatral Action, were never called by the
Ancients *Epifodick Fables* ; becaufe thofe *Drammas*
which contain but one Story, are as much Epifodick
as the others ; that is, they have as many Acts or
Recitals between the *Chorufes*, as we have already
fufficiently explain'd.

Chapter the Third.

Of the Chorufes *of the Ancients.*

WE have faid already, That *Tragedy* in its firft
Original was nothing but a Sacred Hymn
fung and danced to the Honour of *Bacchus* ; and that
by little and little the *Epifodes*, which we call *Acts*,
were added between each *Chorus*. And we know likewife, that now adays *Tragedy* has quite loft its *Chorufes*,
as *Comedy* had loft his, even before the Age of *Plautus*.   So that it may feem to fome, that a Difcourfe
of *Chorufes* may be now an unneceffary thing for the
Practice

Practice of our Stage. But befides that they may one day be re-eſtabliſh'd upon our Theatres, when we are well inform'd what they were amongſt the Ancients, I think it very neceſſary for me to explain here my Thoughts about them , and which will ſcarce be found any where elſe.

To take the *Chorus* not as it was at firſt, when alone it made the whole Tragedy; but as it was in the time of *Sophocles* and *Euripides*, that is to ſay, in its perfection among the *Grecians*, I think we may define the *Chorus* thus.

The Chorus *is a Troop of Actors, repreſenting the Aſſembly or Body of thoſe Perſons who either were preſent, or probably might be ſo, upon that Place or Scene where the Action is ſuppos'd to be tranſacted.*

Theſe Words are of importance, and we are not to proceed without well weighing of them. Thus we ſee, that in the *Hecuba* of *Euripides*, the *Chorus* is of *Trojan* Women who were Slaves in the Camp, it being moſt probable that they were at the Tents of *Hecuba*, who was under the ſame Captivity with them. And in the *Cyclops* the *Chorus* is of *Satyrs*, and that very ingeniouſly contriv'd ; for no other ſort of Men cou'd venture to ſtay before the Den of cruel *Polyphemus*. In the *Antigone* of *Sophocles* the *Chorus* is of the Old Men of *Thebes*, becauſe being ſent for by *Creon* to Council, none could more reaſonably be thought to be before his Palace. In the *Ajax* the *Chorus* is of Seamen of *Salamis*, who come very naturally before the Tent of their Prince, to endeavour to do him ſome Service, upon the noiſe of his being furious and mad. In the *Prometheus* of *Æſchylus* the Nymphs of the Ocean make the *Chorus*, becauſe in probability hardly any other

Perſons

Perfons could be fuppos'd near that unfortunate Man, who was faftned to a Rock far from the commerce of the reft of Mankind ; and alfo in the Seven before *Thebes* , the Young Women of the Town make the **Chorus**, becaufe it was more reafonable to affemble them before the Palace, and make them ftay there full of fears and apprehenfions, lamenting the Calamity of the War, than to have plac'd Men there, who are fuppos'd neceffary to the defence of their Countrey. And from this we may judge likewife with what Induftry and Ingenuity *Ariftophanes*, in his Play againft *Socrates* , makes a *Chorus* of Clouds, becaufe he fuppofes *Socrates* to invoke them to appear at his *Sophifms*; as in another place he has made a *Chorus* of Birds, which two *Athenians* come and entertain in a place full of Trees, and out of the way, talking to them about building a Town in the Air. I make no Citations here out of thofe Trage-dies which go under the name of *Seneca* , becaufe they are very ill Models to imitate ; and particularly, the *Chorufes* are very faulty : for fometimes they fee all that's done upon the Scene, hear all that's faid, and fpeak very properly to all ; and at other times one would think they were blind, deaf, and dumb. In many of thofe *Drammas* one can hardly tell who they reprefent, how they were drefs'd, nor what Reafon brings them upon the Stage, nor why they are of one Sex, more than of another. Indeed the Verfes are fine, full of Thoughts, and overload-ed with Conceit ; but may in moft places be very well fpar'd, without fpoiling any thing, either in the Sence, or in the Reprefentation of the Poem. Be-fides, the *Thebaida* has none at all, whether it be loft by the fault of the Copyifts and our Printers,

which

which I can hardly believe, becaufe there would at leaft have remain d fome fragments, confidering that they were pieces inferted into the very body of the Poem in many places ; fo that I am apt to believe that the Author made none at all for that Play ; and this with fome other conjectures, has given me occafion to doubt of the truth of what *Scaliger* affirms fo pofitively ; to wit, that Tragedy never was without *Chorus's* ; for I incline to think that in the time of the debauch'd and loofe Emperours, where *Mimes*, *Embolimes*, and *Buffoons* came in for Interludes in Tragedy, as well as in Comedy, the *Chorus* ceas'd by little and little to be a part of the *Drammatick Poem*, and became only a Troup of Muficians and Dancers, to mark the Intervals of the Acts; but thofe four Greek Poets,whofe works we have, have been much more exact in their *Chorus's* than the Author of *Seneca's* Tragedys, as underftanding a great deal better than he, the Art of compofing fuch *Poems ;* and out of them likewife it is that we learn that the *Chorus* might be compos'd of all forts of perfons, without diftinction either of Age or Sex,nay of living creatures. or infenfible things, as *Ariftophanes* has done, from which we may likewife obferve, that they who thought the *Chorus* reprefented the people were fomething out; for we fee that in his *Knights* the people of *Athens* is acting, fpeaking and judging the conteft between *Cleo* and *Agoracritus*, and that the *Chorus* is of *Athenian* Knights,perfectly diftinguifh'd from thofe who reprefent the people.

And when *Ariftotle* and *Scaliger* after him name the *Chorus* a *kind of idle Client, which gives but fmall affiftance to thofe he pretends to help.* It muft be underftood only in comparifon of the other Actors,

[Q]   who

who are generally more bufie ; as alfo becaufe the *Chorus* never forfakes the place of the Scene ; whereas the other Actors often perform great things off of the Stage ; but yet the Greek Poets have never chofen for their *Chorus* either idle people (though they might be eafily fuppos'd prefent) or thofe who had no concern in the bufinefs in hand, becaufe all that they could have faid or done would have been weak and languifhing, of fmall, or no effect upon the Spectators, who do not willingly hear unconcern'd perfons in a Tragedy. Befides, according to the Art of Poetry, both of *Ariftotle* and *Horace*, the *Chorus*, befides its finging, ought to act a part of fome concern, and advance and forward the Affairs of the Stage, as other Actors do ; and therefore it is obfervable, that when the Subject did naturally furnifh the Poet with a *Chorus*, he never borrowed it any where elfe ; as in the *Rhæfus* of *Euripides*, where the Scene is before the Tents of the Generals of the *Trojan* Army, and all things coming to pafs in the night. The Guard makes the *Chorus*, becaufe it would have been againft probabilty that any other perfons fhould have been affembled there at that time. Nay, if the Principal Actors themfelves were enough in number, they made the *Chorus* of them, as in the *Suppliants* of *Euripides*, where the feven Princes of *Argos*, that implore *Thefeus*'s help to bury the dead bodies of their Husbands before *Thebes*, make the *Chorus* themfelves.

But if they were put to invent a *Chorus*, they always did it conformably to the nature of their Subject, and to the Rules of probability. This *Ariftophanes* has ingenioufly enough obferv'd in Comedy, as where he makes a *Chorus* of Frogs to fing while *Bacchus*

chus paffing the *Stix in Carons* Bark ; and another of Wafps in the houfe of *Philocleon*, whofe Son would hinder him from going abroad ; for though thofe are very ridiculous Imaginations, yet they are Comical; well enough invented in mirth, and are not againft the Rules of his Art.

From hence we may likewife judg why the *Chorus* was at laft left out in new Comedy, and of this I think no body hitherto has given a true reafon. *Horace* thinks that the malignity and fatyrical humour of the Poets was the caufe of it ; for they made the *Chorus*'s abufe people fo feverely, that the Magiftrates forbid them at laft to ufe any at all ; but I think, that if the Rules of probability had not likewife feconded this prohibition, the Poets would have preferv'd their *Chorus* ftill, with conformity to their Subject, and that without too much Satyr ; therefore I imagine the thing came to pafs thus.

Comedy took its model and conftitution from Tragedy ; and when the downright abufing of living perfons was prohibited, they generally invented feigned Subjects, which they govern'd according to the Rules of Tragedy ; but as they were neceffitated to draw Pictures of the life of the Vulgar, and were confin'd by confequent to mean Events, they generally chofe the place of their Scene in fome Streets before the houfes of thofe whom they fuppos'd concern'd in the Story ; and it was not very probable that there fhould be a Troup of people in fuch a place managing an Intrigue of inconfiderable perfons from morning to night. Comedy loft of its felf infenfibly the *Chorus*, which it could not preferve with any probability.

Comedy therefore having loft its *Chorus* long be-fore Tragedy, that which was called new Comedy receiv'd Dances, Mufick, and Buffoons, in the room of the *Chorus*, as more proper for the genius of Co-mical Poetry.

Since therefore we are now fully inform'd what the *Chorus* was, let us fee how it acted upon the Stage.

At firft it was plac'd a little lower than the Theatre, and was feated by it felf, from whence it rofe to fing and dance; afterwards it was plac'd up on the Stage it felf, and at laft it came upon the very Scene, that is, behind the Hangings or Decoration, as may be feen in *Scaliger, Caftelvetro,* and other Au-thors, with many other things which I forbear to repeat here.

But we may obferve befides, thar the *Chorus* did not ordinarily appear upon the Stage, till after the *Prologue,* that is, as we have explain'd it, till after one or many Scenes, which open'd the Play, and were preparatives to the better underftanding of the piece, not being reckon'd among the Acts or Epi-fods. This too is to be underftood only in ftrictnefs; for fometimes there was no *Prologue,* and all that pafs'd before the coming on of the *Chorus* was the firft Act, and to be reckon'd of the body of the Trage-dy, as in the *Ajax* of *Sophocles*; at other times the *Chorus* its felf opened the Stage, as in the *Rhæfus* of *Furipides,* becaufe being compos'd of the Guards, which had watch'd all night, 'twas not probable any fhould be there before them.

We muft obferve befides, that when the *Chorus* once came on in regularity, they were not fuppos'd to go off till the end of the Play ; and this appears

by

by all the Greek Tragedys, where the *Chorus* often
shews the Pallace or Houfe to ftrangers, complains,
or feems aftonifhed at fudden noifes made within; by
all which it may be concluded, it ftayed all along upon the Stage. 'Tis true, that fometimes we may
obferve it to come in and out, but that is extraordinarily, and by fome remarkable Artifice of the Poet,
who has a mind that fome Action or other fhould be
perform'd upon the Stage without witnefs: As when
Sophocles has a mind that *Ajax* fhould kill himfelf
upon the Stage, he fends out the *Chorus* under pretext of affifting *Tecmeffa,* who is endeavouring to find
out *Ajax,* to prevent the Effects of his fury (he having juft left her with a Sword in his hand.)

Another reafon the Poets have of fending out the
Chorus is, when 'tis probable that they who reprefent the *Chorus* have done an action which could not
naturally have been perform'd upon the Stage: So in
the *Oratrices,* or pleading Women of *Ariftophanes,*
the Women which compofe the *Chorus,* go out at
the end of the firft Act in Mens difguife, to go to the
Council to have it there decreed, that the Government of *Athens* fhall be put into their hands; and at
the end of the fecond Act, they come back upon the
Scene to bring their Husbands cloths which they had
ftolen in the night : Where by the by we may take
notice of the Ignorance of fome of our Pedants in
their Latine Tragedys, when at the end of each Act
they bring on a fingle Actor to reprefent the *Chorus,*
and declaim fome fcurvy Verfes of Morality, bringing him on, and driving him off as they pleafe, thinking thereby to fulfil *Ariftotles* Rules, and perfectly
imitate the Antients; whereas their *Chorus* was compos'd of many perfons, who fung and danced with
great

great Art, and were always brought upon the Stage for fome good reafon; nor are we to imagine, as fome have done, that the *Chorus* fung and danc'd always; for that was only when there was need to mark the Intervals of the Acts. In other places the *Chorus* was confidered as any other Actor, and the *Corypheus,* or chief of them us'd to hold Difcourfe for all the reft; or elfe being divided in two (as fometimes it was half on one fide of the Stage, and half on the other) the Chiefs of each fide difcours'd together of the Affairs of the Stage, as is to be feen in the *Agamemnon* of *Æfchylus* upon the death of that King.

We fee likewife fometimes that the *Chorus* after fome Difcourfes falls a finging, or is commanded to do it, by which it appears, it did not fing before ; The Example is precife in the feven before *Thebes,* where Prince *Eteocles,* after having difcourfed with the *Chorus* a good while, bids him at laft leave off talking, and fing, to know now whether they all danc'd, and whether the fame perfons danc'd that fung, and if they danc'd and played on Inftruments together, and of what fort is that great diverfity of Song we find among the Antients, all this I fay cannot contribute any thing to the compofition of a Drammatick Poem ; and therefore need not be examin'd, but in order to inftruct our Mufick, in cafe we fhould have a mind to bring the *Chorus*'s upon our Theatres.

But we muft not forget here, that the chief Actors did frequently mingle with the *Chorus,* as *Electra* in *Euripides* and *Sophocles.* Queen *Æthra,* with King *Adraftus* in the *Supplicants* of *Euripides* ; and in thefe cafes I am of Opinion, that thofe Actors were the *Coryphæi's.*

Some

Sometimes there was divers *Chorus*'s, when it was not probable that the fame perfons could be twice upon the Stage, as in *Chriftophanes*, when *Bacchus* paffes the River *Stix*, to go to the Pallace of *Pluto*, the *Chorus* is made by Frogs ; but when he is at the Gate of the Pallace, the *Chorus* is made by the Priefts, and the fraternity of his Myfteries.

Sometimes likewife the *Chorus* did not come back time enough at the end of an Act, being ingag'd fome-where elfe, and then that Act was mark'd by fome *Mime*, Mufick Dance or buffooning, taken from the Subject, as in the *Oratrices* of *Ariftophanes,* the Wo-men being all elfewhere at the end of the fourth Act, the Poet makes a farce of two old Women, and a young Girl, who fing and dance to Inftruments, in expectation of fome Man to come by, and are al-ready difputing who fhall have him to make him obey the Womens Laws.

From all thefe Obfervations it is moft apparent, that the *Chorus* is nothing but what we have defcrib'd it to be; and that we have much reafon to wonder that the Learned, who have afforded us fo many cu-riofities upon the Drammatick Poem, have not never-thelefs difcover'd any thing like this to us, though very important, to underftand antient Tragedy, and juftifie the probability of all the Rules of the Theatre.

For firft, if the Antient Greek Poets have made but few *Monologues* upon the Stage, it is becaufe it was not always eafie to find a pretext to fend out the *Chorus*, and to have it come in again ; and on the other fide, a man could not in probability be fup-pos'd to fpeak aloud of fecret things, without being heard by perfons who were fo near him.

Secondly,

Secondly, The Ancient Poets feldom make any of their Actors die upon the Stage, becaufe it was not probable, that fo many Perfons as compos'd the *Chorus*, fhould fee fuch a thing done, and not endeavour to hinder it. Thus *Æfchylus* makes *Agamemnon* be kill'd in his Palace, and his Crys and dying Groans to be heard without by the *Chorus*, which deliberates whether they fhall call the People, or break in to his Relief; when *Clytemneftra* her felf comes out, and owns the Murder, and its manner, fhewing them likewife her Husbands dead Body; which has made fome imagine, that *Agamemnon* was kill'd upon the Stage. On the other fide, *Sophocles* makes the *Chorus* leave the Stage, and brings on *Ajax* in a fedate, calm Refolution of dying; where after having fpoke a moft paffionate *Monologue*, he kills himfelf with his own Sword, from which none could hinder him, he being alone upon the Stage. And by the by, that may ferve to oppofe to thofe who fo peremptorily maintain, that the Ancients never fhed any Blood upon the Stage; for they have both done it, and avoided it, and ftill with decency and probability.

Thirdly, The *Chorus* oblig'd a Poet to a Continuity of Action; for if the Action ceas'd, it was not probable the *Chorus* fhould ftay there any longer, its Bufinefs being onely depending upon the Action. Thus we fee, that as foon as *Ajax* s Fury feem'd to be a little over, the *Chorus*, which was made up of his Subjects, who came to enquire of his Condition, has a defign to be gone; but is ftopp'd by a Meffenger, who tells them the Arrival of *Teucer*, *Ajax*'s Brother, and the danger that *Minerva* had put *Ajax* in all that day.

Moreover,

Moreover, we may here conclude, That the *Chorus* oblig'd the Poet infenfibly to a neceffity of keeping the Unity of the Scene ; for fince it was regularly to ftay from the beginning of the *Dramma* to the end, without going out, tis moft undoubted, that the Place could not change : for it would have been moft ridiculous, that Perfons who never ftirr'd, fhould have been tranfported from *Europe* to *Afia*, or from *Athens* to *Thebes*, without ever having difappear'd from the Spectators Eyes ; and therefore thofe Poets, whenever they did make the *Chorus* go off from the Stage, were very careful to make them tell where they went, that it might not be imagin'd that in carrying off the *Chorus*, they meant to tranfport the Scene too.

And not onely the Unity of Place, but likewife the Meafure of Time convenient to the Drammatick Poem, may be learn'd from the *Chorufes* : for if the Poet had comprehended in his Play a Year, a Month, or a Week, how could he make the Spectators believe, that People who had always been in their Eye, fhould have pafs'd fo long a time without either eating, drinking, or fleeping I know it will be anfwered, That there is an Illufion to be allow'd upon the Stage ; and I own it . But the Spectators muft ftill be deceiv'd, fo as not to perceive that they are fo; and though they know before-hand that they are to be deceiv'd, yet it muft not be done fo grofsly as to be perceiv'd without reflection, and at firft fight.   Therefore that which in our days has help'd thefe irregular Plays to pafs upon us, was the Intervals of the Acts, where none remaining upon the Stage, and our Mufick not being look'd upon as a Continuation of the Action, the Spectator's Imagination

[R]   gination

gination was at liberty to help the Poet, and to
ſhorten Years and Months into Moments, the Eyes
having nothing before them to contradict this Imagination.

From hence then it reſults naturally, That the
time of the *Dramma* ought to be very ſhort, as we
have ſhew'd in a Chapter on purpoſe.

To make an end of this Matter, we muſt obſerve,
That the *Choruſes* made all the Grandeur and Magnificence of the ancient Tragedies; not onely becauſe
the Stage was always full, but becauſe there was
need of making a vaſt Expence : for there was a
great number of Actors, Muſicians, Dancers, Clothes,
and often very coſtly Machins, as in the *Clouds* of
Ariſtophanes; and it was among the *Grecians* an honourable Profeſſion to inſtruct and direct the *Choruſes*, as appears by *Plato* the Philoſopher, who follow'd that Employment the beſt part of his Youth;
and *Ariſtophanes*, we find, had the direction of his
Choruſes, particularly of that of the Clouds. The
Richeſt of the Nobility often bore the Charge; as
Dio, in favour of *Plato*, who at firſt was one of the
Tragick Poets. The Magiſtrates likewiſe, to make
the time of their Adminiſtration more Solemn,
did the ſame thing. Sometimes the State it ſelf,
when they would do an extraordinary Honour to
ſome of their Tragick Poets, order'd, that the
Charges of the *Chorus* ſhould be allow'd by the Publick Treaſury: And this the *Athenians* have often
done. And I believe, that when the Great Men
forſook the Care of the Stage, it ſoon fell into Contempt, the *Choruſes* being retrench'd, by the impoſ-
ſibility that the Players and Poets were in to anſwer
ſuch an Expence; and afterwards, the Ignorance of
following

following Ages thought fit to look upon them as uſeleſs, and unfit to be put in practice. New Comedy it ſelf loſt its *Choruſes*, even in the moſt flouriſhing Drammatick Age ; but that was rather becauſe it was much harder to give *Choruſes* their due Probability in Comedy, than in Tragedy, though its *Mimes*, Muſicians, Embolaires, and ſuch like, were not of a leſs Magnificence than the *Choruſes* of Tragedy it ſelf; and thoſe who were the Maſters and Directors in them, had as much Fame when they ſucceeded, as either *Æſopus*, or *Roſcius*, or any of the Chief Actors of the Age. This may be ſeen by ſome ancient Inſcriptions of *Terence*'s Comedies, and other very conſiderable Proofs in Antiquity.

If then our Age could ſuffer the re-eſtabliſhment of the *Chorus*, as being the moſt glorious and magnificent Ornament of Tragedy, our Poets ought in the firſt place to ſtudy the Art of the Ancients in that point, how ingeniouſly they invented them, how neceſſarily they brought them on, and how agreeably they made them ſpeak and act; and then the King, or our Great Lords, ſhould be at the Expence: Which I think not the hardeſt to compaſs, conſidering the Profuſion we have ſeen in Ballets, Balls, and Tragedies in this Kingdom.

And laſtly, It would be neceſſary to have Muſicians and Dancers capable of executing the Inventions of the Poets, after the way of thoſe lively ſpeaking Dances of the Ancients, which, to ſay truth, I think impoſſible for us *Frenchmen* to attain to, and I believe it very hard for the *Italians*. Therefore I ſhall not expatiate here upon the Method of adding *Choruſes* to our Tragedies, nor ſay what might be left out, and what taken from the Ancients, in conformity to

R 2   our

our Cuftoms ; for that would deferve a particular
Treatife,   I pafs now to things more neceflary to the
true Underftanding of the Drammatick Poem, and
the Practice of the Stage.

<hr />

Chapter the Fourth.

Of the ancient Actors or firft Reciters of Epifodes,
againft the Opinion of fome Modern Writers.

THough in all this Work I have had no other
Defign than to inftruct the Poet in many Particulars which I thought very important for the making of a *Dramma* ; yet being carried, by my own
Study and Enquiries, into the Difcovery of an Errour
of fome of our Moderns, about the ancient Reciters
of Tragedy, I could do no lefs than endeavour to re-
ctifie that Miftake, though it do not perfectly regard
my firft Defign, which was onely to deliver Precepts
about Drammatick Poetry.   But if my Readers are
curious enough to be willing to know fome Circumftances about the progrefs of Tragedy, I fuppofe
this Difcourfe may not be difagreeable to them.

We have laid down, as a moft conftant Truth, That
for many Years Tragedy was nothing but a Pagan
Religious Hymn, fung and danced in the Honour of
Bacchus ; That *Thefpis* introduc'd an Actor to recite
fomething Forreign to that Subject, which was call'd
an *Epifode* ; That *Æfchylus* brought on two Actors,
and *Sophocles* three, with other Ornaments, which
brought Tragedy to its perfection.   And this we
have juftified by the Teftimonies of *Ariftotle, Dia-*
genes

genes Laertius, **Athenæus,** *Plutarch,* **Donatus,** and many other ancient Writers ; to whom I may add all those who since have writ of Drammatick Poesie. But *Castelvetro,* **Ricoboni,** and some others, are of opinion, that the *Chorus* signifies sometimes the Band of Comedians or Tragedians, and that 'tis in that sense that we must understand that Passage of *Diogenes Laertius,* in the Life of *Plato,* which says, *That formerly the* Chorus *alone acted the whole Tragedy* : By which, says *Castelvetro,* *it appears, that the* Histrions *acted formerly without Musick or Dancing.* And as one Absurdity generally engages us in another, to maintain this Errour, he commits a greater, when he adds, *That the Actor introduc'd by* Thespis *was a* Buffoon *who used to Sing, and Dance, and play upon some Instrument, and that Æschilus after him brought on two such, separating Dancing from the Singing, and playing upon Instruments, and that* Sophocles *at last brought on three Actors for these three things.* So that he pretends, that before *Thespis* the *Chorus* was a Troop of Players or Actors, and that those brought on by *Thespis,* *Æschilus,* and *Sophocles* were not so, but Singers and Dancers which certainly is both false and ridiculous. First, there is no passage in any of the Ancients that can be cited to prove, that they who associated themselves to Act Plays were ever called by the Word *Chorus,* but by that of *Company* : We have many Examples of this in *Plautus,* who very often makes them appear under this Name at the end of his Plays to thank the Spectators, and in Terence. *Ambivius Turpio* complains, *That the Poets carry'd to other Companies those Plays that were easy to represent* ; besides, it is so far from being true, that antiently the

Plays

Plays were acted by *Hiftrions* without Dancing or
Mufick; that on the contrary 'tis moft certain, that
they were originally danced and fung by a *Chorus*
of Muficians without *Actors* or *Hiftrions*.

To Illuftrate fully the truth, I think that it is a
ftrange miftake to fay that the *Chorus* of which *Diogenes, Athenæus,* and *Donatus* do fpeak, when they
fay, *That Tragedy was at firft acted by the* Chorus
was a Company of *Comedians,* or reciting Reprefen-
tatours without either Dance or Mufick, for one
need only read thofe Authors to be convinced of the
contrary; and when *Athenæus* faies, *That Tragedy
had none of thofe* Hiftrions *which the* Greeks *call* Hy-
pocrites, or, Reprefenters of other Men; he cannot be underftood of Buffooning, Dancing or Singing
Actors, becaufe the *Greeks* had a great many of
them, in Tragedy; particularly in that which
was called *Satyrical Tragedy.* Befides, in the time,
and before the time of *Thefpis,* they ufed a little fort of
Stage called *Eileos,* where was placed a Mufician to
anfwer the reft of the *Chorus,* and as Tragedy was
then nothing but a Sacred Hymn in the honour of
Bacchus, the *Chorus* was compofed of thofe who
were Minifters to his Ceremonies, and who were
hir'd for Money often to Sing and Dance in great
Feafts, fo that if the Actor brought on by *Thefpis,*
had done nothing but Sing and Dance without reciting, he had done nothing new, and the Priefts of
Bacchus would not have had reafon to complain of it,
but there is more in it ftill, for even in the time of *Thefpis* the *Chorufes* were compofed of Dancers and Singers, and *Athenæus* faies, that he and *Pratinas,* and *Phri-
nicus* with other Poets of that time, were Nicknam'd
Dancers, becaufe they fitted their Poetry to the Dance of
the

the *Choruſes* whom they uſed to teach with care themſelves, to repreſent well in Dancing, that which
they had expreſſed in Verſe.

This *Pratinas* was a *Tragick Poet* who lived a little
after *Theſpis,* and was contemporary with *Æſchylus,* and as *Athenæus* tells us, he writ as an obſervation of his time, *That when the People ſaw the Players of Inſtruments come upon the Stage without Dancing
with the reſt of the* Chorus, *and the* Chorus *ſing and
dance without playing upon Inſtruments, they were
angry at it, as a piece of Novelty againſt a received
cuſtom.* By which it appears, that the Diviſion of
Muſick from Dancing, which was then made by the
Poets, was a change in the *Chorus,* and not an Introducing of new *Interludes;* theſe *Choruſes* were
compoſed of ſuch great numbers, that *Æſchylus* was
forc'd to leſſen them, as we have it from *Ariſtotle,*
and this he did after the repreſentation of his *Eume-
nides,* and that *Chorus* is well diſtinguiſhed from the
Perſons who recited. If then it were or could be
true, that in the time of *Theſpis* the *Chorus* was the
company of *Comedians,* or *Hiſtrions,* we muſt be
told how that Name was transferr'd from the Reciters to the Muſicians, and who firſt brought into
Tragedy that great number of Dancers and Singers
of which we could not be ignorant, the *Greeks* having
been pretty well informed of their own Hiſtory ever
ſince the ſettling of the *Olympiads,* which was
near three hundred years before that time.

To this we may add as very conſiderable, that
which *Ariſtotle,* and *Diogenes Laertius* ſay, *That by
the means of the three Actors introduc'd by thoſe three
lights of the Stage,* Theſpis, Æſchylus, and Sophocles, *Tragedy received all its ſplendour, and its laſt perfection;*

section; for if before them there were companies of
Players that reprefented reciting, as they have done
fince, and that thefe three Actors added, were only to fing, dance, or play upon the Inftruments ;
fure thefe Authors would not have judg'd that fo
great a thing as to make the perfection of Tragedy confift in it ; and when in thefe latter times,
Tragedy having recovered its glory without all this
Mufick, *Mimiking*, and *Dancing*; did ever any one
yet object the want of that for a fault, and that its
true fplendour confifted in thofe ridiculous Interludes ? Befides *Thefpis* brought fo great a change
upon Ancient Tragedy, that he was called the Inventor of it, and if there had been before his time,
whole companies of reciting Comedians, I doubt
whether he would have deferv'd that name for only
adding a Buffooning Actor to the reft.

There is yet another thing to confirm this, which
in my opinion is important enough, which is, That
if before *Thefpis's* time there had been Stage Players,
or *Hiftrions*, they muft have acted without a Stage,
and without Clothes conformable to their parts,
and without any decoration, for all thefe things
were moft certainly brought in by thofe three Poets,
and in different times.

And it is moreover true, that *Æfchylus* having Introduc'd the Second Actor, divided the recitals of
his Actours upon the Stage, and *Ariftotle* for this
reafon calls the Firft Actors part, *The Principal Difcourfe*, or the *Principal Canto*; and *Philoftrates*
fpeaking of this Second Actor of *Æfchylus* writes,
*That by this means he took off from the Stage thofe
long and tedious* Monodias *of a fingle Actor, putting
in their room a* Dialogue *of* Difcourfe *of different
Actors.*

Actors. So *Scaliger* writes, that at the beginning Tragedy was *Monoprofope,* that is, of One Actor, and that *Æfchilus* brought in the Difcourfe of two, by which it appears that thefe Actors were Reciters and not Singers or Dancers, but to finifh the proof of this matter we mult know that by the general Interpretation of all the Greek and Latine Authors that writ fince thefe three Poets; the *Hiftrion,* or Player introduc'd by *Thefpis* is named *Protagonift,* that introduced by *Æfchylus Deuteragonift,* and the Third added by *Sophocles Tritagonift*; that is, Firft, Second, and Third Actor, and not Dancer or Mufician. By the Firft they underftood that Actor who in Tragedy reprefented the chief Perfon of the *Dramma,* and had the chiefeft part, as appearing moft upon the Scene, and by the two others they underftood thofe who acted the fecond and third parts of the Stage. Upon this *Cicero* writes, *That amongft the* Greeks *he that has the fecond or third part, though he happen to have a ftronger voice than the firft Actor, yet he moderates it that he may not drown the firft.* And *Porphyrius* fays, *That the* Tritagonifts *always acted with a low voice* ; and 'tis in that fenfe that thefe names have in other cafes been applied to thofe Perfons who had the firft, fecond, and third parts, which made *Demofthenes* to affront *Æfchynes* call him *Tritagonift,* infinuating thereby, that he had been a Player, and that only of the third rank, and no body will fay, that in all thefe comparifons there was any thought of thefe Actors being Muficians or Dancers.

Indeed fomething like the imagination of *Caftelvetro* has happened in *Comedy* : for where it was firft received in *Rome,* it had no *Chorus* but *Interludes* of

S   Singers

Singers, Dancers, and Players upon Inftruments, who altogether marked the intervals of the Acts, and according to my opinion, were tranflated to the Stage from the *Ludi Scenici*, or Scenical Games.

That they fung danc'd, and play'd upon Inftruments all at once, appears by *Livius Andronicus*, who being grown old took an occafion from the weaknefs of his voice to have a youth fing for him, which made his dancing fo much the more agreeable, as being freed from the conftraint of managing his motions to his voice: Some while after he laid afide his Inftruments likewife, and then having his Arms at liberty to give the full grace to his dancing, he brought that Art to great perfection. This he did in Imitation of the *Greeks*, for we fee in *Lucian*, that in Tragedy thefe three Actions were formerly united and performed by the fame Perfon of which the furprifal of the people mentioned by *Pratinas*, and which we have already alledged, is a fufficient proof.

Not but that there are fome paffages in Ancient Authors which feem to fay, that formerly *Tragedies* and *Comedies* were fung and danc'd, and that fo Artificially that the Mufick and the poftures gave fenfible Images of the things expreffed by the Verfes; but this was either becaufe the Mufical Games (even in *Plato*) comprehended under them all the Exercifes of Poetry even to the Drammatick; or elfe, becaufe the Hymns of *Bacchus* which were originally at firft both Tragedy and Comedy, were always accompanied with Mufick and Dances, or becaufe in the intervals of the Acts they had people who reprefented by their dancing; thefe things which had been fpoken in the Act, as is to be feen in *Plutarch*

and

and *Lucian*, or rather, moſt probably, becauſe not only they had at the ſame time, and in the ſame places, Actors who recited Tragedy, but likewiſe *Choruſes* for Tragedy ; and *Mimes* for *Comedy*, who ſung and danc'd to the ſound of Inſtruments with poſtures which repreſented the Perſons both of Men and Gods.

Let us then conclude, that before the Age of *Theſpis* the *Chorus* was nothing but a company of Muſicians ſinging and dancing Tragedy as a Hymn in the honour of *Bacchus*, and that *Theſpis* brought on the Firſt Actor, who by reciting, divided the ſinging of the *Chorus*, and gave a beginning to the *Epiſodes*, and of this truth beſides Ancient Authors we have for *Guarantees* many modern ones, as *Robortel, Piccolomini, Bernardo Segni, Scaliger, Benius, Eugubinus, Voſſius, Heinſius, Victorius*, and other Interpreters of *Ariſtotle* who have all proved this Aſſertion, though by reaſons differing from thoſe which we have here declared.

Chapter the Fifth.

Of Tragicomedy.

THis New Word which ſeems to have been introduc'd to ſignifie ſome new ſort of *Drammatick* Poem, obliges me to explain it more clearly, and at length, then any of our Modern Authors have done, and to that end I muſt ſhew all that in our Plays is different from, or conformable to the Works of the Ancients.

The Stage by little and little being come to its last perfection, became a sensible and moving Image of all humane life: Now there being three sorts of conditions or ways of living, that of Great persons in the Courts of Kings, that of Citizens, and Gentry in Towns, and that of the Country people in the Country, the Stage has likewise receiv'd three kinds of Drammatick Poems, to wit, *Tragedy*, *Comedy*, and *Pastoral*.

Tragedy represented the Life of Princes and great People full of disquiets, suspicions, troubles, rebellions, wars, murders, and all sorts of violent passions, and mighty adventures; whence it was well call'd by *Theophrastus*, The State of an Heroick Fortune.

Now to distinguish Tragedys by their *Catastrophe*, they were of two sorts; the one were calamitous and bloody in their Events, ending generally by the death, or some great misfortune of the *Hero*; the others were more happy, and concluded by the felicity of the chief persons upon the Stage, and yet because the Poets out of complaisance to the *Athenians*, who loved spectacles of horrour, ended often their Tragedys by unfortunate *Catastrophes*; many people have thought that the word *Tragical* never signifi'd any thing but some sad, bloody Event; and that a Drammatick Poem could not be call'd a *Tragedy*, if the *Catastrophe* did not contain the death of the chief persons in the Play; but they are mistaken, that word, in its true signification, meaning nothing else but a *Magnificent, serious, grave Poem, conformable to the Agitations and sudden turns of the fortune of great people.* And accordingly in the nineteen Tragedys of *Euripides*, many of them have a happy conclusion; and which is very remarkable is, that the *Orestes*,
which

which begins with fury and rage, and runs upon such strong Passions and Incidents, that they seem to promise nothing but a fatal, bloody Event; it nevertheless terminated by the entire content and satisfaction of all the Actors, *Helena* being plac'd among the Gods, and *Apollo* obliging *Orestes* and *Pylades* to marry *Hermione* and *Electra*, *which made one of the Antients say, that that Play had a Comical Catastrophe*; but in that he is much mistaken, as well as *Victorius* and *Stiblinus*, who say the same thing of the *Electra* and *Alceste*.

Comedy was the picture of the Actions of the people, in which were generally represented the Debaucheries of young people, with the tricks and acts of Slaves and Courtezans, full of Railleries and Jests, and ending in Marriages, or some other pleasant Adventure of common life; and this Poem was so much confin'd to represent a popular life, that the style of it was to be low and mean, the expressions taken out of the mouths of ordinary people; the passions were to be short, and without violence. In a word, all the Intrigues were to be upheld by flight and cunning, and not by the sublime and marvellous part of humane life; therefore *Scaliger* is in the right to find fault with *Plautus* for making *Aleesimark* appear with a Dagger, and a design to kill himself, because that is an undertaking too generous for the Comick Theatre. *Donatus* likewise blames *Terence* for making his passions too strong and lasting, with expressions something too noble for his Art, and *Comedy* its self does not always in *Plautus* end happily as may be seen in divers of his Plays.

Pastoral or *Satyr* had a mixture of serious and pleasant; *Hero*'s and *Satyrs* were its Actors; and
the

this fort of Poem ought to be confider'd two ways; at firft it was nothing but a little Poem call'd *Idyllium*, or *Eclogue*, fung or recited by one man alone, and feldom by two or more; and they were generally Shepherds, Gardners, Husbandmen, Satyrs, Nymphs, and all forts of Country people; there was nothing but complaints of Lovers, cruelties of Shepherdefles, difputes for Singing, Embufcadoes of Satyrs, and ravifhing of Nymphs, with fuch like diverting, eafy Adventures; but the Poems were all loofe pieces, without any ftory, or neceffity of Action. We have many Examples in *Theocritus* and *Virgil*, and many Modern Poets have imitated them in Latine. In the Reign of *Henry* the Second in *France*, divers *French* Poets made *Eclogues* in their own Language, of which we have fome Examples in *Ronfard*.

The other fort was a Drammatick Poem, carryed on according to the Rules of the Stage, where *Hero*'s and Satyrs were mingled together, reprefenting both grave and pleafant, ridiculous things; and for that reafon this Poem had the name of *Satyrical Tragedy*.

This fort of Poem had not any courfe among the *Romans*, at leaft that ever I could obferve either in their Hiftorians or Poets; that which they call'd *Satyr*, being only a Copy of Verfes made to flander or reprove, and never us'd for the Stage, but with the *Mimes*, and by way of *Interlude*.

But among the Græcians, Satyrical Tragedy was highly valued; for at the Feafts of *Bacchus*, call'd *Chytres*, the Poets us'd to vye with each other, and difpute for the Prize by this fort of Poem. *Athenæus*, *Plato*, *Plutarch*, and *Suidas*, alledg many Examples of this kind, and we have fome fragments, but

but no entire Poem of this kind, except the *Polyphe-mus* of *Euripides* : And I incline to think that his *Alcefte* is one of that kind too, by reaſon that *Hercules* is very pleaſant there with a Slave, and does very Comical Actions ; but I ſhall wait the Opinion of the Learned, before I ſhall determine any thing in that Point.

These three ſorts of Poems are not now upon the Stage, in the ſame manner as they were antiently; for to begin with *Paſtorals*, they are now a Drammatick Poem, according to the Rules of all other *Dramma's*, compos'd of five Acts, and many agreeable Events and Intrigues, but all regarding a Country life ; ſo that we have borrowed the matter of the *Eclogues* from the Antients, and applyed it to the Rules of *Satyrical Tragedy*.

Comedy among us has remain'd long, not only in meanneſs and obſcurity, but look'd upon as infamous, being chang'd into that ſort of *Farce*, which we ſtill retain at the end of ſome of our Tragedys; though they are certainly things without Art, or Grace, and only recommendable to the Raſcally ſort of Mankind, who delight in obſcene, infamous words and actions. I know indeed that ſometimes our Poets have endeavour'd to reſtore the Comedy of the Antients, either by tranſlating their Works, or by otherwiſe imitating them, but that has ſeldom happened, and then without ſucceſs too, for many reaſons; but particularly, for not having choſen Subjects that had any conformity with our manners and cuſtoms ; or for not having chang'd in the Works of the Antients, that which was not ſo conformable to our Sentiments : Neither can we ſay that the Comedy of the *Italians* has ſucceeded to thoſe of *Plautus* and *Terence*, for they

they have obferv'd neither the matter nor form of
them ; their Subjects are always mingled with ferious Adventures, and *burlesk* ones, *Hero*'s and *Har-
lequins* ; and generally they confift but of three
Acts, without any order of Scenes, nor any thing of
the Conduct of the Antients. And indeed I cannot
but admire how it comes to pafs, that the Defcen-
dents of the *Romans* fhould be fo unlearned in the Art
of their Fathers.

As for Tragedy, it has been preferv'd a little better
among us, becaufe the manners of our Nobility being ferious and heroick, they have with more pleafure feen upon the Stage the Adventures of fuch perfons, and have fhew'd no difpofition at all to that
mixture of ferious and burlesk which we blame in
the *Italians*. But befides the Niceties of the Art, which
as well as the *Italians*, we have long been ignorant
of; we have done two things, one of which is very
reafonable, and the other without any good grounds.
The firft is, that we have rejected all thofe Storys
full of *horrour* and *cruelty*, which made the pleafure
of the *Roman* and *Athenian* Stages ; and for this
very reafon one of the nobleft Tragedys that we
Alboin. have, and the moft worthy of a Græcian *Theatre*,
could never fucceed well upon ours, but gave always
fome difguft both at Court, and to the people. I have
already given a reafon for it in another place. But
the fecond thing which we do without any ground
at all is, that we have taken away the name of
Tragedy from all thofe Plays where the *Cataftrophe*
is happy, and without blood, though both the Subject and Perfons are heroick, and have given them
the name of *Tragicomedys*. I do not wel know whether our Poet *Garnier* was the firft that brought it

up,

up, but he gave that name to his *Bradamante,* which many since that have imitated.

I shall not absolutely fall out with this name, but I shall shew that it is at least superfluous, since the word Tragedy signifies as well those Plays that end in joy, as those that end in blood ; provided still the Adventures be of Illustrious persons.   And besides, the signification of the word *Tragicomedy* is not true in the sense we use it ; for in those Plays that we apply it to, there is nothing at all Comical, all is grave and heroick, nothing popular and burlesk.

But moreover, this title alone may destroy all the beauty of a Play, which consisting particularly in the **Peripetia,** or return of Affairs, it may discover that too soon ; since the most agreeable thing in a *Dramma* is, that out of many sad and Tragick appearances, the Event should at last be happy, against the Expectation of the whole Audience ; but when once the word *Tragicomedy* is prefix'd, the Catastrophe is presently known, and the Audience the less concern'd with all the Incidents that trouble the designs of the chief Actors ; so that all their *Pathetick* complaints do but weakly move the Spectator, who is prepossessed with an Opinion that all will end well; whereas if we were ignorant of the Event, we should tremble for them, and be likewise more delighted with the return of good Fortune that should deliver them.

One thing which surprises me the most in this occasion is, that there are men of Learning and Parts, who out of complaisance to popular Errours, do maintain that this was a word us'd by the *Romans* ; for, for my part I cannot imagine where they can find that a *Dramma,* containing the Adventures of heroick persons, and ending in a happy *Catastrophe,* had the name of *Tragicomedy.* We see nothing of this in what remains of the Works of the Antients, nor in those who have compil'd fragments, or written their own sense about the Art and Maxims of the Stage. 'Tis true that *Plautus* in the Prologue to his *Amphytrio,* uses the word *Tragicomedy;* but as he is the only *Roman* that has us'd it, so has he done it in a sense very remote from the use we make of it. That he is the only Poet of the Antients that has us'd this word, is out of dispute; and our Moderns cannot alledge any other *Roman* Author, while the *Roman* Tongue was a living Language; so that *Plautus* was the Coiner of this word, which also fell with him, and died in its Cradle long before the *Roman* Language; but if others after him had made use of it in the sense he employs it, that could not authorize the word *Tragicomedy,* as it is now employ'd; and quite contrary,'tis by *Plautus,* that we will shew the mistake of its signification, and the ill use that is made of it.

To understand this well, we must repeat here, that *Tragedy* and *Comedy* were two Poems so distinct, that not only the Adventures, Persons, and Stile of the one, had nothing common with the other; but even the *Tragedians* never acted Comedys, nor the *Comedians Tragedy:* They were as it were two different Trades or Professions; and accordingly Story gives us the names of divers Actors, who excell'd in the one or the other, but never, or at least very rarely of any that excell'd in both.

We are to take notice besides, that the *Mimes, Pantomimes, Embolarii,* the *Buffoons,* the *Dancers, Musicians, Players of Instruments,*nay even the *Actors* of the *Atellane Fables* (which were the modestest of all)

all) were not admitted among thofe who acted *Tragedys*, nor likewife among the Comedians, or thofe who acted *Comedy* ; both thefe being reputed much more honourable than the Actors of thofe *Farces* and *Interludes* ; but the chief diftinctive mark of thefe two Poems was the matter of their *Incidents*, and the condition of the perfons in each Poem ; for where Gods and Kings acted according to their gravity and dignity, that was call'd *Tragedy* ; but when the *Intrigues* of the Stage were founded upon the tricks and behaviour of young *Debauchees*, Women and Slaves, that was Comedy. And if we feek a further reafon for this, it will appear that the Hymn or Song of *Bacchus*, which was fung and danc'd before his Altars, having been transferr'd from the Country, to Towns and Citys, the Subject of it was always taken by the Poets out of illuftrious and ferious Storys and Fables, and treated in a grave and fublime ftyle; but the very fame Hymn remaining in the Country Villages, took its Subject from the common people, and their actions ; and being treated in a low, familiar ftyle, was call'd Comedy, though that name too at firft was common to both forts of Poems, till their Characters being fo very different, made them be diftinguifh'd by different names. Now let us fee in what fenfe it is that *Plautus* employs the word Tragicomedy in the Prologue of his *Amphytrion*, where *Mercury* fpeaks ; and having defir'd from the people a favourable Audience, continues in thefe words. *After this I will explain to you the Subject of this Tragedy, What, you frown, becaufe I have call'd this Play a Tragedy ? but I am a God, and therefore can change it prefently if you will, and without altering a Verfe of it make it a Comedy.* Then having jeft-

[T 2] ed

ed a little, he goes on; *I will by a mixture make it a Tragicomedy; for I do not think it reasonable that a Play should be call'd all Comedy, where Gods and Kings come and act; how shall we do then since a Slave too is one of the chief Actors? why, as I told you, we will make it a Tragicomedy.*

After such plain and intelligible words, I cannot imagine how any body can say, that *Plautus* had us'd the word *Tragicomedy*, as we use it; for he never dreamt of that signification; all that he says is a jest, wherein he joyns the names of those two Poems, as he had done the persons by which the great distinction that was between them does more evidently appear; and that therefore we have very ill apply'd that name to a Poem, where all the Persons and Adventures are heroick. 'Tis for this that *Plautus* never call'd his *Amphytrio* a *Tragicomedy*, but because his Gods and Kings do not act according to their dignity, but rather very far from it, playing the fool almost continually, insomuch that *Jupiter* and *Amphytrio* go to Fifty-cuffs; he therefore often boldly calls it Comedy, in many places of his Prologue. *Jupiter*, says he, *will act himself in this Comedy*, and by and by, *Hearken now to the Argument of this Comedy*; so that his Interpreters and Commentators have not also call'd it by any other name, no more than such Antients as speak of *Plautus* and his Works; as *Cicero, Quintilian, Varro, Aulus Gellius, Volcatius* in his Treatise of the Comick Poets, *Servius, Sextus, Pompeius, Macrobius, Rufinus, Donatus, Petrus Crinitus, Lilius Geraldus*, in his History of Poets, *Scaliger* in his *Poetica*; none of these, I say, have called his *Amphytrio*, no more than all his other Plays any thing else but a *Comedy*. And when *Vossius* explains

this

this word of Tragicomedy, he fays, *Plautus* gives it
to his *Amphytrio*, becaufe he in that Play mingles
the dignity of perfons with the lownefs of Comical
Difcourfes; and *Feftus* making a divifion of the
Fables among the *Romans*, fays, that the *Tabernariæ*,
were fuch as admitted of perfons of Quality, mingled
with people of mean Extraction, upon which *Voffius*
adds, that the *Amphytrio* of *Plautus* is of that fort,
and that fuch a Play may be call'd *Tragicomedy*, or
Hilaro-Comedy, which is a new word invented by that
Author. And *Scaliger* before him, fpeaking of the
name of Tragicomedy given to this Play, fays, It is
done in *Raillery*, becaufe the Poet had made a mixture of the meannefs of Comedy, with the dignity
of great perfons; let us not therefore affirm any longer, that this word Tragicomedy was us'd by the
Antients in our fenfe; for *Plautus* is the only one
that has it, and that in a quite different fenfe from
ours, who by that word do mean *a Drammatick
Poem, of which the Subject is Heroick, and the End
or Cataftrophe happy*; and that indeed is a noble and
agreeable fort of Tragedy much us'd by the Antients.

The fame fault, in my Opinion, is committed by
thofe who would have the *Hilaro-Tragedia* to be a
Dramma, or Theatral piece in ufe among the Greeks,
and of the nature of that which we call *Tragicomedy*,
which feems not to be very probable. *Suidas* indeed
does fay, that *Rintho*, a Comick Poet, invented a fort
of Poetry call'd by him *Hilaro-Tragedia*; but to conclude from thence, that it was a regular Drammatick
Poem, of which the Subject was Heroick, and the
End happy, feems againft all appearance, firft, becaufe that it was a Comick *Poet* that invented it, and
they

they feldom or never undertook to treat any grave
Subjects; or when they did, it was always to turn
them into *Ridicule*, as this *Amphytrio* of *Plautus*, and
the Comedys of *Ariflophanes*. *Suidas* calls this Play
of his a *Farce*. *Hefichius* calls the Author Jeſter and
Laugher; and *Varro* puts the name of *Riortho* for a
Jeſter. Befides, this Invention of his had no progreſs,
and we have not heard ever fince, of any regular
Dramma that has carryed this title, nor of any Poet
that fucceeded him in this kind.

What I ſhould think then of this *Hilaro-Tragedia*
is, that it was a little piece of Poetry, of the number
of thoſe call'd *Mimes*, wherein were mingled ſerious
and pleafant things, fung with Voices and Inſtruments, and danc'd upon the Stage with geſtures, ex-
preſſing the fenfe of each word, according to that
wonderful way of the Antients, fo little known in
our days; and this feems to be fo much the more
probable, becauſe *Voſſius* fays, that the *Hilaroedia* is
the fame with the *Hilaro-Tragedia*; and 'tis certain,
that that, and the *Magedia*, were two Poems of that
fort, fung and danc'd upon the Stage by thoſe who
were thence call'd *Hilaroedians*, and *Magedians*; and
they were not Drammatick Poems repreſented by
Tragedians or *Comedians*, as fome by miſtake have
imagin'd, for the *Hilaroedians* (who were likewiſe
call'd *Simoedians* from one *Simon Mages*, who ex-
celled in that Art) did dance and fing a piece of Poetry agreeable, but ferious; and though not fo ferious as *Tragedy*, yet much of the fame nature; and
as for the *Magedians*, they at firſt recited only Dif-
courſes of Magick or natural Cauſes, ſuch as is the
Pharmaceutra of *Theocritus* and *Virgil*; but in pro-
ceſs of time they came to act all fort of laſcivious
Farces

Farces in the Comick Character, but much below it.
The *Magedians* reprefented Men in Womens cloths ;
but there were another fort who reprefented only
Women in Mens cloths, and thofe were call'd the
Lifoedians Athenæus remarks many more parti-
culars about them not proper to our Subject.

But that none may have caufe to wonder at what
I fay about *Hilaro-Tragedy*, we muft obferve that
moft of the Poems of the Antients were fung and
danc'd with ingenious Geftures, either in their
Temples, or upon the Theatres, or at their Feafts In
a word, in all publick Pomps and Shows, either fa-
cred or profane. Sometimes they took *Odes* and
Idylliums, and other fmall pieces of Poetry, as *Mna-
fion* did by the *Jambicks* of *Simonides*, and fome others
by the Verfes of *Phocilides*, and other Poets. The
Lacedemonians did the fame thing by the Songs of
Thaletas and *Aleman*, and the *Pæans* of *Dionifiodo-
rus*, at the celebration of the Feaft for the *Tyrean*
Victory. Sometimes they took a *Cento* out of fome
great work, as out of *Hefiod* or *Homer* ; and thefe reciters were call'd *Homeriftes*, being firft brought upon
the Stage by *Demetrius Phalereus*; and one *Hermodo-
rus* was famous among them.

We find alfo by a certain *Jafon*, cited by *Athenæus*,
that in the great Theatre of *Alexandria*, *Hegefias* the
Comedian was a famous Actor of thofe Poems, written by *Herodotus Logominus*, a noted Poet of thofe
times, different from the Hiftorian of that name.

Nay, there were people who us'd to fing and dance
fome parts of Tragedys and Comedys at Feafts, and
great Entertainments ; and fometimes the entire Plays
were thus fung and danc'd, not only in the time
when Tragedys and Comedys confifted of the Hymn
of

of *Bacchus*, (of which we have spoke in its proper place) but even since they were reduc'd into Rules, and made up of many *Episodes* inserted between the *Chorus's*, as we have them now.

From whence we see *Aristotle* calls *Æschylus's Dancer Divine*, for having so rarely danc'd a Play of his call'd the *Seven* before *Thebes* ; and we see *Seneca* makes use of *Pylades*, a rare Tragedian Dancer: and *Batyllus* as rare a one for Comedy, to insinuate, that no one ought to undertake any thing but what they are excellent in, if they mean to succeed. 'Twas this *Pylades* who rais'd a Dispute before the people of *Rome* against *Hylus* his own Scholar, which of them two represented *Agamemnon* best, either *Hylus*, who to make him great, rais'd himself upon his Toes, or *Pylades*, who made him pensive and thoughtful, as being the best *Idæa* of a Prince that was to take care of his Subjects good. *Plutarch* likewise in his *Table Conversations* makes two great Discourses about this ingenious way of representing by motions and postures, persons and actions, insinuating that Poetry is nothing but a speaking Dance, and Dancing a dumb kind of Poetry, and condemning at the same time the Dances of *Pylades* in publick Feasts, as being too serious and passionate.

But, though these Discourses about the Antients may be agreeable and useful, they carry me too far from my Subject, upon which I have already been too tædious to explain only the word *Tragicomedy*, our Poets may reflect whether they think fit to use it still in its vulgar acceptation, or whether according to the true notion of Tragedy, they will use this word indifferently in all those *Dramma's*, of which the persons are Heroick, whether the *Catastrophes* be
happy

happy or fatal, that fo they may hinder the Spectator from difcovering the Event of their Plays beforehand.

An Analyfis, or Examen of the firft Tragedy of So=phocles, entituled Ajax, *upon the Rules deli=ver'd for the practice of the Stage.*

IF the Curious that have read thefe Remarks, are willing to receive fome fatisfaction for their pains, and to judg equitably of the labour I have undergone, it will be neceffary for them to read in the Original this *Dramma,* which I am going to examine, and till then, if they condemn or praife me any where, I muft except againft them as unfit either to cenfure or applaud my Endeavours. All *Criticifms* have this property, that they oblige the Readers to view the piece they *criticize;* for if they have not prefent in their minds all thofe particulars, upon which the Rules are to be applyed, they are fubject to doubt of the beauties and faults that are fhew'd, and of the truth of all the Criticks Obfervations. I am not ignorant that fuch a Difcourfe is none of the moft agreeable of its felf, and therefore ought not to impofe the reading of another Book; but there is no way to make this Lecture eafie, but by taking in both. It may be a bolder man than my felf would tell you, that thefe Remarks, though by the crabbednefs of their *Criticifm* they may fail of pleafing one way, yet they will in fome meafure atone for that, by fhewing the hidden graces, and the great dexterity of thofe great Mafters which have hitherto been

[V]   little

little taken notice of, or at least regarded as casual beauties.

Supposing therefore that my Reader has just read *Sophocles's Ajax*, I begin to examine it by the *Subject*; for 'tis there that the Poet himself ought always to begin.

The subject of this Poem is nothing but the just Indignation of *Ajax* against his Country men the *Græcians*, for preferring *Vlysses* before himself in their dispute about the armour of *Achilles*. This affront in the person of a King and the bravest man of the whole army unjustly and basely us'd by those whom he had so valiantly defended, and that by those Generals who could not be ignorant of his great Actions done in their presence, could not but be most highly resented and therefore afforded a noble Theme for great passions. The fund, I confess, seems to be sterile, and to promise little; but there lies the greatest art of chusing such improvable subjects, to give the Poets Imagination the greater Play; who it may be upon this Anger alone Invented both his rage and manner of dying, for I do not find History to have positively determined either of them: *Ovid* speaks onely of his Anger, and some have said that he was killed by *Paris*; others that he was stifled in mud by the *Trojans*, because he was Invulnerable, otherwise; for my part, I believe that those who tell his death *Sophocles's* way, have had it from him, which is no new thing in Theatral stories, the very Fables, from thence having by the Poets Inventions passed at last for Authentick Histories.

These two Incidents then I think to be the Poets Invention, who in that has with great Art, followed the Rules of probability, for a Soul as fierce and
passionate

paffionate for Glory as that of *Ajax*, might well entertain the refolution of being reveng'd upon his
Judges and his Competitour, and thereupon run mad ;
After which coming to himfelf again, and feeing the
extravagant and fruitlefs Effects of his tranfport, he
might well kill himfelf out of fhame and fome remainder of rage. That which makes this ftill feem to
be the Poets Invention, is the prohibition that *Mene-*
laus and *Agamemnon* lay upon *Teucer Ajax*'s Brother,
that he fhould not bury *Ajax*'s dead body, for 'tis
very probable that thofe two Princes were not fo in-
humane; but *Sophocles* added that to create the greater
compaffion for *Ajax*'s calamity, feeing his brother
hardly permitted to pay him thofe funeral rites which
were due to fo great a man and a King ; in this indeed he makes fomething bold with the generofity of
Menelaus and *Agamemnon*, but *Ajax* is his *Hero* to
whom he Sacrifices all things; and this refufal of theirs
to let him be folemnly Interred againft the law of all
Civiliz'd Nations, contributes not a little to perfwade that they had ufed him Unjuftly in the point
of *Achilles*'s Armour, all which, makes him ftill be
the more pityed; not but that thofe *princes* might have
fome fhadow of reafon for their feverity, confidering
Ajax as one who had meditated the ruine of the chief
Captains of the *Græcian* Army, and made himfelf as it
were a publick Rebel whofe punifhment among them
was to be prohibited the folemnity of fepulture. I am
not Ignorant, That *Cointus Calaber*, an Epick Poet,
makes them much more generous and with him they
perform honourable obfequies to his body. And in that
he aims at preferving the dignity of his Poem and
Hero's, as *Sophocles* does of his, befides this Ingenious
Fiction in his Subject he brings in *Tecmeffa Ajax*'s

                                                    Wife

Wife whence he draws three or four very paſſionate Scenes; now let us ſee what other changes he makes to adjuſt the time and place neceſſary for the compoſition of his Poem.

As for the time, he ſhews that indeed there needs no longer a one for the repreſentation than for the real action. Since in the third Act 'tis ſaid, *That Minerva's Anger againſt* Ajax *is to laſt but a day, and that if they could but watch him for one day, he might avoid deſtroying himſelf.* Now *Ajax* after this is all alone, and kills himſelf, by which we may naturally conjecture, that the Play ends the ſame day that his madneſs began; for all that's done after his death, is nothing but a conteſtation about his being buried, which is ſoon over, as happening near the dead body; and to ſhew that he does not employ the whole day upon his Stage, he opens his Theater in the morning, after *Ajax* had already run through the whole *Græcian* Camp, exercis'd his fury upon the Flocks of Sheep, and carry'd ſome of thoſe Animals bound into his Tent, which takes up naturally more time than is ſpent from the hour that *Ulyſſes* comes to ſpy what *Ajax* did, to the time that *Teucer* carrys away his dead body to have it bury'd; ſo that a ſmall part of the day is taken up by his Actors.

The only Incidents in this piece is the return of *Teucer,* who was in *Myſia* with an Army; and that this coming of his might not appear affected, he makes *Ajax* complain of the long ſtay of his Brother, who ſhould have been back long before, and who was expected by him with great impatience; ſo that when *Teucer* comes at laſt, that does not appear ſo much a contrivance of the Poets to make him be there to diſpute about his Brothers Obſequies, as a
natural

natural effect; the Spectatours being so prepared that they are wishing for his return of themselves before he comes, that he might save *Ajax*'s life, in which we may observe another change that *Sophocles* makes in the Story by this absence of *Teucer*, the reason of which change is, that if *Teucer* had been present in the Camp during his brothers Madness, the Scene being before *Ajax*'s Tent, 'tis very probable that *Teucer* would have taken care to secure him, whereas all other Authors who speak of this adventure, as *Cointus Calaber* particularly, leave *Teucer* in the Army, but not able to save his brother, because he was gone out of his Tent to kill and Massacre the Flocks of Sheep, and no body knew what was become of him.

Observe moreover with what art he chooses the place of his Theater. In following the Fable as it is generally receiv'd, none of the Actors have any Stable or particular place. *Ajax* is abroad in the Fields; *Teucer*, *Ulysses*, *Menelaus*, and *Agamemnon* are in the Camp; his Wife *Tecmessa* laments with her litt'e Son in his Tents, and his Subjects the *Salaminians* are either upon their Ships, or abroad to seek out their Prince. There was nevertheless a necessity of bringing all these people together, and to make them appear in one and the same place with probability, and thus he brings it to pass.

He places his Stage before *Ajax*'s Tent as being the most probable place where all things should come to pass; particularly considering that there was a necessity of making an afflicted Lady appear before the Audience, it would nor have been decent to place her any where else, nor to make her run about the Fields after a Mad-man; but because likewise he

was

was refolv'd to bring the body of *Ajax* upon the
Stage, that he might the better fhew the Paffions
of *Tecmeffa* and *Teucer*, and the conteftation about his
burial; he fuppofes that there was a Wood Clofe
by the Tent, and to make that fuppofition the more
likely, he places *Ajax*'s Tent the laft of all the
Camp, which is very artificially intimated in the
firft Verfes that *Minerva* fpeaks, and to fhew that the
Wood is hard by his Tent, he makes the *Salaminians* hear from the Camp, the voice of *Tecmeffa*, when
fhe falls into loud complaints in the Wood upon finding the Dead Body : Then to bring *Ajax*, who was
the chief Actor, to his Tent, he fuppofes againft the
receiv'd Fable, that he did not immediately kill himfelf after the flaughter of the Sheep; but that he
brought into his Tent, a great Ram which he took
for *Ulyffes*, and other Creatures which he took for
the Chief Captains among the *Græcians* with an in-
tent to make them linger under the torment of his
Stripes.

But let us fee in particular how each Actor is
brought upon the Stage, and goes off according to
reafon. *Ulyffes* comes to fpy what *Ajax* was doing,
and *Minerva* to affift him againft the fury of *Ajax*,
Ajax appears by the command of *Minerva* to give *U-
lyffes* the content of feeing his Enemy in the condition that fhe had put him; *Ajax* returns to his
Tent to whip the Ram that he took for *Ulyffes*, then
Minerva and *Ulyffes* go off of the Stage where they
have nothing more to do, and that's the Firft Act.
In the Second Act *Tecmeffa* comes out of her Tent to
defire fuccour from the *Salaminians*, who are the
Chorus in this Tragedy, and then opens her Tent to
go in again, where appears *Ajax* in the midft of the
flaughter'd

flaughter'd Beafts, but fomewhat come to himfelf, which gives fubject to very fine Difcourfes between him, his Wife, and his Friends. In the Third Act he comes out of his Tent feigning to go wafh him-felf in the Sea to purify himfelf ; but indeed to hide the Sword that *Hector* gave him ; his Wife comes out to follow him, but by his command retires into her Tent again, and he goes on. Then appears a Meffenger, who bringing the news of the return of *Teucer*, orders from him that *Ajax* be carefully kept ; upon this news *Tecmeffa* goes out again, and defires the *Salami-nians* to help her to look *Ajax*, which they do very willingly, and fo ends the third Act. In the Fourth Act *Ajax* appears in the Wood near his Tent, making complaints of his misfortunes, and fo falling upon his Sword, the Hilt whereof he had put into the ground, which circumftance fhews that his Death was at the fame time an effect of fhame for what he had done, and fome remainder of the rage he was poffeffed with ; at the very moment that he expires the *Salaminians* come upon the Stage from different parts weary, and vex'd that they had fought him in vain, and *Tecmeffa* who alone had gone towards the Wood, finds *Ajax* juft expiring, and cries out, which being heard by the *Salaminians* they go to her : In the mean time the feeking of him with fo much noife had eafily made every body think that he was gone out of the way on purpofe to kill himfelf, and fame which or-dinarily fore-runs great events, having carried the news of his death to *Teucer* obliges him to leave the *Greeks* with whom he was wrangling about his Bro-ther, and come to his Tent to hear fome news of him ; and at the fame time almoft *Menelaus* who had likewife heard the news of his death comes thither to

forbid

forbid his being buried ; then goes back to tell *Aga-memnon* of *Teucers* difobedience to his Commands ; who at the fame time goes out to find a burying place for his Brother, having firft fhut up *Tecmeſſa* with her Maids. In the Ffith Aƈt *Agamemnon* comes himfelf to put his Orders in execution ; and *Teucer* who fees him afar off, comes back to be near his Brothers dead Body, to defend it ; *Ulyſſes* arrives to appeafe *Aga-memnon*, who at laft yields and goes out ; *Teucer* de-fires *Ulyſſes* to withdraw, left his prefence trouble the deceafed Ghoft or *Manes* of *Ajax* who had been his Enemy ; he does fo, and *Teucer* carries off his Bro-thers Body : Now all thefe pretexts and colours for the going off, and coming on of all the Aƈtors, are without doubt very natural and probable ; but the Art with which the Poet brings all to pafs, is fo fine, and fo ingenious, that one cannot fay that he affeƈts fo much as a word in it all, every thing being fo well contriv'd, that all appears neceſſary, and therein lies the fecret of the Art.

You do not neither fee any Aƈtor upon the Stage whofe name you do not prefently know, or at leaft their quality or concern as much as is neceſſary to prepare the Attention of the Speƈtators. At the opening of the Stage *Minerva* (eafily known to the Ancients by the marks of her Divinity) difcovers *Ulyſſes's* name who comes to her, and the defign he has to fpy what *Ajax* does ; and when *Ajax* ap-pears, one fees in what condition he is, for *Miner-va* declares it, and calls him by his name. The *Chorus* in its firft Verfes fhews, that it is made up of *Ajax's* Friends, the chief of them faying, *That he had been always partner of the good and ill Fortune of that Prince*, hardly has *Tecmeſſa* fpoke three lines, but

but the *Chorus* asking her about *Ajax,* ſhe tells them that ſhe can beſt inform them, being from his Miſtreſs and Slave become his lawful Wife. The Meſſenger is preſently known by his Dreſs, and by the firſt words he ſpeaks. When *Teucer* comes in the Fourth Act, the *Chorus* ſays they hear his voice, and his name alone is enough to raiſe the expectation of ſome generous Sentiment from him, and the *Chorus* bids him conſider what to ſay to *Menelaus* who draws near, and by that prepares an incident of ſome new trouble. When *Agamemnon* arrives, *Teucer* ſays, *That he came back quickly, becauſe he had ſeen* Agamemnon *at a diſtance with the marks of Anger in his Countenance.* Thus by the Poets moſt agreeable Artifice, the ſpectators are not uncertain in the knowledge of the Actors, and their deſigns, which always ought to be; except where the ignorance of their Names and Intereſts is to produce ſome rare effect in the incidents of the *Dramma.*

Could theſe Acts have been more judicioufly divided? The firſt contains *Ajax*'s fury, the ſecond his repentance, the third the preparations for his death, the fourth his death, and the fifth the Diſpute about his burial, not that theſe Actions are meerly ſingle, for they are accompanied with many circumſtances which much embelliſh, and altogether compoſe the Acts; and as for the Scenes they are extreamly well knit together, as becauſe there always remains ſome body of the precedent Scene in that which follows except in the Third Act, where the Meſſenger who brings the Order to watch *Ajax,* and not to abandon him, arrives upon the Stage juſt as *Ajax* goes off, which is one way of uniting a Scene, when he that comes on ſeeks him that gois off. And in the Fourth Act,

[X]   though

though *Ajax* talks no longer with the *Chorus* which comes back juft upon the point he kills himfelf, yet thofe two Scenes are united by the time, and the fpectacle of his dead body, which remains as an Actor to whom the others arrive. As for the Intervals of the Acts, they are fo neceffary and fo well fill'd by what is done off of the Stage, that the continuity of the Action is moft manifeft; for in the firft Interval, *Ulyffes* tells the *Greeks* what he has learn'd concerning *Ajax*, and *Ajax* continues his Madnefs in his Tent: In the Second *Ajax* feeks for *Hectors* Sword; and in the fame Interval *Teucer* comes to the Camp and fends a Meffenger according to *Calchas*'s advice. Between the Third and Fourth Act there is no Interval, becaufe the *Chorus* is gone off of the Stage which remaining empty, makes very well the diftinction of thofe two Acts; not that *Ajax* had been doing of nothing all that while, for he fays himfelf that he had been fitting his Sword to kill himfelf: The Fourth Interval contains the return of *Menelaus* to *Agamemnon*, with their Difcourfe about *Teucers*'s difobedience, and the care that *Teucer* takes to find a fit place to bury his Brother in; fo that from the firft opening of the Stage there is not one moment that the Actors are not bufie each according to their Defigns.

Confider befides how well he has chofen the *Chorus* in this piece, and how induftrioufly he makes him Act. He makes his *Chorus* of *Salaminians*, who more probably then any others might be fuppofed to come to *Ajax*, their Princes Tent upon the news of his madnefs, as alfo to pity his diftraction with their own ill fortune; neverthelefs he does not bring them upon the Stage at the beginning, as he

does

does his *Chorus* in other Plays, becaufe they were not to hear the Difcourfe between *Minerva* and *Ulyf-fes*, and befides too they could not without fear have been in *Ajax*'s prefence fince *Ulyffes* himfelf thinks himfelf not fafe near him, though under the protecti-on of *Minerva*; but he brings them on at the end of the Firft Act, and makes them go off again at the end of the Third Act under pretext of looking after *Ajax*; but indeed becaufe that having a defign to make *Ajax* kill himfelf upon the Stage, it would not have been probable that his Subjects fhould have feen him undertake fuch a thing and not hinder him.

To take this Tragedy according to the truth of the Action It feems not that the Poet has done any thing in favour of the Spectatours, fo naturally do all things fall out, and are depending of each other, and yet his making the *Chorus* go out that *Ajax* may kill himfelf upon the Stage, is contriv'd on purpofe to fhew the *Audience* a generous Action worthy their compaffion, and to move them yet to more tendernefs, the very body of fo great a *Hero* is deny'd burial.

We cannot but admire befides, the Art of his Nar-rations, for he makes *Minerva* tell the Defign which *Ajax* had fecretly refolv'd upon the Night before againft all the Græcian Princes, and how fhe had made him run mad to hinder the execution of it, which are things that *Minerva* alone could know; and then he makes *Tecmeffa* tell the remainder of what he had done when he was in his Tent. This divifion pro-duces two different effects upon the Stage; the firft a Sentiment of Admiration for the care that *Minerva* takes of *Ulyffes*, but with furprize for fo great a

misfortune

misfortune in the Perfon of *Ajax*. The other is a Sentiment of Pitty, when the Spectatours fee a Lady beautiful and well beloved fitting near a Mad-man her Husband. We muft not neither let flip the Narration which *Tecmeffa* makes fummarily of the ruine of her Family, and the death of her Parents, her Captivity, and then happy Marriage with *Ajax*; nor that of *Teucer* about the exchange that *Ajax* made of a Belt with *Hector* for a Sword which he received from him; the firft having ferv'd to faften the Body of *Hector* to the Chariot of *Achilles*, and the other having been the Inftrument of *Ajax's* Death, for though both thefe Narrations are inferted in the moft lively paffions of the perfons that make them yet are they touched with fo much Art, that they do not at all weaken the Paffions, but quite contrary heighten them by giving an Image of fome new misfortunes; befides that all the ftory of *Ajax's* Country, his Family, and his Warlike Exploits are induftrioufly told in different places without any affectation, and only for a more perfect underftanding of the Subject.

I do not knew whether the Conteftation of *Ajax's* Sepulture would be agreeable and pathetick in our age, but I make no queftion but that in *Sophocles's* time it muft have taken extreamly; for then it was a mark of the higheft Infamy, and the extreameft misfortune that could befal any body to be forbid burial, and without doubt the Spectatours were moved with great compaffion feeing the body of fo great a Prince ready to receive fuch unworthy ufage by the effect of *Minervas's* anger and as the Difcourfes of the two Princes, *Agamemnon* and *Menelaus* feem well grounded upon reafons of State to deprive

prive him of the honour of Sepulture; and on the other fide, the reafons of *Teucer* have Piety and Generofity on their fide, I believe that this debate which was conformable to the manners and cuftoms of the Ancients muft needs have been very agreeable to them, particularly confidering that *Euripides* has founded the Tragedy of the *Suppliants* in honour of the *Athenians* upon that fole confideration; and that it is not probable that fo great a Poet would have taken a weak Subject to eftablifh the glory of his Country.

As for the fhew or fpectacle he might have made *Ajax* appear in all his Madnefs; but befides that it is a Paffion below a *Hero*, except fome great caufe excite it, and that the effects of it are Illuftrious; I believe he avoided doing of it, becaufe it would have been hard to reprefent him making a great flaughter among the Sheep and Goats without making him ridiculous and fo deprive the *Hero* of that compaffion due to fo great a Calamity; therefore to fhew the deplorable condition of fo great a Prince, and yet not to rob the Stage of any thing of ornament, he makes him appear in his frenzy indeed, but fomething abated by the prefence of *Minerva* (which is a Figure of the rage of Great Men, which ought not to be quite abandoned by prudence, as the madnefs of the vulgar is) and fo fhews him fitting in his Tent in the firft abatement of his fury, having thofe flaughter'd Animals all about him with his Wife, his little Son, and his Friends in a mournful pofture near him; all which does in my opinion afford a well invented fpectacle, apt to raife compaffion; when *Ajax* comes alittle to himfelf, and that all his looks, words, and actions have the character of

fhame

fhame, courage, and fury painted in them, the better to manifeft the excefs of his mifery ; add to this the tears and complaints of his Wife, the prefence of a little Infant who cannot fpeak it felf, but whofe prefence gives occafion to many tender expreffions ; and laftly, the heavy confolations of his Friends, I fay, that it is hard, but all this muft produce a very pathetick and moving fhew. After this the Poet brings him to his Senfes entirely, but then the prophetick words of *Calchas* which threaten him that day particularly with death, bring new terrour upon the Stage, and that fo much the ftronger, becaufe the Spectatours thought him fafe by being returned to his Senfes. After this he dies by his own hand and his very Sepulture becomes a Subject of conteftation ; all thefe are new Objects of Compaffion which fhew us the maftery of the Poet in fupplying his Stage with variety by changing continually the Face of things.

A Project for Re-eftablifhing the French Theater.

THe Caufes which hinder the French Theater, from continuing the Progrefs it had made fome years ago in Cardinal *Richelieu*'s time may be reduced to fix.

1. The common belief that to frequent Plays is a fin againft the Rules of Chriftianity.

2. The Infamy with which the Laws have noted thofe who make an open profeffion of being Players.

3. The failings and errours committed in the reprefentation of Plays. 4. The

4. The Ill Plays which are indifferently acted with the good.

5. Ill Decorations.

6. Diforders committed by the Spectatours.

To begin by that *Generally received Opinion.* 'Tis true that the Ancient Fathers of the Church always forbid Chriftians to frequent the Theaters for two reafons.

The firft, (which few have taken notice of) was becaufe that the reprefentation of Plays was Anciently an Act of Religion, making a part of the Cult and Worfhip performed to the Gods of the Heathens; this is out of difpute, and may be eafily proved, if need were, by a thoufand Teftimonies of the Ancient Writers of Antiquity; the Firft Fathers of the Church condemned therefore the Chriftians that affifted at thofe Spectacles as being participant of Idolatry, which they had renounc'd by their Baptifm, as we may fee in the writings of *Minutius Felix*, *Tertullian*, St. *Cyprian*, St. *Auftin*, *Lactantius*, and others.

The fecond Reafon was founded upon the Indecencies and obfcenities faid and committed there by the *Mimes, Pantomimes*, Dancers, and others who acted their *Dythirambes* , *Phales* , *Itiphales* , *Priapeas* and other impure reprefentations which were proper to the Cult of *Bacchus*, to whom the Theater was Confecrated as to its Author, and to *Venus* as the companion of *Bacchus*. As to the firft Reafon then of the Pagan Religion, that ceafes now, fince Plays are no longer a piece of Worfhip, but rather an Innocent Recreation without any Impious Ceremonies in honour of the Idols, but the Publick muft be well informed of this.

As

As for the fecond Reafon, though in Cardinal *Richelieu*'s time all *Obfcenity* was banifhed from the Stage in his prefence, yet the Publick Theaters do retain fomething of thofe Indecencies in *Farces* and other Poems where the Authors endeavouring to pleafe the rabble reprefent Impudent Stories, and fet them out with filthy jefts ; which is a thing that ChriftianReligion juftly condemns,and which all good Men abhor ; and till that be taken away, and the Publick Theater as pure as it was in *Cardinal Richelieu*'s prefence, Plays will be look'd upon to be againft good Manners and the ftrictnefs of the Gofpel

As to the Infamy of thofe who take up the profeffion of Players, it was juftly inflicted upon them formerly, but now is no longer fo.

To underftand this point, we muft know that there was two forts of Actors among the Ancients, the *Mimes*, and *Dancers*, and the *Comedians* or *Players*, who are thofe that now act among us, and as thefe two forts of people were very different in the things that they reprefented as well as in the manner, places, and habits of reprefenting, fo were they very differently efteemed.

The firft in the later end of the *Roman* Empire were declared Infamous though at firft they were not fo, neither among them nor amongft the *Græcians*.

But the *Comedians* and *Tragedians* never were fo difgrac'd, but on the contrary, always us'd with civility and kindnefs by all perfons of worth and quality, which may be made out by many proofs, but particularly by this,that the *Drammatick* Poets themfelves acted often the chief parts in their own Plays, though fome of them have been Generals of Armys, and

and had other noble employments in the State; and if it has happen'd that the Actors have in some Reigns at *Rome* been us'd somewhat severely, it was by Maxim of State, for having sided openly with Princes reputed Tyrants, but not at all for being Enemies to good Morals.

In *France* our first Acting begun in Churches, representing then only holy Storys, but it soon degenerated into buffooning and satyr, both of them as opposite to good Government, as to the purity of the Christian Religion. Amongst these Actors who were nam'd *Basochiens* and *Bastelours*, *Comedy* remain'd with as much shame as ignorance for many Ages; the Libertinism of that sort of life drawing away many young men of good Families, our Princes very justly noted them with infamy, to hinder by that means young Debauchees from continuing in a Society which was made incapable of keeping company with any other honourable sort of men; and from this likewise followed, that persons of quality scorn'd to contribute any thing to so mean a diversion, and were far from imitating the Antients in their generous liberality to *Comedians.*

From these two Considerations arises a third, which still stops the progress of *Drammatick* Poesie, which is *the fault of Representation.*

The Esteem that the Antients had Plays in, made many of the most excellent Wits apply themselves that way, and the Glory of the Magistrates, as well as the Fortune of the *Choragues* or Undertakers being depending upon the success of the Play, they did take great care in chusing their Actors, and instructing of them in the perfect performance of their parts, so that they attain'd to have many rare Actors in all

[Y]   kinds,

kinds; whereas with us very few ingenuoufly bred, have mounted the Stage, being hindered from fo doing, either by the fear of committing a fin, or by the apprehenfion of incurring the Infamy affix'd to the profeffion by the Laws, from whence it has follow'd, that thofe who did undertake it, being ignorant of their duty, perform'd it very ill in all its parts; nay, fo little knowing they were in their own Tongue, that they often expreffed very imperfectly, what they were to fay; and if there did fometimes rife up an Actor worthy of the Antient Theatre, he was fo ill feconded, that upon his failing any way, the Stage was ready to fink, and that even in our days has brought Plays towards their decay.

The fourth Caufe is founded upon ill *Dramma*'s or Plays, and this does not fo much regard our Modern Poets, who, to fay truth, have gain'd a very juft applaufe by many excellent pieces of theirs; but yet fomething may be faid, which is this;

The Antients could not leave us any ftore of ill *Dramma*'s, becaufe all their Plays were feen and examin'd by the Magiftrates; and befides, their Poets were not mercenary, but wrought for glory as much as for gain, there being a folemn Prize appointed for their reward, which was deliver'd with great Ceremony at their greateft Feftivals, to thofe who had beft fatisfied the Judges, and the Spectators; but we are far enough from that Method.

In the beginning of our Plays, as our Poetry was bad, fo was the reft of the Play, as to the Rules of the Stage; I have feen fome of eight and forty Acts or Scenes, without any other diftinction. In the time of *Ronfard*, Comedy was a little more regular, being cultivated by *Jodelle*, *Garnier*, *Belleau*, and fome
                                                          others,

others, who contented rhemfelves with making fine Difcourfes, but without Art, nor any contrivance in the Reprefentation. *Hardy* did quite contrary, endeavouring to pleafe the people by the variety of things reprefented, but without any knowledge of the Rules, which his Poverty did not give him leave to fpend any time to ftudy.   At laft *Cardinal Riche-lieu* encouraging by his noble generofity the Induftry and Labour of our Poets, brought Plays to the State, where we now fee them far enough from their true perfection, nay, and fomething decay'd fince his time.

For, as every day there appears new Poets animated either by the defire of glory or reward, and that they cannot all be excellent, we fee often fuch Plays as ought not to be acted, which proceeds from the little experience and prefumption of thofe new Poets, as alfo from the ignorance of the *Actors*, who being capable of judging only of fome things, are neverthelefs the only Judges of all *Dramma*'s, whether they fhall be acted or no; add to that the little care they take to have their Plays review'd and repeated in the prefence of intelligent perfons, before they come to be acted publickly.   For there is no fmall difficulty to judg of the fuccefs of a Play, by the reading of it alone; for very often thofe Plays which read worft, are the beft, when they come to be reprefented; and on the contrary, likewife thofe which feem admirable to the Reader, are often very defective upon the Stage, and the reafon of this is, the difference that there is between conceiving an Action as you read, and feeing the fame thing reprefented to your Eyes.   Things fine to fay are not always fo to fee; and the pleafure of Reading makes

[Y 2]   fome

some things agreeable, which the vehemency of
Action makes otherwise ; as likewise some that appear weak in reading, are strengthened by Action;
all which faults in the representation, as they lessen
the Excellency of the Plays, so they discredit both
Poets and Actors, and keep the people in the Opinion that the Stage is not capable of much improve-
ment.

The fifth Cause about the *Decorations* is likewise
important among the Antients, the Magistrates, and
other great Men, who us'd to give publick Spectacles to the people, either by the obligation of
their place, or to gain publick favour, us'd to be
at the charge of the Decorations, the Players contributing nothing towards it, and by that means
those Ornaments were not only magnificent, but
perfectly answer'd the Poets Intentions.   But now,
that our Players, though not very well in their
Affairs, nevertheless must undergo all the charge ;
they cannot be blam'd if they endeavour to do it
as cheap as may be; but then the Decorations must
be imperfect, and altogether below the dignity of
the Poets Invention.

As for the Disorders of the Spectators, we may
consider, that nothing was more safe and quiet,than
the Antient Theatres, the Magistrates being always
present, and every thing done by their orders; but
amongst us there is no order at all, but any sorts of
people wear Swords in the Pit, and other places, and
therewith attack very often many peaceable Spectators, who have no other defence than the Authority
of the Laws.   Among the *Greeks* and *Romans,* the
Women were so safe in the publick Theatres, that
they often brought their Children with them ;
but

but with us a company of young Debauchees come in, and commit a hundred Infolencies, frighting the Women, and often killing thofe who take their protection.

We may add to that, that the Seats of the Spectators were fo conveniently plac'd among the Antients, that every one was plac'd conveniently, and there could be no diforder in changing of place; whereas now the Pit and Boxes are equally inconvenient; the Pit having no rifing, nor no Seat, and the Boxes being too far off, and ill fituated; fo that what with the diforders of the Pit, and inconvenience of the Boxes, the Theatres are much forfaken by the better fort of people.

To remedy all thefe Diforders, it will be neceffary firft, that the King be pleas'd to fet forth a Declaration, which fhall fhew on one hand how that Plays being no longer an Act of Religion and Idolatry, as they were formerly, but only a publick diverfion; and on the other hand, that the Reprefentations being now perform'd with decency, and the Players themfelves living fober, and not of debauch'd lives, (as they were when the Edicts were made, by which they are declar'd infamous) His Majefty doth upon thefe confiderations make void all thofe former Laws, forbidding them ftill neverthelefs to do or fay any thing upon the Stage againft decency or good manners, under fuch and fuch penalties, as of being driven from the Stage, and reputed infamous again. And to preferve that Modefty which is neceffary, it fhall be likewife ordered, that no fingle Woman fhall act, if they have not their Father or Mother in the Company, and that all Widdows fhall be oblig'd to marry within fix

months

months after their year is out for mourning; and in that year fhall not act except they are married again.

And for the Execution of thefe orders his Majefty may be pleaf'd to fettle a perfon of probity and capacity to be as it were an Overfeer, Intendant or great Mafter of the Theatres and other publick Entertainments in *France* who fhall take care that the Stage be free from all Scandal, and fhall likewife give an Account of the life and actions of the Players. By this means the two firft caufes which hinder the *Re-eftablifhment* of the Stage muft ceafe; for all fcandal and obfcenities being banifhed, there will be no fcruple of Confcience in affifting at Plays; and the Players will befides be in fo good a reputation, as not to fear any reproaches from the fober fort of people. It was by fuch a declaration as this that the *Roman* Emperours re-eft ablifh'd the Theater when it was fallen into Corruption.

The third caufe muft likewife ceafe, for the profeffion of Actor being once made reputable, all thofe who have any Inclination that way will the eafilyer take to it; and befides, the Overfeer may himfelf felect out of the Schools, and the Companys of Country Players fuch as fhall be fitting, and oblige them to ftudy the reprefentation of fpectacles as well as the Recitals and Expreffions of the Poet, that fo the whole action may be perfect; and to this end none fhall be admitted but by the Kings Letters Patents delivered to the Actor by the Intendant General of the Theatres, who fhall give a certificate of his capacity and probity, after having tryed him in many ways. By this means there will always be excellent Actors, and the Reprefentations will no longer be defective.

The

The 4th cause which regards the Poets themselves does require some distinction for those of them who have already the approbation of the publick by the Excellency and number of their works, shall be obliged onely to shew their Plays to the Overseer General to see that there be no *Obscenities* nor any thing against decency in them, all the rest to remain untouched, at the hazard of the reputation they have already acquired.

But as for the new Poets, their plays shall be throughly Examin'd by the Overseer and reformed according to his orders, by which means the Stage will not be loaded with ill *Dramma's,* nor the Players burdened with rewarding such as afterwards can be of no use to them.

As for the *Decorations,* they shall be perform'd by the care of the same Overseer, who shall employ understanding and able Workmen at the publick charge, and not at the Players costs, who shall have no Expence to bear but that of their clothes, and the reward they shall give the Authors.

As for the sixth Cause, which concerns the conveniency and safety of the Spectators, the King shall forbid all Pages and Footmen to enter the Play-house upon pain of death, and prohibit likewise all other persons, of what quality soever, to wear their Swords there, nor any offensive Arms, upon the same penalty, it being reasonable that that safety which cannot be had here, out of respect to the place, as it is in Churches and Pallaces, be obtain'd by the equality of the Assistants ; and for this reason some of the Kings Guards shall be plac'd at the doors of the Play house, to take notice of any that shall go about to contravene this Order.

And

And for the greater conveniency of the Spectators, the Pit fhall be rais'd, and fill'd with Seats, that fhall overlook the Stage, which will hinder the quarrelling of the *Hectors*, there being not room for them to fight.

But to perfect the magnificence of the Stage, the Overfeer fhall look out a fpot of ground, fpacious and convenient to build one according to the Model of the Antients, fo that it be capable of the nobleft Reprefentations, and the Seats fo diftinguifh'd, as that the common people need not mingle with thofe of the beft fafhion; and round about which fhall be built houfes to lodg two Troups or Companies of Players *gratis*, which I fuppofe may be enough for the City of *Paris*.

And for the buying of the place, conftruction of the Theatre, lodging the Players, charge of the Decorations, and the Penfions of the two Houfes, as the King now gives them, with a Sallary For the Overfeer, and other fuch charges, there will a Fund be provided, without touching any of the Kings ftanding Revenue.

Thus there will be Remedys found for all the defects of the Theatre, which will be magnificent in all its parts, and worthy of the greatnefs of the Court of *France*, and the City of *Paris*, and the people will likewife have fome *Idæa* of thofe marvellous Reprefentations which have been upon the Stage of the *Palais Cardinal*, and that of the *little Bourbon*, and by confequent will be lefs envious and difcontented at the magnificent pleafures of the Court, and the great people.

F I N I S.